FIRST TO FIGHT

FIRST TO FIGHT

The U.S. Marines in World War I

OSCAR E. GILBERT AND ROMAIN V. CANSIÈRE

Philadelphia & Oxford

Published in the United States of America and Great Britain in 2017 by
CASEMATE PUBLISHERS
1950 Lawrence Road, Havertown, PA 19083, USA
and
The Old Music Hall, 106–108 Cowley Road, Oxford OX4 1JE, UK

Hardcover Edition: ISBN 978-1-61200-508-9
Digital Edition: ISBN 978-1-61200-509-6 (epub)

A CIP record for this book is available from the British Library

Printed and bound in the United States of America

For a complete list of Casemate titles, please contact:

CASEMATE PUBLISHERS (US)
Telephone (610) 853-9131
Fax (610) 853-9146
Email: casemate@casematepublishers.com
www.casematepublishers.com

CASEMATE PUBLISHERS (UK)
Telephone (01865) 241249
Email: casemate-uk@casematepublishers.co.uk
www.casematepublishers.co.uk

To Colonel Edward L. Bale Jr., USMC (ret.),
for help and advice
provided for over a quarter of a century.

Contents

Acknowledgements

Interlibrary Loan Services were provided by the Harris County (Texas) Public Library, Katy Branch. Rare and other books, as well as other materials, were provided by: Moffett Library, Midwestern University, Wichita Falls TX; Montgomery County Public Library, Conroe TX; Library of the University of Missouri - St. Louis MO; The Grey Research Center, MCB Quantico; Texas A&M University Library, College Station TX; Fondren Library, Rice University, Houston TX; The University of Michigan, Ann Arbor MI; and The University of West Florida John C. Pace Library, Pensacola FL. The *Service Historique de la Défense* provided French sources, mainly through their archives available online via the website www.memoiredeshommes.sga.defense.gouv.fr. Additional French resource materials were provided by the *Musée de la Grande Guerre, Meaux*; *Association du Souvenir de Sommepy-Tahure; Centre d'Interprétation 14–18, Suippes;* and the *Musée de la Mémoire de Belleau 1914–1918*. Unpublished interviews were provided by the U.S. Marine Corps History Division, MCB Quantico, with special thanks to Dr. Fred Allison. Archival photographs were provided by The U.S. Marine Corps History Division, MCB, Quantico, The Library of Congress, and the US Navy. Special thanks to Kara Newcomer and Annette Ammerman, USMC History Division; Stéphanie Derynck of *Musée de la Grande Guerre, Meaux*; Jean Myslinsky and Bernard Nodet from Bouresches; David Bedford and Constant Lebastard from the American Battlefield Monuments Commission (sites of Romagne sous Montfaucon and Belleau respectively). Thanks to Catherine R. Gilbert for archival research assistance and editing; and to Caroline Barbot and Christiane Cansière for field assistance.

Authors' Preface

This project grew out of two prior projects, and the realization that much information about the World War I Marine Corps has been greatly mythologized over the past century. For most readers the Battle of Belleau Wood—considered the "birth of the modern Marine Corps"—is World War I. However Belleau Wood was by no means the only contribution of the Fourth (Marine) Brigade to the land fighting in France. Belleau Wood did, however, cement the reputation of the Marine Brigade as a unit that could achieve the impossible. This fueled a rivalry between the Marine Brigade and the Army's Third Brigade that made the Second Division arguably one of the most ferocious Allied divisions on the Western Front. As a result, they would be called upon to fight both under French tactical control, and in every major action of the American Expeditionary Force for the remainder of the war.

Perhaps because it was fought under French control, the Battle of Blanc Mont Ridge in October 1918 is now one of the almost forgotten battles of history. Its strategic importance in unhinging the German front east of the Ardennes range was the subject of considerable professional literature until the early 1930s. In the opinion of Marines who fought in both battles, Blanc Mont was the worse of the two. At Blanc Mont the Marine Brigade was assigned the most difficult task, attacking a dominating enemy-held ridge, heavily fortified over the course of four years, across several kilometers of open terrain subject to observed artillery and long-range machine-gun fire, and with shallow bedrock that offered no opportunity to dig in if the attack faltered. The result was best summed up by an Army officer of the Second Division's Third Brigade: "The French troops that we relieved here had been trying to advance their lines for some time, gaining ground one day, only to lose it the next. They told us that it was no use trying to advance because it could not be done. However, we did not know that it could not be done, so we went ahead and did it."

Less well known are the contributions of the Marine aviators of the First Aviation Force that served with the British Royal Air Force in northern France and Belgium. Least well known by far are the contributions of the 1st Aeronautic Company and a small contingent of Marine artillerymen to the defense of the Portuguese Azores, crucial to interrupting German U-boat activities in the central Atlantic. Marines also served aboard capital ships of the US Navy in the North Atlantic and North Sea, helping bottle up the German High Seas Fleet.

The existing literature of the Great War can in large part be divided into two broad categories: the summation of the strategic "big picture", and the memoirs and experiences of the men on the Western Front. It is a rich literature, and one that could fill years of reading. In this study we have tried to merge the "big picture" with personal experiences, and in the latter case we have relied heavily upon both published memoirs, and interviews—most previously unpublished—conducted by the Marine Corps Historical Division under the direction of Benis Frank.

The Marine Brigade was part of a composite Army–Marine Corps division, and artillery, medical services above regimental level, and other services were provided by supporting Army components of the division. Experiences of soldiers in these units are incorporated as appropriate.

Accounts of American units in the Western Front battles have often ignored the role played by cooperating French forces, and in many the American accounts of the actions do not jibe with French military records. In these cases we have relied upon archival French military records to reconcile the discrepancies.

In the final analysis, this is but a tiny slice of the varied and important contributions of the United States Marine Corps in the Great War.

Ed Gilbert, Katy, Texas, August 2017
Romain Cansière, Puimoisson, France, August 2017

CHAPTER I

Background to War

> Sometimes people call me an idealist. Well, that is the way I know I am an American. America is the only idealistic nation in the world.
>
> PRESIDENT WOODROW WILSON

For most of its early institutional history the United States Marine Corps filled many of the functions of the British Royal Marines upon which it was patterned: shipboard and naval security, and providing skilled manpower to strengthen naval landing parties. Yet almost from its inception the Corps had been forced by circumstance to function as infantry in land warfare. The most notable examples were in the Battle of Bladensberg in defense of Washington against a British raid in August 1814, and in a raid on the British camp on the night of December 23/24, 1814 prior to the decisive Battle of New Orleans.

When the United States became a colonial power in the aftermath of the 1898 Spanish-American War, the Marines found themselves thrust into a new role as America's "colonial infantry" and "the State Department's troops" The Corps almost never fielded any force larger than a company, the primary exception being Huntington's Battalion in Cuba during the Spanish-American War. (Typically operating as extemporized numbered companies, the Corps did not even have a system for naming larger formations—hence the name.)[1]

Another role stemmed from the Navy's adoption of concepts presented in Alfred Thayer Mahan's 1890 book *The Influence of Sea Power upon History*, when the Navy began development of a battleship navy appropriate to a global power. Germany was then perceived as the main potential foe, with a need to defend the new and extraordinarily important Panama Canal then under construction. In the aftermath of the 1904–1905 Russo-Japanese War an aggressively expansionist Japan suddenly emerged as a potential threat to America's Pacific possessions.

Relatively safe behind the Atlantic and Pacific moats, America maintained a sizeable navy. But most Americans were immigrants or immediate descendants of European immigrants who held strong distrust of standing armies that in Europe had all too often been used to subjugate the population. In 1914 the tiny US Army was 5% the size of France's army, 9% the size of Germany's.

As early as 1900 the Navy General Board and the Secretary of the Navy ordered the Marine Corps to establish an Advanced Base Force of Marines primarily to secure bases in Cuba and the Dominican Republic (the approaches to the Panama Canal) against attack.

In 1903 the new Secretary of the Navy, Franklin Roosevelt, established the Joint Board as a planning body to coordinate between the Navy and Army. The Army quickly expressed opposition to the advanced base defense role, with no intent to seize or defend naval bases. Congress had also appropriated funds for a large battle fleet but only a limited number of support vessels, fueling the need for a capability to capture and defend the necessary bases. Over the following decades the Marine Corps would struggle to establish an expeditionary force in the face of bureaucratic foes and a stingy Congress.

The first real test of the Corps' new expeditionary force capabilities came in 1914. Mexico was in the grip of revolution. Conspirators connected to General Victoriano Huerta assassinated the new president, Francisco Madera, Madera's brother, and the Vice-President, and seized the reins of power. Known as *El Chacal* ("The Jackal") or *El Usurpador* ("The Usurper"), Huerta's brutal regime was based on oppression of the people, if necessary by violence.

Instability in Mexico was threatening both the global oil supply and access to the new Panama Canal. President Woodrow Wilson was also something of a moral crusader, and he lifted an arms embargo against the Constitutionalist forces in an attempt to force Huerta from power.

(In 1914 Mexico was the third largest exporter of oil. Though it produced only 7% of the global supply, several major European nations were heavily dependent upon Mexican production.) Wilson continued to ratchet up the pressure on Huerta, stationing a Marine Corps regiment under Colonel John Lejeune offshore, and resurrecting Army plans for a land invasion. Tensions grew when Mexican forces detained a few American sailors in Tampico. The sailors were quickly released and an apology offered, but Huerta balked at the terms of the demanded apology.

On April 18, 1914, the American consul in Veracruz reported that a German ship with 200 modern machine guns and fifteen million rounds of ammunition to support the Huerta regime would soon dock there. The Germans still wished to establish an alliance with Mexico that would also further their influence in Central America and the Caribbean. Veracruz was, not coincidentally, also Mexico's primary shipping port for crude oil.

For Wilson, it was the last straw. The Navy began to hurriedly concentrate a force off Veracruz.

Still seeking appeasement, Huerta ordered his troops not to resist an American landing, but the local commander had already sent soldiers to the docks, armed the local militia, and even released and armed prisoners from the jail. The naval landing force was quickly pinned down, but the Marines—more accustomed to such fighting—took to the rooftops to eliminate the snipers that formed the main resistance.

Captain Frederick M. "Fritz" Wise who had suffered under the Corps' slow peacetime advancement for fifteen years, seeing extensive expeditionary and sea service, as well as combat in the Boxer Rebellion, arrived on the second day of the fighting; he commented that "All the Advance Base business on which we had been drilling and maneuvering for months had been dropped. We were plain infantry now."

The Marine reinforcements were instructed to systematically clear the city block by block. The process was not greatly different from that in the twenty-first century. "Each company was allotted a city block [wide swath] with orders to comb it from the water front straight through to the inland edge of the town, disarming all Mexicans we found, confiscating all arms. When one block was finished we were to wait until each company had cleaned up its block, and then advance all together on the next block. We started.

"We found the blocks were built solid. Walls flush with the streets. Patios inside. Flat roofs. We started with the first house. The heavy wooden doors were locked and barred. Marines with sledge hammers were ready. We smashed the doors and went in.

"Not a shot was fired at us. We never found an armed Mexican. We did find a few old rifles and pistols. We picked them up and went along. It took us most of the afternoon."

Other landing parties had been in the town since early morning, and "Here and there we encountered parties of them. Our men were under orders not to shoot without a target. Others weren't under quite so rigid discipline. All over the town around us wild shooting was going on all afternoon. It was the damnedest mêlée I ever saw in my life." Members of other patrols warned them that few Mexicans were being encountered, but they "also warned us to be awfully careful about American sailors—they would shoot at anything." Wise was later told that a surgeon reported that "out of the nineteen Americans killed at Vera Cruz, thirteen deaths were due to wild shooting by our own people."

Clearing one house Wise went onto the roof, and "suddenly I heard bullets whizzing all around me. The plaster on that parapet flew on both sides of me. I flopped. The shooting continued. It was a miracle I wasn't hit. From where I lay I could see a group of American sailors on the roof of a high building which I took to be the Diligencia. Evidently they took me for a Mexican sniper." Wise slithered along behind the parapet until he was able to drop back through the roof's trapdoor into the building and send a runner to ask the sailors to please not shoot at them. That night one of Wise's NCOs was killed by a sailor.

By the next day there were three Marine regiments in the city, and later Army units arrived and began the task of fortifying the small city. Both sides settled into an uneasy truce.[2]

By April 22 the landing parties and naval gunfire had subdued any organized resistance. At War Department request, a Marine brigade—infantry and artillery—under Lejeune remained to police the city for eight months while American and Mexican negotiators argued. The conflict simply sputtered out, and in July 1914 Huerta resigned his office and went into exile.

The performance of American forces had in general been less than sterling, but the press gave heavy coverage to the Marines, virtually ignoring the sailors of the landing force. The exercise demonstrated that the Corps could quickly organize a regimental-scale expeditionary force by combing available troops from base security personnel, ships' guards, and a core of an advanced base force, all transported aboard naval vessels.

The Corps continued to struggle with the problems of growth from the nuclei of shipboard detachments, and the separate numbered companies that constituted most of the Corps' manpower was an artifact of that system. In October 1916 the 49th Company—a typical unit—disembarked from the battleship USS *Nebraska* at Portsmouth, Virginia, to begin a seven-month stint as a guard company. Plagued by rapid turnover of officers and senior NCOs as men were transferred to and from other duties in the expanding Corps, the company languished. Absorbing large numbers of recruits from among the crews of vessels impounded by the United States, the company quickly became known as a sort of "foreign legion", with many recruits who did not speak English. As for practical field training—there was none.[3]

President Wilson was determined to avoid entanglement in the European war that erupted in August 1914. As Germany grew increasingly isolated and beleaguered, she turned to unrestricted submarine warfare in early 1915, and the sinking of the passenger liners SS *Lusitania* and SS *Arabic* with heavy loss of life (among them American citizens) were the most egregious incidents. Still Wilson resisted, narrowly winning re-election in November 1916 on the slogan "He kept us out of war."

Imperial Germany's foreign policy was rather ham-fisted, and the worst provocation by far was the so-called Zimmermann telegram. Confident in the security of German diplomatic codes, in January 1917 the German Foreign Secretary wired instructions to the German ambassador in Mexico City. The cable was intercepted and decoded by the British:

FROM 2nd from London #5747

We intend to begin on the first of February unrestricted submarine warfare. We shall endeavor in spite of this to keep the United States of America neutral. In the event of this not succeeding, we make Mexico a proposal of alliance on the following basis: make war together, make peace together, generous financial support and an understanding on our part that Mexico is to reconquer the lost territory in Texas, New Mexico, and Arizona. The settlement in detail is left to you. You will inform the President of the above most secretly as soon as the outbreak of war with the United States is certain and add the suggestion that he should, on his own initiative, invite Japan to immediate adherence and at the same time mediate between Japan and ourselves. Please call to the President's attention to the fact that the ruthless employment of our submarines now offers the prospect of compelling England in a few months to make peace.
Signed, ZIMMERMANN.[4]

The United States began interning German vessels in February 1917, but the British delayed showing the telegram to Wilson until February 24. Wilson was already exasperated by Germany's refusal to end unrestricted submarine warfare, and the clear German disinterest in ending the war by negotiation. The Zimmermann telegram was one provocation too many, but still Wilson vacillated. On April 2 he finally asked Congress for a declaration of war.

When war was eventually declared the Navy was the service best prepared for it as it had been the primary guarantor of American neutrality behind its Atlantic moat.

The Mexican intervention provided some limited combat experience for many future Army officers from John Pershing and George C. Marshall, to Douglas MacArthur and George Patton. The tiny American Army, though potentially one of the most formidable in the world, would require many months to mobilize and train into a capable combat force.

The Marine Corps, dragged along by the Navy's insistence upon the advanced base force role, and with a demonstrated capability to quickly mobilize a land combat force and transport it overseas, suddenly found itself thrust into a new land combat role that would alter its future forever.

CHAPTER 2

Making Marines

> The first day I was at camp I was afraid I was going to die. The next two weeks my sole fear was that I wasn't going to die. And after that I knew I'd never die because I'd become so hard that nothing could kill me.
>
> ANONYMOUS MARINE[1]

For most of its institutional history the Marines trained recruits in a very different fashion from national armies.

Armies traditionally trained recruits by immersion in the unit in which they would serve. The recruit was assigned to a unit, and the officers and NCOs of the unit would whip him into shape by whatever means thought necessary. The same officers and NCOs would lead him into battle and the soldier—though he might be transferred between units and sub-units (less often than for officers and senior NCOs)—strongly identified with the unit. This was the case with the Regular US Army.

In the pressure of building a large organization for war, the US Army actually developed three armies. There was the old, pre-war Regular Army, made up of proud regiments that could trace their lineage back more than a century. These units recruited on a nationwide basis. The new National Army—regionally recruited or conscripted men—was organized into newly created units, with men trained in the same manner. The National Guard consisted of pre-war state militias, controlled by the governors of the various states and absorbed into the National Army in time of war. Though many Guard units had long and sometimes distinguished histories, officers were far too often selected and promoted on the basis of political connections rather than professional ability. Training—usually on scheduled drill days and in summer encampments—often consisted of socializing and skylarking about the countryside.

The Marine Corps had traditionally recruited and trained in very small numbers, chiefly individuals who volunteered from port cities or through local advertisement in places like post offices.

All too many recruits were indigents or the scrapings of port cities, seeking "three hots and a cot." The individual recruit was sent for a brief period of training at places like the Philadelphia Navy Yard, where most of his training was in basic skills like drill, dress, and rifle marksmanship. The individual's advanced training in skills like naval gunnery (in that era Marines manned the secondary batteries on battleships and cruisers) was conducted on the job within his assigned unit.

The enormous expansion of the Corps following the passage of the 1916 Naval Appropriations Act necessitated major changes in the way the Corps recruited and trained. The Act provided for an active-duty strength of 597 officers and 14,981 men; the President could increase the strength to 693 officers and 17,400 enlisted by executive order, which he promptly did on March 26. In August Congress authorized the creation of a Naval Reserve of unlimited strength, to include a Marine Corps Reserve. The Marine Corps Reserve would eventually incorporate women Marines, and inactive personnel. The total strength of the Reserve at war's end was 277 women; 463 officers of whom 360 were newly commissioned second lieutenants; 33 warrant officers and specialist clerks; and 6,483 enlisted men including officer trainees.[2]

This expansion necessitated considerable expansion of recruiting efforts, and recruitment became nationwide through post offices and newly established recruiting offices in urban areas. The recruitment process was often quite aggressive as the recruiters strove to meet requirements. The new Recruiting Policy Bureau in New York City began to beat the publicity drum, providing newspapers with information extolling Marine virtues, advertising the preparedness of the Corps for war, and recruiting appeals.[3]

Albert L. Jensen was an Iowa farm boy who did not get along with his parents, so in 1916, at age 16, he ran away. He worked at a number of jobs, including as a chicken-plucker, until he grew tired of the cold and made his way to Omaha. The Corps was aggressively recruiting as part of the expansion, and as Jensen got off the train he was met by a Marine sergeant in dress blues who asked where he was going. "I said, 'I'm not going anywhere. I just come into the city.'" After a brief conversation the recruiter asked, "Why don't you enlist in the Marine Corps?" The recruiter talked about the coming war, and finally "He gave me a ticket, and said, 'You can stay up here at this hotel'" and promised to talk to him the next day. The next morning Jensen gave in.[4]

Joseph E. Rendinell was a young electrician in a steel mill when the US declared war, and he announced his decision to enlist. His mother was grief-stricken, but Rendinell waited until June 1 to quit his job, and went to stay at a hotel in Cleveland to avoid his mother. He went to enlist in the Navy, but "The first man I met was a U.S. Marine [a Sergeant Fuller]. He sure looked fine, too. He showed me the Marines' posters, first to fight on land and sea & I was so impressed that I signed. He was a fast worker alright."

His co-worker Dave Felch had already enlisted in the Navy, but the recruiter told him he would "fix it up O.K." Felch was underweight, so Fuller instructed him "Between now and the time you go to Cleveland, eat all the bananas you can hold and drink all the milk and water you can get down" to pass the physical.[5]

Recruiters had other factors that worked in their favor. The opportunity to serve afloat and in exotic locales had always appealed to the adventurous. The distinctive and finely tailored dress blue uniform was a powerful recruiting tool—though most would never wear it.

While the War Department struggled to develop a conscription system—the Selective Service Act of May 1917 that would build the National Army—the Corps was already advertising tales of Marine valor. Recruits were also assured of overseas service in the event of war, and the Corps was careful to note that in the event of war the individual's term of service was for the duration of hostilities as opposed to the fixed—and often lengthy—terms of service offered by the Regular Army. And of course voluntary enlistment avoided any stigma associated with being a conscript.

When war was declared on April 6, 1917 the strength of the Corps stood at 462 officers, 79 warrant officers, and 13,214 enlisted men. Of these, 187 officers and 4,546 enlisted men were scattered across the globe on various duties, and 49 officers and 2,187 men were assigned to ships' detachments. Congress authorized a new manpower ceiling of 30,000 in May 1917.[6]

With the declaration of war the recruiting offices were inundated with volunteers, and the publicity campaign proved so fruitful that the Corps could be extremely selective in its choice of recruits. To standardize the manpower pool to avoid supply problems, recruits were required to be between 18 and 36 years of age, from 5 ft 5 in. and 6 ft 2 in. in height, between 130 and 245 pounds in weight, unmarried (or have a letter of permission from the spouse), be a native-born or naturalized citizen, literate, have no addictions, and of high moral character and mental fitness. About three-quarters of applicants were rejected, primarily for medical reasons.[7]

Many men found ways to work around the medical and age restrictions. Thomas Jackson had suffered a ruptured appendix and could not complete his pre-med studies in the spring of 1917. He first tried enlisting in the Army on the theory that service in the medical corps would be useful in medical school. He was turned away. The Navy medical officer who conducted his physical was the same physician who had treated him in the hospital; he was told to come back in a year. The Marines told him that if he could complete boot camp, he would be accepted. Jackson was accepted and went on to play football for the Mare Island team.[8]

The most common enlistment issue was underage enlistees. Wilburt S. Brown was born in Massachusetts in 1902, and with a friend decided to enlist in 1918. The two obtained copies of their birth certificates and altered the birth dates with ink eradicator but "It was not a very good job really and we should have known it wouldn't fool anybody. As a matter of fact, I was scared that it wouldn't." On the morning of his enlistment the recruiter was about to dispute the document's authenticity. Brown snatched the paper back, and said "Well, I'll go up and get another one.

"But I had noticed an old lady up at the Bureau of Vital Statistics at the State House who was wearing very, very heavy glasses, a nice garrulous old lady." Returning to the records office, "I got this old gal, and made put like I was all out of breath. I said 'They want it on that little card form instead of this certificate. Could you please copy this for me?' And she said, 'Well, isn't that strange! Usually they want the certificate.' So she started copying not noticing what had been done by myself and my friend." The simple ploy worked, though the recruiter probably did not inspect the document too closely.[9]

Recruiting efforts were sufficiently successful that until the end of the war they continued to reject a high proportion of applicants.

In the enthusiasm for war, the students of several universities enlisted en masse. At the University of Minnesota five hundred students enlisted as a group, no doubt encouraged by the presence of Lieutenant Carleton S. Wallace, the former captain of the track team, attired in his dress blue uniform. The result was that the Sixth Marines and Sixth Machine Gun Battalion in particular were two of the most highly educated units in history. An astonishing 60% had at least some college education at a time when about three percent of the male populace was college-educated.[10]

Gerald Thomas said that "There was a little bit of everything. We had artisans. We had college boys. We had kiddoes. We had just everything in that regiment ... Each company had about five or six, maybe 10, pre-War, non-commissioned officers; but they peeled off early," assigned as trainers or replacements in other units.[11]

The vast majority of recruits predictably came from more populous states or those with some connection to marine or fresh-water navigation, with about half from just nine states: New York (6,782), Ohio (4, 968), Illinois (4,959), Pennsylvania (4,365), Missouri (3,721), and Minnesota (2,581). Odd statistical anomalies included Florida (110) and Maine (24), with sparsely populated Montana somehow contributing 1,205 recruits.[12]

The wealth of manpower resulting from the recruiting bonanza would take time to be felt, so a desperate effort began to comb out men from ship's detachments and shore duties to form the Fifth Marines.

The new responsibilities in France did not relieve the Corps of its existing responsibilities, primarily fulfilling its commitments for naval security, and these absorbed considerable manpower. Most were in the continental US: at headquarters, administrative, and training establishments, and naval base security and the core of two Advance Base Forces were held for possible duty in securing the strategic oil fields in Mexico (6,481 total). The next biggest commitment was to shipboard detachments not just on battleships and cruisers, but gunboats, the presidential yacht, and even one submarine (2,236 men). There were sizeable garrisons at Guantanamo Bay, in the US Virgin Islands, Pearl Harbor, Guam, Cavite and Olongapo (the Philippines), Managua (Nicaragua), and Peking (2,095). Other detachments staffed the Haitian Gendarmerie (684), Dominican Guardia Nacional, and a small Advanced Base Force in Santo Domingo (1,925 men).[13]

Under the exigencies of war the legislative or official strength quickly became a meaningless number. At the end of June 1918 the authorized strength was 1,323 officers and 30,000 men. The actual strength was 1,424 officers and 57,298 men.[14]

Through most of the war, the Marines continued to enlist a disproportionate number of highly educated and intelligent recruits, whom the Army thought could be better utilized as specialists. On August 8, 1918 the President signed an Executive Order terminating direct enlistment in the Marine Corps, including the Reserve. From that date the Corps would draw its manpower from the Selective Service pool, though draftees had to volunteer for Marine Corps service. (Because of the late date, none of these "voluntary inductees" served in combat in France.)[15]

A few enlisted men were exempted from recruit training due to prior experience. By 1912 Walter S. Gaspar of Wisconsin had served in the Iowa National Guard and a one-year tour in the Navy. Unsatisfied with civilian life he then enlisted in the Marines. Exempted from boot camp, he served on the Presidential Yacht (PY-1) *Mayflower*, and over three years at sea on the battleship USS *Texas* before requesting transfer to Quantico as a gunnery sergeant.[16]

The recruit training facilities at the Philadelphia Navy Yard (capacity 2,500 recruits) and a temporary recruit barracks at Norfolk, VA (capacity 500), were wholly inadequate for the greatly expanded Corps. Two large training facilities were constructed at Paris Island, SC,* a former quarantine station and disciplinary barracks, and Mare Island, actually a swampy peninsula in San Pablo Bay northeast of San Francisco. In its expansion effort, the Marine Corps developed a different training policy. The enlistees would be trained by NCOs at recruit depots or "boot camps". Once training was completed, the recruit companies would become numbered companies, led by the officers and NCOs who had trained the recruits. Later in the war each recruit would be assigned to a numbered company in a replacement battalion, but once in France he would be reassigned as a replacement in an existing company, led by different officers and NCOs.

Merwyn R. Silverthorn was a student at a land-grant university and was therefore required to take officer training. As a student, when his Minnesota National Guard artillery unit (consisting almost entirely of college students) was nationalized in the summer of 1916, he was an enlisted man stationed in Brownsville, Texas. "Due to my infractions of regulations, I spent most of my time on stable police, which was a job that appealed to me more than polishing up the 3-inch field pieces." Like most, he was released to be back in school by September. He thought enlisted service useful because it taught him "what not to do." He never completed his studies and enlisted in April 1917.

Minnesota provided a disproportionately large number of recruits. Silverthorn's eyesight was below standard, so he chatted with the recruiting NCO while covertly memorizing the eye chart on the nearby wall.

After a lengthy rail trip the batch of Minnesota recruits reported for recruit training at Mare Island. For reasons unknown, there recruits were given a longer course of instruction than at other recruit training camps.[17]

The recruit received 8 weeks of training at Parris Island. At Mare Island recruit training was initially 12 weeks, shortened to 9 weeks (April 29, 1917) and eventually 8 weeks (June 22, 1918). Of the total recruits, some 46,000 (81%) passed through Paris Island.[18]

Several other recruits joined Albert Jensen in Kansas City, and the group grew steadily larger as they traveled toward Parris Island. In

* Only later did the modern spelling of Parris come into common use.

Chicago Jensen wandered away and bought a beer for the free food that (in those days) went with it. As he was eating, another recruit wandered in. "He was a little older than I was. One of the first things he said was, 'When we get back to the office, don't let any of the guys know what we were doing.' I said, 'Well what difference does that make?' He said, 'Kid, you sure are green. Half of those guys are bums. They don't have any money.'" The older recruit advised him not to let the others know he had money, about $600, an absurdly large amount of cash in those days and about $12,000 in today's value. "Oh boy, was that good information. I never did let them know I had money."[19]

For many the trip to Parris Island was their first away from home. Those from inland origins went by train, housed in bug-ridden hotels paid for by the government, at train stops. Rendinell recalled that on the train trip south gambling, drunkenness, vandalism and general carousing took place. Then at a small railways station "We saw a Marine Sgt. talking to our escort & then this Marine took charge but didn't say a thing till we started to raise a rough house & Oh, Boy, from then on we sure knew we were in the Marine Corps. He sure was tough. Offered to lick any guy in the car. He had us sitting in our seats like school boys. That .45 he had looked too big anyhow."[20]

Others arrived from port cities aboard ships that docked at Savannah, Georgia, or Charleston, South Carolina. Private (later general) Melvin L. Krulewitch arrived from New York. "As its [the ancient side-wheeler *Savannah*] gangplank hit the dock, out belched a motley horde of sweating, stinking, stumbling recruits, who were assailed immediately by the hoarse commands of Marine sergeants...." All were herded onto equally old train cars. The final stop was inappropriately named Port Royal, South Carolina, described by Rendinell as "a few old houses and a barge ... A gov't tug come along side and our tough sgt marched us on two by two."[21]

The final stage of the journey to Parris Island was aboard a barge pushed by an old tugboat. The men had not eaten all day, and dinner was beans with mustard and pickles, bread, and coffee or tea.[22]

Christian F. Schilt was the son of an Illinois farmer but decided that "there a hell of a lot of work to it, and I thought I would go in for some other vocation." As a college student in June 1917 he was a clerk and driver for his congressman in Washington, saw the Marine Corps Band, and decided to enlist. At Parris Island "they took away all my clothes and marched me right up to the shower and they assigned me a Marine Corps uniform...." The recruit's clothing was mailed home. One of the things that struck Schilt was the shortage of tents, with some men forced to sleep outside until more tents arrived.[23]

When Wilburt Brown arrived at Parris Island a Lieutenant Edwin C. Denby* informed him that his forged documents had been found out, but that his parents could give permission to enlist. "My folks did give it, and they allowed me to stay in the Marine Corps. I actually was not eighteen years old until after the First World War was over." Denby would later be the CO of a replacement draft battalion that included Brown.[24]

New arrivals were greeted with verbal and physical abuse by the "old timers" who had been on the island a few days longer. They were also promptly given the first of many harangues about the history and merits of the Corps. The recruits were issued the bare necessities—a cup and a mess kit—and marched to the chow hall. There "The first fellow passed out bread, the next slum. It looked as though it was made of beef stew, boiled potatoes, hash, dish rags, and a few old shoes mixed together, as close as I could tell." Over the rest of his term of service each Marine would subsist largely on the slum—short for slumgullion—a crude stew made of whatever ingredients were available.

Next "I held out my cup & he poured hot coffee all over my hand & it certainly was hot. To make a long story short I did not have any supper; that dam fool burnt my hand & I dropped everything."[25]

The next morning they were rousted out by raging drill instructors for what Private Levi Hemrick called "just the first of many pain-wracked mornings." Breakfast was what they would soon come to recognize as more staples of the Corps' diet: "hen fruit, spuds, punk, piss, and sow belly". In their new vocabulary nasty-smelling scrambled eggs, potatoes boiled whole, bread, acidic black coffee, and fried fat pork.[26]

---

*Denby, a politician from Michigan, had enlisted as a private but was a major by 1919. He was later Secretary of the Navy and deeply involved in the Teapot Dome scandal.

William W. Rogers had enlisted from Ohio, and was more impressed by the "wormy grits". He had enlisted after the Army had rejected him, but "After I had been there about two weeks, I got a letter to report … for officer training camp." After conversations with his sergeant and captain, he decided to forget about being an officer.

The first phase of the recruit's new life was quarantine. Batches of men were herded into large tents, where they would wait out the incubation period of any disease from measles to gonorrhea. The quarantine period did not always work as planned. Albert Jensen had been on the island for several weeks and was about to shoot for qualification with the rifle when he came down with measles. He was recycled, graduating with another platoon.[27]

In this period the men were used as general labor, and learned more new vocabulary. Yacht drill, or peeling potatoes for the slum, and submarine drill, washing pots. Rendinell: "The rest of the gang got hooked on police detail. My buddy thought he was going to be a cop and he swelled all up. Sure he was a cop—with a rake and shovel."[28]

The oyster shell drill, carrying buckets of oyster shells from the beach to surface streets, was fixed in the minds of most recruits. Christian Schilt: "we had to carry a certain number of buckets of shells every day, after our drilling was over. I think it was three or four buckets, which really was good for you, it made you use your muscles, and some of 'em certainly needed it."[29]

McDonald's most memorable event early in boot camp was the simple way in which the Marines dealt with religion. On their first Sunday the drill instructor informed them that the one thing they were not compelled to do was to attend church. "I said to myself, 'Hooray! It's something you don't have to do.' So he said, 'Now, we have three denominations; we have Protestant, Jewish, and Catholic. Now the Catholics will take one step to the left, Protestants one step forward, and the Jews one step to the rear; the rest of you fall out and fall in again right over here, right back of me.'" The churchgoers were marched away, and the rest began to leave. "He said, 'Just wait a minute! Were you dismissed?'"

The drill instructor promptly produced a thick copy of "Rocks and Shoals" (actual title *Articles for Government of the United States Navy*), the regulations governing conduct and punishment for infractions of naval regulations, and proceeded to read at length. "The sun was pouring down upon us, we were perspiring. And finally the crew came back from church and we were still standing there … 'Now you're dismissed'"

One of McDonald's fellow atheists said "I never was at church a day in my life, Mac … but whatever church you go to next Sunday, I'm gonna go to church."[30]

At Parris Island the conditions themselves were part of the hardening process. Recruit Sheldon R. Gearhart wrote home: "A week ago to-day it was 132 degrees in the sun. You know this island is nothing but sand, sand, sand. You can grit your teeth any time, I don't care when, and grate on it. It's in your chow, on the sheets, and in your eyes. It blows and drifts just like snow, and it's just like snow to walk in—you sink in."[31]

Recruit training was not intended to prepare recruits for combat duty, but emphasized discipline, close-order drill, physical fitness, and rifle marksmanship. The level of practical training was inconsistent, and varied during the course of the war as troops were rushed into service.

Christian Schilt remembered the routine as "rather strenuous. We got up about 4.30 in the morning, as I remember, took a physical exercise, and had a drill; then we had classroom studies, and kept going for about three months as I remember."[32]

The physical fitness training consisted of marching, running, manual labor, and "Swedish exercises", what are today called calisthenics. Private Ruben Jaffe wrote to his recruiter that "in the 'Swedish' I have heard big men sobbing through gritted teeth." There was also rifle drill, holding the heavy rifle in awkward positions until the cramps became agony.[33]

Joseph Rendinell described a typical days as "Drill, drill, drill, early morning to late at night. Day after day, Sunday & every other day for 3 weeks … Seven mile hike out to the maneuvering grounds. Ninety in the shade & no shade.

"More drill. Up at 5 A.M., drill until 12. Dinner. From 1 P.M. to 3 P.M. out on beach with our water buckets picking oyster shells to carry them a mile, making road. Checked for every bucket or trip we made, too. 3 P.M. to 4 P.M., wash clothes. Supper at 6 P.M. and drill till 8 P.M. Fall out.

"Next day same, & so on."

Like most, Rendinell liked rifle training the best, though the bone-bending contortions in the firing postures were not much appreciated. His first round missed the target completely. "The coach sat on my back & said, 'Squeeze that trigger, don't pull it. Keep your eyes open, too. Now fire.'" On qualification day he qualified as sharpshooter, and "I sure was one happy boy. That meant three dollars more a month."

European armies of the era de-emphasized marksmanship in favor of massed fire. In contrast, the Marines paid the individual "beer money": an additional $2 per month for marksman qualification, $3 for sharpshooter, and $5 for expert.

After rifle qualification it was back to manual labor. Rendinell was offered a permanent position as an electrician at Parris Island, but declined. "I told them 'No, I enlisted to fight the Germans.'"[34]

As the fighting chewed through hundreds of men, the training cycle was shortened to speed recruits into the replacement pipeline. Author William Manchester wrote that his father, a replacement wounded at Soissons, spent "less than four weeks as a recruit on Parris Island, the Corps' boot camp, and most of that had been occupied building a road. Somehow he had qualified as a sharpshooter with the Springfield 1903 rifle; otherwise he was untrained and unprepared for the fighting in France."[35]

In early 1917 the Corps was still procuring officers as it always had. The required small numbers of officers were traditionally supplied by the US Naval Academy or recruited from selected universities, and trained at the Philadelphia Navy Yard. Officer recruitment was soon perceived as a particular problem, and the Commandant aggressively recruited from military colleges and state universities. This pool provided about 37% of officer candidates for a sampling period immediately following the outbreak of war, followed by meritorious promotion of NCOs and warrant officers (28%), civilians with prior military training (18%), and civilians passing a competitive examination. These officer candidates had to pass an officer training course, and those who failed could either be discharged or serve as enlisted men. After an initial recruitment period new officers came from the Naval Academy, but the vast majority through meritorious promotion.[36]

The training experience for pre-war officers was completely different from those who followed. Louis R. Jones enlisted out of high school in 1914, lying about his age, since he was 19. Jones wanted to be an officer, but the cash-strapped Corps was awarding few commissions even to Naval Academy graduates. The usual recourse for those of limited education was to spend 2 years on active duty as an enlisted man before applying for a provisional commission. His boot training was at the Portsmouth Virginia Navy Yard, with subsequent clerical duties until 1917 when he was given a provisional commission and transferred to the Sixth Marines at Quantico.[37]

DeWitt Peck was one of the few Naval Academy graduates, Class of 1915. Some of his midshipmen's classmen were at sea on the obligatory summer cruise when Archduke Ferdinand was assassinated in Sarajevo. The long-obsolete Maine-class battleship *Missouri* (BB-11) had been returned to service as a training ship and was in the harbor at Naples when the news came. Officers were uncertain as to proper mourning dress uniforms, so the captain quickly put back out to sea and headed for England.

On liberty in London, the junior officers were tracked down and ordered to report back aboard at Gravesend. "We found out later that the ship had been advised by the British admiralty to get clear of the English Channel. We were out in the Atlantic when England declared war."

After completing his officer training at Norfolk and field training at Gettysburg, Pennsylvania, Peck was ordered to duty in Haiti, and later Cuba where the Marine Corps still maintained a sizeable presence.[38]

Another source of a few officer candidates and recruits was the naval militias of selected states. Naval militias dated from the War of Independence when the infant nation was a confederacy. Each former colony maintained its own land militia for self-defense, and some with strong seafaring traditions raised naval militias for both offensive and defensive operations.

In 1913 Massachusetts re-organized its naval militia, and soon afterward created the First Marine Company. William A. Worton had attended the officer academy for the state's land militia. In November 1915 he enlisted as a naval militiaman, and in March 1916 was commissioned as an officer. These formations were generally organized only during wartime, but the Massachusetts Naval Militia actually had a good deal of seagoing experience, from weekend voyages and annual cruises aboard the obsolete battleship USS *Kearsarge*.

Worton had decided to return to school, but war was now looming. In March 1917 the Naval Militia was federalized and Worton was eventually ordered to the new base at Quantico. [39]

Career officer Fritz Wise had been waiting many years for such an opportunity, and shamelessly used his connections to be assigned to the new expeditionary force. His first assigned task in Philadelphia was to go through eight companies of Marines hurriedly returned from Haiti and Santo Domingo. His instructions were to cull each down to 40 of the best men, and the companies would then be filled out with new recruits.

For the professionals of the "old Corps", the process was one of disappointment. "A bunch of those men were broken-hearted when they learned they couldn't go. Some of the old sergeants, when they heard the bad news, headed straight for me. I told them they were too old; that they couldn't stand the gaff in France; that it was a young man's game. The only one I relented on was First Sergeant James Gallivan," an elderly veteran of 47.

"He waylaid me in the Yard one day. 'I hear, sor, that you're not goin' t' take me t' France,' he said.'

"That's right," I replied.

"'There's room in France for both av us, sor,' he assured me." Wise kept the old man and "It was one of the best decisions I ever made."[40]

When the Corps could not meet its officer requirements through the traditional means, Commandant Barnett sent letters to the presidents of state and private universities, and state military schools, offering commissions to the top ten seniors in each graduating class.

Graves Blanchard Erskine was a "dirt farmer's son", interested in following an uncle into medicine. In 1917 he was student at Louisiana State University, and a member of the Louisiana National Guard, who had briefly served as a sergeant trumpeter in the 1st Louisiana Infantry on the Mexican border. He enlisted in the Marine Corps Reserve in early 1917, and reported for active duty in July 1918. Nineteen years old, he was frustrated when his Guard unit was not called into Federal service, and his school commandant suggested he apply for one of the 10 positions offered to each state university although he knew nothing about the Marines. Although underage, he was given a waiver and provisional commission because of his Guard experience. Provisional commissions were valid for 2 years, at which time the candidate would be evaluated for a regular commission.[41]

Lemuel Shepherd was a student at Virginia Military Institute, and like the other cadets he was impressed by Commandant George Barnett's uniform and bearing when he inspected the cadets in June 1916. He applied too late for one of the "top–ten" commissions, but got the school commandant to select him as an alternate, since Shepherd was convinced that two of the selected candidates were not physically fit enough. When word got around, a dozen cadets in all signed up to fill the two extra slots: given the storied reputation of VMI, all were selected.

Officer candidates had to travel to Washington at their own expense, so Shepherd borrowed the train fare but had to ride the crowded night train for six hours standing up. Shepherd was 12 pounds under the minimum weight for his height, but the physical examination by a Navy surgeon named Bobo Dessez was perfunctory. "After he looked us over he took our blood pressure and then said to me 'Get down over here and stick up your ass'" for a hemorrhoid examination. "'Have you ever had a dose of clap?' 'No, sir.' 'You pass.'"

Regular provisional commission required the approval of Congress, but Reserve commissions were effective immediately, so the group opted for Reserve commissions. It was arranged that the new officers would graduate from VMI early, on May 3, 1917, a significant date. On that day in 1863, just before the battle of Chancellorsville, Thomas J. "Stonewall" Jackson (a former instructor at the school) looked over several officers of his command and said, "I see that a number of my commanders are VMI men. VMI will be heard from today." Shepherd and the others took it as a sort of omen.[42]

Clifton B. Cates was the son of a successful farmer and cotton ginner who had completed law school at the University of Tennessee in 1916, and was preparing for the state bar examination. By coincidence he ran into the son of the president of the university. "And I asked him, 'Has your dad had any calls for people going into the service?' And he said, 'Not that I know of.' I said 'Well, if he does, put my name down.'

"About 2 weeks later I saw him and he said, 'Dad has a letter from the Marine Corps wanting eight Second Lieutenant reservists. Do you want to apply?' And I said, 'What in the hell is that outfit?' I really didn't know. And I said, 'Yes, put my name down.' And that's the way it started."

A major problem with the breakneck pace of expansion was that no one knew quite what to do with all the new officer candidates. Cates: "We were ordered to appear at the Marine Barracks in Washington for a physical examination on the 21st day of May [1917]. There were about, I'd say two hundred other college kids there, and we reported at nine o'clock. They said, come back this afternoon; come back tomorrow at nine o'clock; come back in the afternoon at one o'clock. So that went on for three days and we were all running out of money. In fact we had run out and they appointed a committee of three to go in to see the Commanding Officer.... So we went in and I explained to him—I was the spokesman—and I said, 'Major, we've been here three days now and we're all running out of money and if we can't get examined, we're going back home tonight.' And he pounded the desk and said, 'What the hell is this? Insubordination before you get into the Marine Corps? Get out of here!'

"So we got out, but as I went out I said, 'If we're not examined this afternoon, we're going back.' So we were examined that afternoon."[43]

Officer candidate training first commenced at various sites (Mare Island, CA, San Diego, CA, Parris Island, SC, and Winthrop, MD). Alfred H. Noble was a student at a private military school, St. John's College, in Annapolis, Maryland. In the summer of 1916 he had served as a "combination of mule nurse and machine gunner" in the Maryland National Guard garrison at Eagle Pass, Texas, but saw no action against Pancho Villa's bandits before being released to return to school for the fall term. Impressed with the military bearing and uniforms of the Marines he saw around Annapolis, in April 1917 he enlisted at Washington.[44]

In officer training at Parris Island, Noble's first duty was to don his new white dress uniform and present his calling card to the base commandant, but "fortunately he didn't want to see all of us, and we were very much relieved."[45]

In July 1917 officer training was centralized at the new base at Quantico, VA.

In general, the training of new officers in the US came so late that the vast majority of new officers in France (604) came through meritorious promotion of NCOs and attendance at Marine Corps or Army officer courses in France.

To accommodate both advanced field training and centralized officer training, the Corps leased, and later purchased, a large tract of land surrounding the sleepy backwater town of Quantico, VA. The Overseas Depot, established in May 1918, was for organizing and training formations to be sent to France. Two French and four Canadian officers with combat experience on the Western Front were added as advisors.[46]

Colonel John Archer Lejeune assumed command of the new base in April 1917. Lejeune's rise had already been meteoric, following the usual path of service in the Spanish-American War, sea duty, expeditionary duty, the Veracruz expedition in the US-Mexico crisis, and a tour as assistant to Commandant Barnett. Lejeune, like many, was exceedingly vocal about getting to France.

The functions of Quantico included not just training, but overseeing the organization of expeditionary regiments for possible intervention in Mexico, and the organization of the Corps' motorized artillery regiment. Lejeune's difficulties were exacerbated by having to commute by train from Washington, the closest placed he could find housing for his wife, and the brutal winter of 1917/1918 when temperatures often plunged to −17°F (−27°C). Lejeune: "I never felt colder weather anywhere. The Potomac River was frozen over and the ice was so thick that many of the great 14-inch shells fired from the Naval Proving Ground at Indian Head ricocheted on the ice and finally came to rest opposite Quantico. Frequently the men would walk out on the ice, haul then ashore, and place them on the company streets as ornaments…."[47]

When not frozen, the new base was, in everyone's descriptions, a sea of mud where the men lived in tents until wood and tarpaper buildings could be quickly thrown together. Graves Erskine: "As I recall they said they had 10,000 workmen there. You could hear the hammers going all night long, it was a round the clock operation."

The base had four Jeffrey Quad trucks, and one day Erskine saw one stuck in the mud on the main street, Barnett Avenue. When another arrived to pull it out, it got stuck. Finally four mules extricated the trucks. "So I think most of us got the impression that this [mechanization] thing was not here to stay."[48]

The hundreds of mules and horses that pulled the various transport likely did not greatly decrease the odor or number of flies in the hot Southern summers.

The base did not take shape as quickly as might have been expected. Leo D. Hermle had enlisted from university, trained at Mare Island, and was an officer in a battalion shipped from there about October 25, 1917. He was surprised to find that "Quantico still had stumps on Barnett Avenue."[49]

Erskine was assigned to the first officer candidate class at Quantico, and one night drew the duty of Fire Patrol Officer. He decided to meet base commander Lejeune, the "Cajun Colonel". "I shined myself up, it was a muddy and rainy day, and I cleaned up every place so I'd look real snappy when I got out there, and he let me stand in the doorway about five minutes before he spoke to me. He was looking at me, and I was putting on my best military brace, and finally he looked up and said, 'All right, Napoleon, come in and tell me what you want.'

"I made my fire patrol report for the night. Then when he got up his shoes were muddy and his puttees were dirty and his pants were too big in the seat, and I wondered, 'I don't think I'd ever get away with that.'

"But he was a very fine man. A very fine man. You couldn't help but have confidence when that fellow was standing around talking to you."[50]

The staff at the Quantico base was struggling not just with training, but with organizational problems. Lejeune was charged with assembling a fighting force on a scale never before seen in the Corps, and the history of operating in small independent units added to the confusion. The new pattern of the Marine Corps rifle company was large and unwieldy, and the headquarters, supply, and support functions totally inadequate. There were no centralized mess facilities, so the three-man company mess section was burdened with feeding a 250-man company three meals a day. In an effort to streamline the company, the platoons were divided into two half-platoons, a 17-man first section of riflemen and hand-bombers, and a 12-man second section of automatic rifle teams and rifle grenadiers.[51]

In reality much of the training was unrealistic, emphasizing tactical maneuvers that dated back to the American Civil War. Foremost among them was the "wave attack" in which successive linear formations moved forward toward the enemy. It was a tactic tailor-made to suffer heavy loses to machine-gun fire. Also lacking were training in such crucial skills as map reading, moving in defilade, scouting, and realistic chemical warfare.

At Quantico there were Canadian and Scots officers who were veterans of the fighting in France, whose greatest accomplishment was that "They had been in action and of course they scared us to death, particularly on the gas question. They said, 'If you get one sniff of mustard gas, you'd die.'"

Training so many men so quickly was beyond even Lejeune's prodigious abilities to properly oversee. The curriculum at the Quantico base was supposed to prepare the men for open warfare as opposed to trench warfare, since the Americans hoped to restore mobility to the battlefield. As a result training primarily emphasized open warfare (80% of training) as opposed to trench warfare. Rendinell recorded that training included "baynote drills, throwing hand grenades, machine-gun drill, digging trenches, cutting trees & building dugouts. Were taught how to charge over trenches, how to cut enemy bob wire without making any noise, how to lay our own bob wire. Taught the international Morris [Morse] code, dot and dash signaling, receive & send messages, firing Lewis machine guns on the rifle range. How to dismantle & rebuild machine guns blindfolded. Paraded three times a week for Allied diplomats, guard duty once a week. That's the training we got at Quantico."[52]

Machine gunners, who by now were considered specialists, were eventually sent to additional training at Ithaca, New York.[53]

Merwyn Silverthorn particularly recalled signals training, a half-hour per day. "Signal communication consisted of getting out in front of your tent, and the man who lived in the tent across the little company street was your partner. You would signal to him in Semaphore by arm or wigwag by arm—we didn't have flags—and he would reply. It was up to you to learn the alphabet. The result was that none of us knew the alphabet, and we stood around on one foot and the other, accomplishing nothing whatsoever...." In an example of military efficiency, Silverthorn was transferred to the Headquarters Company 3/5 as the corporal in charge of a battalion signals section. "Well, that caused lot of consternation among the signalmen and in my own mind." The First Sergeant took Silverthorn aside and quickly taught him the alphabet. "So I, having memorized the alphabet the night before, lined up the signalmen and said, 'Now, men, the first thing you do is to learn the alphabet.' And I stayed about two days ahead of them ..."[54]

The training of officers was even more naïve than that of enlisted men, if such a thing were possible. After his fundamental training at Parris Island, Clifton Cates was assigned to lead the 4th Platoon, 96th Company, Second Battalion, Sixth Marines at Quantico. He opined that "I spent at least half my time in trying to learn the Semaphore and the Morse code, and what good is that for a second lieutenant. And of course, we had a lot of close order drill. We had some extended order drill and we dug trenches and we threw dummy grenades. Some of the training was good but a lot of it wasn't worth much." He thought that the signals training was particularly useless, since officers did not do the signaling.[55]

Graves Erskine, with his military experience, was more straightforward. He decided to resign his commission to fight as an enlisted man. Instead Lieutenant Presley M. Rixey lectured him at length. "Finally he said, 'Have you got anything to say?' I said. 'Yes, that's why I am getting out of this outfit, I haven't learned a damn thing since I've been here, I am getting pushed around.' He said, 'What are you going to do?' I said, 'I am going to Canada and join the Black Watch.' And that's exactly what I planned to do." Rixey disapproved the request and reassigned him to the Captain Randolph T. Zanes's 79th Company.[56]

Zane's company seemed to have more than its share of characters, even by Marine Corps standards, and one was Lieutenant Evans Spalding, the cosmopolitan son of a railway executive who had already served with the Red Cross in France. Zane had taken over from William Worton due to seniority, so Worton was housed with other junior officers. One chill morning in September 1917 Worton was still in bed when Spalding shouted from the adjacent cubicle, "Arthur, what's the uniform of the day?" and Worton replied the khaki summer uniform. When the entire battalion assembled for morning exercises, battalion commander Major Thomas Holcomb instantly spotted Spalding—wearing the green winter uniform complete with fancy but non-regulation riding breeches. "But he rushed over, he galloped over—he didn't like Spalding anyway—and he hollered at the top of his voice, 'Mr. Spalding. Mr. Spalding, where in the hell did you get those breeches.'" Spalding, who affected worldliness and a British accent, "turned and saluted and said: 'Brooks Brothers, Major, Brooks Brothers.' The old man said, 'I'll give you ten minutes to get out of them and get back here.'"

As Holcomb rode away Evans said, "'God, he has no sense of humor, no sense of humor.' That's a true story from the old corps."[57]

CHAPTER 3

Over There

> We got a reputation then that we never had before. We got an international reputation, a European reputation, and a reputation in America. Before, the people who had heard of the marines admired them as a sort of military naval policeman, and that's about all they knew about them.
>
> GENERAL ALFRED H. NOBLE, USMC

Although the Army operated the greater number of troopships, they declined to transport Marines. The regiment was instead transported aboard the Navy transports USS *Henderson* and USS *Hancock*, and the auxiliary cruiser USS *DeKalb*, the former German liner *Prinz Eitel Friedrich*, seized by the US Navy at the outbreak of hostilities. By a peculiarity of regulations, the three ships, as Navy vessels, were considered not as transports but as convoy escorts.[1]

General Pershing and his staff, including two Marine officers, preceded the troops in late May of 1917, and Pershing was widely fêted in Paris. Marines were loaded aboard ships in Philadelphia, and headed for the convoy assembly site in New York. Sergeant Karl McCune on the Hancock described, "Close stuffy quarters below were allotted to the company [55th Company, Fifth Marines], but few decided to sleep there. Everywhere possible on the deck Marines made their bunks."

Then, "Just as the *Hancock* neared the Delaware Bay, a wall of fog settled over the waters. The Bay was barely visible from the deck; fog horns and sirens at regular intervals sounded warning to all ships of their danger. About 10.00 A.M. the *DeKalb* ... hove down upon us. Sirens screeched unceasingly until, a few minutes later, the vague outline of the *DeKalb* passed us by, missing our bow by a matter of feet." It was a portent of things to come for the hard-luck *DeKalb*. Then the engines failed on the *Hancock*, further delaying the trip. In New York harbor the men were hastily shuttled about on boats, reassigned to differing transports. McCune and most troops were assigned to the brand-new *Henderson* for her maiden voyage, while *Hancock* was designated primarily for supplies and equipment.[2]

On June 14 the first contingent—two battalions of the Fifth Marines with 70 officers and 2,689 enlisted men (20% of the infant American Expeditionary Force)—hurriedly sailed just five weeks after the declaration of war.

Fritz Wise: "There were no elaborate farewells. No bands playing. No flag-decorated streets. Nobody knew we were coming."[3]

The *Henderson*, captained by William Steele, had its share of miseries as things kept breaking. Several times the *Henderson* was immobilized by engine problems, but as a new, fast transport was always able to overtake the slower convoy. Lemuel Shepherd: "we had to maintain a watch in the rudder compartment to hand steer the ship when the mechanical transmission didn't work." Leaking oil contaminated rations and water. After some hair-raising combat service in Haiti Roland McDonald found that on the crowded ship "all you could do was walk; the sailors said, 'you can't stay here'" so the men remained in constant motion.[4]

Private Gerald C. Thomas was the son of a farmer and railway worker who had dropped out of his last year of college to enlist. He recalled that even when the *Henderson* was not overcrowded there was insufficient berthing space. "We lived very well, sleeping in hammocks. There were few bunks. This was my first experience with a hammock." But "Our food was not bad."[5]

Wise said that "Nothing seemed to work right on board. The little drinking fountains wouldn't function. She was an oil-burner, but the oil-burning ranges in her galleys wouldn't work until I found a couple of my men who knew how to run them. We entered the submarine zone without even gaskets on the hatches. If we had ever been torpedoed, she would have gone down like a broken china bowl. We made gaskets out of rope."[6]

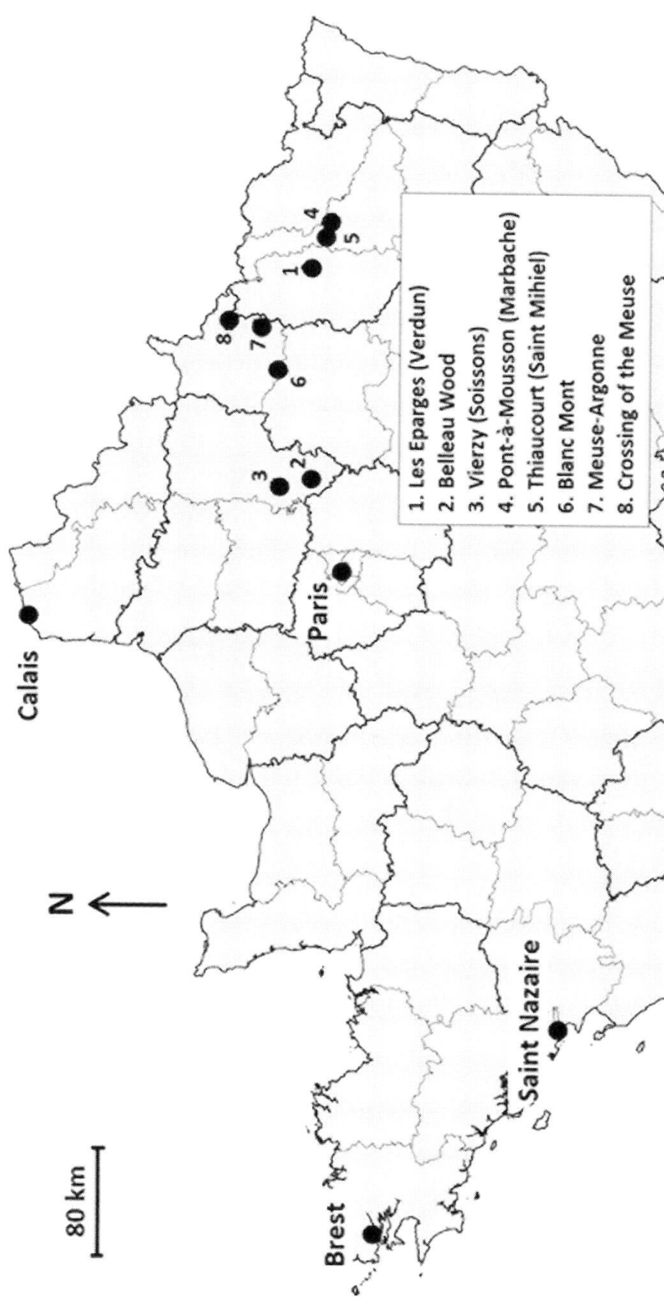

Marines entered France through the ports of Saint Nazaire and Brest, and fought alongside the French on the eastern part of the front. Neither the Army nor the Navy really wanted the Marine aviators, who operated from bases around Calais.

As members of the naval service the Marines were expected to share in the routine operations of the ships such as lookout duty and the ever-present maintenance. Walter Gaspar was one of the few men with seagoing gunnery experience, and spent the trip training the crews of the ship's 5-inch guns.[7]

Shipboard routine quickly grows tedious, relieved only by twice-daily lifeboat drills, watching the ship's gun crews, and twice-daily regimental band concerts.[8]

On June 22 the first convoy group was attacked by a German submarine. The armored cruiser USS *Seattle*, the flagship of the escort force, suffered a jammed rudder and sheared away from the convoy. Just as *Seattle* regained rudder control her lookouts spotted a wake crossing the bow only 50 yards away: it was a submarine running on the surface. Torpedoes passed fore and aft of *DeKalb*, but no ships were hit by torpedoes fired by two submarines. *Seattle*'s and *DeKalb*'s guns opened up on one submarine, but failed to hit it. The remainder of the voyage was uneventful. The three transports arrived off St. Nazaire on June 26 (*DeKalb*), June 27 (*Henderson*) and July 2 (*Hancock*).[9]

As the transports sat in the harbor, "We saw crafts of different nations lying at anchor, and, near the Esplanade at St. Nazaire, the aluminum skeleton of an unfortunate [German] dirigible that had been brought down…."[10]

One frustration common to all the Marines was that they were generally confined to ships tied up in the harbor for days due to a regulation. On the voyage over they remained part of the naval establishment and subject to naval regulations. Before being put ashore they had to be formally transferred to the administrative control of the Army, subject to Army regulations and discipline, and reporting through War Department channels.

As a result of this delay, elements of the Army's Sixteenth Infantry were first ashore.

The First Battalion, Fifth Marines was the first ashore on June 27 from *DeKalb*, followed by the balance of the regiment. However the Marines were the first to leave the docks and move to camps, where the company clerk of the 49th Company "greeted the passing soldiers with 'JUST GETTING IN?'"[11]

Five hundred Army stevedores were too few for the port's traffic, civilian stevedores were slow in arriving, so the Marines were charged with unloading their own transports. Wise was ill with influenza, but Colonel Charles A. Doyen had turned command of the troops on the *Henderson* over to him. "Our first sight of France had been through a driving rain. In that rain we landed and took our stuff ashore, unloading the ship, the usual Marine stuff." Then, "Five miles through the rain we marched out of St. Nazaire to a camp site the British had used in 1914, pitched camp and turned in under canvas."[12]

By July 3 the entire regiment was housed in the tent camp. Pershing still seemed loath to accept the Marines, but part of the regiment was attached to the Army's First Division, and entered training at Gondrecourt as part of the First Division. The Third Battalion remained on guard duty.[13]

The situation at the port continued to be one of massive confusion. One day a motorcycle driven by an Army captain arrived at the camp with a familiar Marine NCO named Thompson in the sidecar. "'What in the hell are you doing here?' I asked him.

"The sergeant replied, 'I'm trying to straighten out a mess called a company of the Transport Corps, of which I am first sergeant, sir,' he said. 'This is my captain. But if you want anything done, you come to ME about it.'

"The captain took it as a matter of course.

"Thompson was right when he spoke of 'a mess called a company of the Transport Corps.' The Army had loaded ships any old way. Motor trucks down at the bottom. Hay and ammunition piled on top. That whole St. Nazaire area was one hell of a mess. We couldn't get motor trucks. We couldn't get much of anything."[14]

Gerald Thomas's 75th Company, Sixth Marines was typical in that it labored in a variety of tasks. "We did guard duty about one day a week in the camp. It was an enormous camp. We worked on a reservoir that was a being dug outside of our camp. But mostly we went down to the piers in St. Nazaire and unloaded ships because there was a great shortage of stevedores. During the next four months we spent many, many days on the pier. We would be up at five o'clock in the morning, and would be at work by seven. We would work until five o'clock and we would go back and get a little chow and we were really ready to hit the sack."[15]

Corporal Merwyn Silverthorn's company continued to serve as stevedores long after other units departed, unloading cargo but without the usual tools that made that backbreaking job easier—even work gloves. There was a great deal of pilfering, particularly of sweets and cigarettes. "Unfortunately, those items came packed in boxes lined with tin, so it was difficult to pilfer those. But by judicious use of a bayonet or a pocket knife, we could penetrate this tin lining." The crews also pilfered food like corned beef and canned beans to supplement limited rations.[16]

Another of the Marines' first duties was purely ceremonial. A handful of men from the 49th Company was selected to march with the Army's First Division in a parade in Paris. The parade wound its way through Paris to great acclaim, and the highlight of the festivities was a wreath laying at the grave of the Marquis de Lafayette where Colonel C. E. Stanton from Pershing's staff announced, "Lafayette, we are here"—a statement later erroneously attributed to Pershing.

One correspondent wrote that "The marines were the pick of the lot, for size and behavior too. The sense of being something special was with the marines from the first. They marched that way. And, set apart by their olive drab as well as by their size and comportment, they gave that First Division's first march in France a quality of real distinction."[17] The Marines were set apart by their tailored forest-green ("olive drab") uniforms, in sharp contrast to the baggy brownish ("khaki drab") Army uniforms.

The Marines were the subject of much curiosity including a constant flow of correspondents and members of Congress ("fact-finding" missions to places like France were a staple of Congressional perquisites even then), and suffered through a series of inspections by senior officers. On August 1 Frederick Wise was told to have his men in formation for inspection by 0930 h, but noon (with no lunch) came and went. Finally at 1630 h they spotted an approaching column of cars, one of which sported a four-star flag. The inspection was by Pershing, Marshal Ferdinand Foch, AEF Chief of Staff General James G. Harbord, and the commander of the First Division, Major General (brevet) William L. Sibert.

Wise had been forewarned that during inspections Pershing had a practice of suddenly turning and looking back over his shoulder to see that the men still had their eyes fixed to the front. None of Wise's men fell into the trap.

"And as Marshal Foch shook hands with me to say goodbye, he said, 'Major Wise, the Marines are the Chasseurs of the American Army.'

"One of Pershing's aides told me that the old man was on the warpath and rabid, as we were the only outfit that was ready for him. I noticed that when Pershing got back into his car, though he shook hands with me, he didn't shake hands with General Sibert. I told myself that old boy's goose is probably cooked." Pershing fired off a letter to Secretary of War Newton Baker: "I hope you will permit me to speak very frankly and quite confidentially, but I fear that we have some general officers who have neither the experience, the energy, nor the aggressive spirit to prepare their units or to handle them under battle conditions, as they exist today. I shall comment in an enclosure on the individuals to whom I refer particularly."[18]

The series of inspections was culminated by one on August 18 by Pershing and Phillipe Henri Pétain, who had played a major role in negotiating an end to the Spring 1917 mutiny in the French Army, and was now "waiting for the [Renault FT] tanks and the Americans."

As in all bureaucracies, the inspection had other, more prosaic, fallout. One correspondent published a story lauding some cream of tartar biscuits that one of Wise's cooks had prepared. "Presently I got one of those thick files of official correspondence—the 'Referred to you' kind." A reader in Chicago demanded to know why Marines were cooking fancy foods "for the revels of officers and war correspondents. He must have pulled a powerful oar someplace. For his complaint had been given attention at Washington by the Secretary of the Navy, Mr. Josephus Daniels, and forwarded through General Headquarters of the A.E.F. The last endorsement requested me to report on the matter.

"I wrote across the document: 'I can't train my men to fight and do my own cooking. Which shall I do?'" That was apparently the end of that matter.

The incident was of more than usual interest to Wise. "I had learned that a good mess is essential to contentment and efficiency. Nothing puts you in a worse humor than poor food." Wise had put his orderly,

Private John McKeown, a veteran from his Santo Domingo days, in charge of the battalion officers' mess. "Marine-like, McKeown never did any work he could make others do." Somehow McKeown arranged the loan of a former hotel chef serving in a nearby French veterinary unit. McKeown was assisted by 16-year-old Private Jimmie Lewis, who roamed the countryside procuring foodstuffs for the mess. But "One day McKeown ran across him near the house and heard him cuss. McKeown took him by the neck, led him into the kitchen, and scrubbed his mouth with yellow soap."[19]

On August 4 the Sixth Marines were stood up, on direction of the President. The tiny fleet of Navy transports shuttled to and fro across the Atlantic, moving more Marines to France. On October 5 the *Henderson* arrived with the First Battalion, Sixth Marines.

On October 23 the Fourth Marine Brigade was established with newly promoted Brigadier General Doyen in command; it became part of the Second Division, while elements continued training at Bourmont. However, Marines continued to be scattered and used as labor troops by the Services of Supply (save one company in England as a security unit); security detachments, and many officers were attached to Army units of the AEF. Doyen was promoted to major general and on October 26 became commanding officer of the Second Division. Doyen, however, was quickly replaced by Army Major General Omar Bundy on November 8.[20]

As the main existing component of the brigade, the Fifth Marines were suffering command disruptions of the Corps' own making. Officers were quickly promoted and replaced. On October 30 Colonel Hiram I. "Hiking Hiram" Bearss assumed command from Doyen. On December 28 Colonel Wendell C. Neville, along with the new First Machine Gun Battalion (soon to be redesignated the 6th Machine Gun Battalion) arrived aboard the *DeKalb*, and on December 31 relieved Bearss.

Many of the Fifth Marines continued to be scattered among the Service of Supply, assigned to any duty senior commanders could dream up. In late October Merwyn Silverthorn was promoted to sergeant, and his signalmen assigned to patrol the railway station at Bordeaux (southwestern France). The Marines occasionally worked with the French police patrolling the slums, duty Silverthorn thought was "sort of a glamorous jot." In December the Headquarters section was disbanded, and Silverthorn was transferred to the 20th Company.

In the meantime those students from the colleges and universities who had enlisted later were the beneficiaries of the Civilian Military Training Corps, and had graduated as "ninety day wonders". Some of Siverthorn's former college classmates were now lieutenants or even captains.[21]

The new composition of the Second Division, with a brigade of Marines and a brigade of Regular Army soldiers inevitably produced internal friction. The 9th and 23rd Infantry that made up the Third Brigade were both proud old regiments with long lineages, and the competition between the two brigades would eventually transform the division into one of the most ferocious on the Western Front. Throughout the war officers would be seen as interchangeable, with Marine officers serving in Army units, and vice versa. Louis Jones summed up the issue of morale within the division as being like squabbling siblings: "we were very close to the 9th and 23rd Infantry—they would fight for us and we would fight for them if some outsiders came!"[22]

Pershing felt sufficiently uncomfortable that on November 10 (the birthday of the Corps) he wrote the Commandant: "I take this opportunity, also, of giving you the reasons for distributing them along our Line Communications which, besides being a compliment to their high state of discipline and excellent soldierly appearance, was the natural thing to do. As the Marine Regiment was an addition alone in the Division and not provided for in the way of transportation and fighting equipment in case the Division should be pushed to the front. When, therefore, service of the rear troops and military and provost guards were needed at our base ports and in Paris it was the Marine Regiment that had to be scattered, in an endeavor to keep the rest of the organized division intact."[23]

The 3/6 sailed out of New York on October 31. There was no liberty for the enlisted men, which mattered little to William Rogers of the 84th Company. "I lost my last five dollars shooting craps, and I had a nickel left and I bought a piece of candy bar with that."[24] Like many, Joseph Rendinell spent much of his time desperately seasick. On the night of November 9 the unlucky *Von Steuben* collided with the USS *Agamemnon*.

The larger *Agamemnon* tore open the bow of *Von Steuben* and scraped down the starboard side. Joseph Rendinell: "We thought sure we were torpedoed. We were thrown against the bulk heads. A rush for life belts. Orders were to wear life belts all the time & we were using ours for cushions. Everyone made a run for the life boats & when we got on deck, there were no life boats." The more experienced company commander calmed the men as the crew set to work building an emergency bulkhead.

Lieutenant Alfred Noble's company was on the *Von Steuben*. The glancing blow "took all the guns off the side of the ship and destroyed all the lifeboats that were swung out, and listed the ship over on one side and frightened everybody almost dead!" Lieutenant Timmerman, in charge of the ship's guard raced around checking his posts. He descended into the pitch-black hold. "And he said, 'Sentry, are you there?' And he heard click, click, click. The sentry was presenting arms!"[25]

William Rogers was Corporal of the Guard, and "So after about fifteen minutes of looking after myself, I finally thought about having some men down in the hold, so I went down and got them."[26]

Von Steuben turned a searchlight on the *Agamemnon* in an effort to help, and "the cruiser *South Carolina* steamed up along side us. 'Put out those damned lights, do you want to be torpedoed?'"

Destroyers were dispatched to escort the damaged ships. After sighting a submarine on the afternoon of November 10 *Von Steuben* docked safely in Brest where "French fishermen sold wine & beer & Cognac brandy, and did a land office business until the skipper ordered them away."[27]

One thing that repeatedly appears in interviews was the delay in 2/6's departure for France, and Thomas Holcomb's seemingly great influence that no one could account for. Worton: "The 2nd was due to sail in November. But the 2nd didn't sail because Mrs. Thomas Holcomb was expecting a baby. So the 3rd Battalion was substituted for us.... The old man wasn't going until that baby arrived. The war had to be held up.

But it didn't make much difference, because there wasn't much doing in France except bad weather when we did get there."[28]

Like the others before them, the Sixth Marines were assigned to Line of Supply, with platoons and squads parceled out building docks, digging ditches, guarding prisoners, unloading all sorts of cargo, and other tasks. Joseph Rendinell was amazed that the French schoolchildren carried bottles of wine with them to school, and the Marines traded cigarettes for wine. The weather was wet and chill, but at least "Plenty of vin rouge and cognac to keep the dampness out of our system."

Thanksgiving Day was a holiday, celebrated by "Slum for dinner. Washed clothes in afternoon." Then on "*Dec. 13, 14 & 15.*—Unloading more coal. Jesus!" Rendinell's diary recorded a litany of such duties until January 8, when they were ordered to rejoin the company.[29]

By early January the Marine Brigade was beginning to assemble as a unit, though many still remained on duty along the Line of Supply, and some had not yet arrived in France. Housing was always a chronic problem in training areas. Rendinell's diary noted that on January 12 "We are in barracks & they moved 10 men out, with me in charge, into a French barn that used to be a chicken coop & pig pen. It was a sight. We all turned to and cleaned it. Got it fixed up fine. Even built a fire place in there out of mud & rocks. Every billet allowed so much wood from the company supply, enough to burn one day if you're stingy with it. Our billets had plenty, believe me. Never mind where we got it. We have real American barbecued chicken every night, too."[30]

Some burdens were made lighter in the billets. In the absence of men, "The women here have to work for a living. Most of the women wash our clothes. They don't charge much either. Two francs [40 cents] for all the clothes you give them.... Every town around here has a public wash house and there everybody does their washing."

Rendinell complained about the "miserable" cold and wet. "Our company commander makes us take our shoes off and rub our feet with snow to keep from getting chilblains. I have to keep moving all the time to keep warm." (Chilblains is an inflammation caused by prolonged exposure to cold, and the old practice of rubbing affected parts with snow is precisely the worst thing to do.)[31]

The balance of the Sixth Marines arrived in bits and pieces as the few transport ships shuttled to and fro across the Atlantic. There were final rounds of carousing before shipping out from Quantico. Graves Erskine said that just before 2/6 shipped out in January 1918 "Some one of the fellows got a civilian friend of his to bring in a suitcase full of liquor. And I had had maybe one or two drinks in my life up to that time. We were all having a hell of a big night; I don't think anybody went to bed that night, and we were raising so much racket that Arthur [Worton], who was very serious about his duty, came in with his sword on and ordered us to pipe down, and we decided that Arthur didn't have much authority, so Jack West and I caught him and nailed his shoes to the floor. So we had our OD [Officer of the Day] nailed down for once."[32]

Not surprisingly, Worton recounted a somewhat different version of the same incident: "the Sergeant of the Guard called me, say around midnight, and said, 'The officers are shooting themselves down there in the officers' quarters.' I said, 'What are you talking about,' but by God I stepped outside and wham, all these sounds, like they were shooting." Worton rode down "and when I got off the horse, the sergeant with me, I told him to stay outside, I didn't know what in the hell I'd find in there—they were all hollering and singing, I knew they were all drunk. I got in there; they were all swacked to the gills. And they were taking these .45 bullets, and we had these big stoves, you know, they were throwing them in there, and of course they were exploding. Fortunately they didn't hit anybody, the iron was able to stop it. But the stuff made a hell of a racket....

"So I said, 'Gentlemen, this must stop.' Somebody grabbed me from behind, tied my hands; they poured liquor down my throat, and, god damn it, they were going to get me in on the party, whether I liked it or not. Fortunately my sergeant, I hadn't come out, he came in, and boy, they got kind of scared of him. So they released me, and I went back again. But I can always remember the next morning, because they had terrible heads, and of course they had to fall out, and I had to break them all out at 5 o'clock in the morning. And they said, 'Oh, for God's sake, use your head, let's delay it, what the hell do we care?' I said, 'Well, you damn well had better get going.' They got up and got out. So, the boys used to play in those days."[33]

Lieutenant Clifton Cates sailed from Philadelphia aboard the USS *Henderson*, he thought en route to France. But instead, the next day the ship was in New York harbor. Despite bitter cold and ten inches of snow and sleet, officers were given shore liberty, and told to report back aboard at 0800 to up-anchor at 0900.

About 0200 Cates grew tired of partying, and checked into a hotel, and asked for an 0600 wake-up call, only to awaken at 0900 hours. "So I was frantic, of course, and I finally got down and cussed the clerk as I went out the door." At the dock he could not see the *Henderson*, but got a ride with a British liberty boat in the fog-shrouded harbor. "The *Henderson* was still there.

That night they allowed us to go ashore again and I said, 'No, sir, not me! I'm not going.'"[34]

Cates thought "The old *Henderson* was rough as billy-hell. It was an exceedingly rough trip."[35]

In the bitter cold and heavy seas some of the routine shipboard duties were hair-raising. Worton: "In those days, they used to put the lieutenants up in the foretop with six Marines as lookouts, you see. You'd stand four hour up there."[36]

Like so many of the green Marines, Graves Erskine had no clue about what to do. One day he was ordered to post sentries around the ship, with orders to report what they saw "and I had one rough time finding out because they used seagoing expressions [ship's interior guards, not lookouts].

"I remember very clearly that one man was supposed to be at the scuttlebutt, and I hadn't the faintest idea what the scuttlebutt was. I was marching along, and I didn't want to show my ignorance to the Marines. I happened to be going along and I saw this spigot and I happened to stop. A sailor had just had a drink of water there, and I said, 'Where is the scuttlebutt?' He looked at me and he said, 'That's it, right there.' So I went to the sentry and gave him his orders about the scuttlebutt."

Erskine continued on his rounds searching in vain for the ship's eyes, until he found Major Holcomb "standing right up on the bow and I sneaked over to him and confided that I could not find the eyes of the ship. He said, 'You are standing on them right now.'" The ship's eyes are the hawse holes at the very front of the ship, an allusion to the ancient Greek practice of painting eyes on the ship's bow. "That was my last sentry post. But it was a very long trip."[37]

On February 6, 1918 the final elements of 2/6 and 3/6 arrived aboard the *Henderson*, only to cool their heels in the harbor at St. Nazaire for 3 days. One glitch in the disembarkation was a goat. Arthur Warton had obtained a goat as a mascot and 2/6 successfully concealed on the voyage. Erskine: "The French found out about this goat and they had a fit over bringing a goat over there. I guess it was a question of inoculations and so forth. So we thought we had lost our goat until we got down on board the train and the goat showed up. These fellows—we had a part of the regimental band—they took the drum head off and put the goat in the drum and tried [apparently successfully] to get him up and put him on board this train. You can't beat a bunch of Marines."[38]

In February Lieutenant Leo Hermle, now the platoon leader of 2nd Platoon, 74th Company, 1/6 was loaded aboard the *Von Stueben*. On the voyage Hermle was assigned to the depth-bomb watch, at the stern, but "We never had to let it go."[39]

The senior officers may have had their concerns, but for many enlisted Marines France was a source of wonderment. Literature professor Paul Fussell has described the 1914–1918 conflict as a "literary war", and Corporal H. W. Elliott was typical. In the throes of a February winter he wrote his father of arriving at a railway station that "This is truly a beautiful section of France, a beautiful spot in a beautiful country … As the minutes passed and the light of dawning day began to peep from behind the hills coloring the sky with the delicate touch of a master artist, we could see, away in the distance, a city of pine boards and tar roofing—our division headquarters in France … a welcome sight to our little group of hungry and boot-sore Americans."[40]

Not until February 10, 1918 was the brigade finally assembled as a unit (save one company still in England), and integrated training could commence. The Marines were first shipped to a training area in the infamous *quarante hommes ou huit chevaux*—40 men or eight horses—from a loading mark stencilled on the sides. The French boxcars reeked of horse manure and urine in the summer, and were drafty and cold in the winter. The only amenity was a thin layer of straw that covered the floor.

En route the Marines continued their incessant foraging. Erskine found that the NCOs had ways of making the officers complicit in this minor thievery. "While we were sidetracked, there was a big cask of wine … and a bunch of officials came down to Col. Lee, who was the senior officer present, and complained that somebody had stolen their wine. I was on the sidetrack there. He turned everybody out, called the officers together and said, 'Somebody has tapped the wine cart over there, and I want you to turn every man out and sample his canteen.'

"Well, they lined them all up, and I had my platoon out there, and every blessed man had the canteen full of white wine. And just as I was leaving the sergeant reached over to me and took mine out. I knew nothing about this thing. He pulled my canteen out and he said, 'You'd better check yours, Lieutenant.' Which I did, and *it* was full. Anyway I reported I didn't find any, and I think everybody reported the same thing. Nobody found any wine."[41]

The training continued to be haphazard at best. From the Fifth Marines the First Battalion for a period remained in St. Nazaire on Provost Marshal duty, while the Third Battalion was briefly shipped to England. Only the Second Battalion received a complete course of training with the 115e Bataillon de Chasseurs Alpin—the "Blue Devils" mountain troops—and some British instructors.[42]

The Marines found that many of the British and French ways of doing things were quite different. Wise described bayonet training: "according to the British instructors, you must put on a fighting face, grunt and curse as you lunged, and literally try to tear the dummy to pieces with the thrust. There was special instruction to bayonet them in the belly wherever possible. If you bayonetted a man you were chasing, you must get him through the kidneys and not in the rump. If your bayonet stuck, shoot it out. The British at that time were crazy about the bayonet. They knew it was going to win the war.

"The French were equally obsessed with the grenade. They knew *it* was going to win the war. So we also got a full dose of training in hand grenade throwing."[43]

The French instructed the Marines in a straight-armed over-hand throw of a grenade that flew in an arc, better suited to dropping the bomb into a trench. The Marines considered the technique girlish, and demonstrated a flat-trajectory baseball throw. The French were not amused. "You must land your bomb in the trenches—they do no more harm than the wind when they fly straight—and you must save your arm so that you can throw all afternoon."[44]

Period photos also depict American Marines demonstrating their rifle marksmanship techniques to the *chasseurs*. Marine emphasis of marksmanship was a source of some contention since European armies emphasized mass firepower.

Wise had placed old Sergeant Gallivan in charge of training some very green young lieutenants, members of Philadelphia society whom Wise had dubbed The Racquet Clubbers. When asked about their performance, Gallivan replied "They're doin' foine, sor. They ask for nothin' and they do as they're told. You'd never know they was gentlemin."[45]

Final training with the Blue Devils was in the harsh winter of 1917/1918 in the Vosges Mountains and their foothills east of Chaumont. Globally it was a record-breaking cold winter. Troops were billeted in several villages, the officers in homes, the men in stables (Erskine: "sometimes the old cow was in there with them"). By this period of the war the *chasseurs* had relinquished their distinctive dark-blue uniforms in favor of the sky-blue of the ordinary *poilu*. Graves Erskine: "I know that on many of the hikes we would have 40 pounds on our backs. We had a blanket but that didn't do much good high up in the Vosges Mountains. I remember more times than once I had icicles in my hair. We'd sleep on the ground."[46]

Shepherd recalled that "There is where the battalion trained all winter. We never saw the sun shine from October to the following March. Rain, snow, cold—I used to get so sick of the place."[47]

Even in billets conditions were severe, with each man allocated 2 kg of firewood per day for all uses including cooking and heating buildings.[48]

Gerald Thomas had benefited from rapid promotion, and was now a sergeant. He was more inured to harsh condition than many, yet distinctly recalled that "We were wet every day, had a miserable life in the training area. The place was icy cold. We didn't bathe very often because the only way you could bathe was to go out and get a bucket of water, stand in the snow, and take a bath. We worked on bayonet, fired grenades, and we hiked. We went on hikes from this camp out to a trench area. We'd be gone about twenty-four hours and go out and spend the night in the trenches until two o'clock in the morning, and then we'd march back to our camp. We remained in those little wooden barracks in Champigneulles from the eighth of January until the fifteenth of March. I couldn't imagine anything more calculated to toughen people. The outfit was so damn mean that they would have fought their own grandmothers." Trench foot, now called immersion foot, was a common affliction in World War I, and "Our feet were wet every night. We dried our socks by sleeping on them. That was the only way that we ever had dry socks. Our boots were cold and wet in the morning, but we put them on again.[49]

Battalion commander Frederick Wise described the routine: "The men got up at reveille in bitter cold. Breakfast. Extended order drill, hiking or rifle range, grenade-throwing, or bayonet work. The rolling kitchens always went with us. We ate where we happened to be at noon. After the meal the work went on. By three o'clock in the afternoon I always got them back to Damblain. They hadn't been near a fire since taps the night before. And that was a cold winter. From three o'clock until taps they could relax and warm up."[50]

After the original contingents were trained, some Americans were retained as instructors. Walter Gaspar was assigned to the Army's School of Musketry at Gondrecourt from October 1917 until May 1918. Gaspar finally escaped when Pershing issued an order that no one could be assigned to duty separate from his parent organization for more than five months.[51]

These separate assignments, sickness, and rapid expansion led to a serious shortage of junior officers. When men began to be commissioned from the ranks, First Sergeant Gallivan grew ambitious and asked Wise, his battalion commander, about a commission. Gallivan was too old, but Wise managed to have him appointed a warrant officer. But some old habits were hard to break. One day Gallivan walked in while a Captain Mike Harvis was breakfasting with Wise and another officer: "'Harvis,' he roared. 'Git on your hind legs! What do you mane by sittin' down with your betthers!'

"And Captain Harvis jumped! He had been a private under Gallivan when Gallivan was a sergeant, and the old authority stayed.

"Gallivan was a Godsend to the younger officers now that he could associate with them on a footing of equality. They looked upon him as an oracle."[52]

In January 1918 the Americans were also required to relinquish their beloved and reliable Lewis machine guns, ostensibly because these more reliable weapons were needed for the air services. The replacements were the Chauchat (pronounced sho-sho by the Americans) automatic rifle and the Hotchkiss heavy machine gun.

Training included the usual rounds of inspection, and by this time Rendinell had taken up chewing tobacco, but like many another, he soon found that chewing had its own hazards. In a morning formation "The lieut kept watching me close & I could not spit. My mouth was full & I wondered would he ever move. He stood right in front of us for about 20 minutes, pretending to give us a little lecture. He was watching me all the time. Finally I had to swallow it to get rid of it. Gee, I was sick for a couple of hours."

But he was learning that a good NCO has ways to strike back. "I told the sgt what happened in ranks the other day. He knew about it all ready because the lieut told him he was going to break me of the habit of chewing in ranks. Yesterday I had a wad in my mouth again and of course the lieut seen me. He stood right in front of where I was and watched me like a dog at a rat hole for about a ½ hour. He never took his eyes off me. I guess he wondered why I did not swallow that. Then he walked off. The wad in my mouth was paper this time."[53]

Bourmont was the prelude to the ultimate training, service in a quiet or *bon secteur* of the front. The Fifth Brigade functioned primarily as a replacement and labor pool and received essentially no advanced training once in France. This was in stark contrast to the 6 months or more of training received by their Army counterparts.

Even service in a *bon secteur* was fraught with danger. Artillery was used for random harassment fire. Alfred Noble: "Sometimes they'd drop a shell about every five minutes and let it go and then come in again in 15 minutes or half an hour, enough to keep you awake and worried. At other times they'd vary it by banging down with a whole battery at a time at some one place they'd found." This fire was intermixed with gas, and some areas like communication trenches were contaminated with mustard gas so that "you wouldn't want to walk through it if it were mustard, you had to climb out and walk around it some way, with your gas mask on … And it slowed things up."[54]

At no time was the brigade ever assembled as a whole, and most of its officers were on detached duty with other Army divisions.[55]

As it turned out these early arrivals in France received the best training, regardless of its shortcomings. The Fifth Brigade functioned primarily as a replacement and labor pool and received essentially no advanced training once in France. This was in stark contrast to the six months or more of training received by their Army counterparts. Later arrivals were thrown into the front lines as replacements with little or no additional training. Replacements and separate battalions continued to arrive until the end of the war, almost entirely carried by the three original transports. The transport USS *Pocahontas* made a single voyage to transport Marines in late October/early November 1918.[56]

In May of 1918 Lejeune finally received the coveted orders to ship out for France. Brigadier General Doyen had been ordered home for health reasons. But Lejeune was thwarted when Commandant Barnett showed him a telegram from Pershing, explaining that "Brigadier James G. Harbord, Chief of Staff of the American Expeditionary Forces, had succeeded him [Doyen] in command of the Marine Brigade, and that if a Brigadier General of Marines were sent to replace Doyen he would not be assigned to command the Marine Brigade, or any other front line unit, but would be detailed to duty behind the lines." Lejeune was a graduate of the Army's War College and was highly regarded by his Army peers, but Pershing was looking out for the careers of his Army subordinates.

Nevertheless, Lejeune accepted "as I would be much nearer the front in any part of France than I was at Quantico, and that if I got that far I felt sure I would be able to obtain a command at the front." One part of his mission would be to continue Barnett's thus far unsuccessful campaign to organize a full Marine division in France, something Pershing would continue to adamantly oppose.[57]

CHAPTER 4

Into the Lines—Les Eparges

Human nerves quickly get accustomed to the most unusual conditions and circumstances and I noticed that quite a number of men actually fell asleep from sheer exhaustion in the trenches, in spite of the roaring of cannon about us and the whiz of shrapnel going over our heads.

PRIVATE FRIEDERICH "FRITZ" KREISLER, AUSTRIAN ARMY

The final phase of each division's training was service in a quiet sector of the front. The Second Division drew the Toulon sector in Les Eparges, with the French 33e, 34e, and 52e Divisions d'Infanterie. To organize defensive zones along the front, and locate them on maps, the French divided the front into sectors. Each sector was given a codename such as "Toulon". Each sector was divided into three sub-sectors (originally one per infantry regiment to fit the triangular organization of the French infantry divisions). Each sub-sector was divided into two *centres de résistance* (centers of resistance), one per battalion, plus one in reserve.

Les Eparges was located southeast of Verdun and was the scene of violent fighting in February 1915. Now it was a *bon secteur*, and both the French and Germans had adopted a strong live-and-let-live attitude.

On March 14, 1918 the now-united brigade began movement from Bourdon to Les Eparges. The division staff would soon learn about the banes of the Great War—poor communications, limited mobility, and logistics. Logistics in a sense had started the war: once set into motion the intricate mobilization plans, controlled by railway logistics, of the combatant countries could not effectively be reversed. Once settled into trench warfare, communications and logistics prevented the combatants from breaking free of its grip. Both sides dreamed of a "breakthrough" and kept cavalry units in readiness to exploit a tactical victory. However, the intricate defensive systems, and most of all the massive artillery bombardments that pulverized roads and rail lines, and churned the earth itself into a mire meters deep, prohibited any exploitation. Even when a rupture of the enemy lines occurred, it was impossible to push supplies and ammunition across the wasteland, and attacks inevitably bogged down for lack of supplies.

Radio sets were bulky and unreliable, and of limited tactical value. Bombardments ripped apart telephone wire nets, and laying new lines was slow and hazardous. Most communication was by human runners, who slowly picked their way across the battlefield; many did not survive to deliver their messages. Carrier pigeons were commonly used, but were often killed or disoriented by the noise and chaos, so messages that did get through often arrived too late to be of practical use. Signals like rockets and flares were of limited value. Blinker lights were seldom useful in the smoke of combat, and semaphore flags were suicidal. It was not uncommon for commanders to have no clue where their units were, and sending aircraft to try and locate them was fairly common.[1]

The movement into the trenches at Les Eparges was typical. On March 16 the first units departed to the training area, their movement hampered by the language barrier between American troops and French railway personnel. Officers traveled in the relative comfort of passenger coaches. Enlisted men were crammed into the infamous *quarante hommes et huit chevaux* boxcars.

Advance parties for this routine movement arrived at Dugny and Souilly on March 14. The first units moved into the trenches in the pre-dawn hours of March 17. Joseph Rendinell recorded in his diary: "*March 15th*—Arrived at Dugny, ten kilometers from Verdun. We come up here in box cars. We were packed so tight it was hard to lay down & stretch our legs without shoving them in some guy's face and there would be an argument. Sgt Richardson would yell. 'Pipe down, you leathernecks' & that would end it for a while. My legs were so numb I could not stand up because 3 Marines laid on them.

"The first stop our train made I left the gang & went in a mule car where there was 8 mules & 5 of us marines. At least there was a little more room and this car had straw too & the marine car had nothing. In the morning we had hardtack & canned tomatoes for breakfast"[2]

The French military rail system was a source of puzzlement and sometimes frustration. For efficiency, the French had implemented what would one day be called unit trains, standardized blocks of cars set for a specific purpose. Brigadier James G. Harbord: "It takes fifty-eight trains to move an American division. All French military trains are exactly alike. They are kept standing on sidetracks ready to move out, and not broken up and scattered or used in the meantime as would be done by a rude railroad system in America. Theirs is most wasteful of cars and time but it has the advantage of having the trains ready when needed.... Their units of troops are different from ours in the proportions of animals to men and in some other particulars, so in using their trains for our troops' shipments we quite often have some empty cars, but they are carried along just the same."[3]

No provision was made for mixed trains of flatcars and boxcars, so in general men and animals traveled by train, while the division's motorized equipment, artillery, and other equipment traveled by road. This was a constant source of confusion, as road convoys were often misrouted or delayed, and troops often arrived hours or days before the heavier equipment—including water carts and field kitchens. In other cases the situation was reversed.

The arrival of a new division was not lost upon the enemy. Frederick Wise's 2/5 was the first to arrive, and did not realize the significance of the aircraft overhead. The French officer assigned as a guide told Wise, "Get out of here as quickly as you can. Those German planes are on reconnaissance work, and the first thing you know this damned place will be shelled." The Marines were quickly marched to a camp; that night the camp was shelled by heavy artillery, but without inflicting any casualties.

Wise was taken on a tour of the positions his battalion was to occupy, a series of strongpoints rather than continuous trenches. There were aprons of barbed wire, old and rusty. "I suppose it had been inactive so long everyone had become careless."

"It is a very, very quiet sector," said the French major. "Like being in rest billets. You'll have no trouble here. Occasionally the Germans stage little trench raids, and they shell every afternoon. But by common consent the men on both sides can climb out of the trenches and stretch their legs for half an hour before sunset without being fired on." There was even a narrow-gauge railway for bringing up supplies and ammunition. Though it was obvious and noisy, the Germans declined to shell it.[4]

Captain Wendell Westover belonged to the Army's 4th Machine Gun Battalion, a unit that would support both brigades as needed. A French officer asked if he would like to visit a forward observation post, so a small group of officers donned the clothing of French *poilus* to avoid being identified as Americans. Looking across a large crater, he saw "a Boche O.P. with the double sentries visible to their waists; thick-set, square-jowled, their ugly but efficient helmets covering their heads like ancient armor."

Westover drew his pistol, but a French sergeant intervened: "*Non, non! S'il vous plait! Prenez garde, mon capitaine.*" Westover outlined the Frenchman's clarity: "One or two less combatants meant nothing to the war. If this sort of thing commenced it would mean constant casualties in that advanced post, to no purpose. One Boche seemed to sense the debate. He held up his hand, raised five fingers, and shook his head, growing suspicious of the unusual number there. We turned and crawled back to the front line."[5]

In this sector the Marines suffered their first known "casualty" when a dud German shell punched a hole in the bass drum of the Fifth Marines band.[6]

The last train departed the training area on March 21, but all components of the Sixth Marines were not into the lines until March 22.[7]

The Marines were to study under French advisors, who quickly taught them what actual life in the trenches was like. Lieutenant Clifton Cates thought, "That was good training, too, because we got in patrolling and we had our baptism of artillery fire, and we got plenty of it, too."

Toul had been chosen for its inactivity, but according to Cates: "you know Americans. When they get in they get trigger happy and we started firing and they fired and they poured it on them."[8]

Corporal James Rendinell: "Each of us has his place in the trench & there are so many men assigned to each dugout and a guard at the entrance for gas duty. If he smells gas, he gives the alarm."[9]

William Rogers spoke rudimentary French and had been appointed as company interpreter, and was given the task of being the gas NCO. One night, "All of a sudden the siren went. Everybody held their breath and put on their gas masks and dashed out. We had a little Frenchman there with us as liaison. The Frenchman went out and he sniffed around, and said *pas de gaz*—no gas.... At that time if a gas alarm, a flare would show up down on the English Channel in about two hours. Somebody had to stop it someplace."[10]

Even in these rest and training sectors the two sides staged periodic raids, not for any real tactical purpose, but for training and to prevent the troops from becoming too lax in the eyes of senior officers.

Rendinell: "In the daytime hardly anybody is in the trenches and only lookouts 50 feet apart. They get relieved every hour. The rest of the boys stay under cover & kill cooties or write home or shoot craps. We never leave go of our rifles and ammunition belts.

"At 6 P.M. we stand to & every man is at his post till 10 o'clock. Then half the company goes in to the dugouts to rest and the others stay on watch but at 2 o'clock the whole outfit stands to till daybreak. Every man is on the firing-step in back of sand bags & we got men in listening posts out in front of our bobbed wire. Four men & a machine-gun & hand grenades." These listening posts were manned all night and it was not enviable duty. Raiders from the other side might pick off the occupants, and in the event of a larger attack they were quickly overrun.

"Gee, how long the night is. The lieut walks up & down the trenches to see everything is O.K. and the boys are all at their place. My eyes got sore looking out in No Man's Land. The bobbed wire posts & stumps of trees looked like they moved & many a time I let fly thinking they was Germans. The early morning hours is when a guy's morale is lowest & that is when the enemies send over their raiding parties."[11]

The watch for raiders was a primary task, as was launching the Marines' own raids to take prisoners. Lieutenant Lemuel Shepherd recalled that considerable emphasis was placed on front-line intelligence. "The two front lines were only a few hundred yards apart and troops manning front line positions were constantly on the alert to guard against a hostile surprise raid or attack ....

"I attended a Platoon Commander's course in the First Corps School at Gondrecourt, where great emphasis was placed on front-line intelligence. The British were good at this. We had a British instructor who placed a great deal of emphasis on observation of enemy movements...."[12]

Sergeant Gerald Thomas had been turned over to Lieutenant Carleton Burr of the 1/6 intelligence section for on-the-job training. After manning observation posts for about a month, "They wanted some training for our scouts so we laid on a patrol to move out from a little destroyed village named Tresavaux, which was down in the front of our battalion. This patrol was laid on principally because the Germans—realizing that there was a new outfit in front of them—wanted to get some prisoners and identify units. So they had been pushing patrols over against our wire, getting ready to make a raid. The French and our own people decided that we would counter this raid. A French officer came up and brought a patrol of about twenty-five soldiers. They were experienced in this kind of business, and this was part of our training. We brought up our fifteen scouts. I accompanied Burr, and we joined the French officer and laid out the patrol. We knew that the Germans were sending men over against our wire to listen there at night, and we were going to sweep out in front of the wire and trap some of them. It was a complicated maneuver, but we all understood what we were supposed to do.

"About midnight we started out from our lines passing through a gap in our wire. We were just starting to fan out when—zingo!—we crashed into a big German patrol. Both of us backed off, started shooting, and called for the defensive barrages that we had planned before. Well, we had a real rough night ... Burr got cut off, and I went back and got him and brought him back into our line. We had several men wounded and one of our men killed. We were very, very lucky."[13]

Hermle returned to his parent regiment after being sent away on separate school duty. "I hung around there two or three days until somebody could tell me where the 6th was." Eventually he was reassigned as Second Platoon Leader in Major Maurice Shearer's 73rd Machine Gun Company, where the most memorable character was First Sergeant Dan

Daly. Daly already had two Medals of Honor, from the 1900 Boxer Rebellion and fighting the Cacos in Haiti in 1915. Daly was one of the best-known characters in the Corps, and had a habit of referring to "his" lieutenants.

The company moved in and out of the front lines, supporting 3/6. Captain Dwight Smith's 82nd Company, 3/6, had suffered unusually heavy officer casualties and only Army officers were available as replacements, so Hermle was reassigned as Executive Officer.

Hermle was badly gassed, with burns on his crotch and feet, and sent to a French hospital, until he was discharged to a replacement battalion where he would remain for months.[14]

The quality of the weapons left a great deal to be desired. On March 28 the War Diary of 2/5 commented that "The [Hotchkiss] Machine Gun ammunition is in poor condition, there being 54 misfires out of 336 rounds fired."[15]

The Marines quickly learned what life in the trenches was like. Corporal Adel Storey (83rd Company, 3/6) wrote home that in the dreary weather "the trenches could not dry up. It is so muddy that I think I am getting web-footed. We are sure getting used to the noted mud of this country, for we eat in mud, sleep in mud, and live in mud, and if there is anything else to do, I guess we do it in mud too."

Captain Roy C. Hilton of the Ninth Infantry's Machine Gun Company wrote that "The dugouts were constructed to accommodate from ten to fifty men, depending on the importance of the particular part of the trench. Bunks were built with one section above another in the dugouts .... The depth of the dugout was from ten to forty feet. Nearly all dugouts were infested with lice, better known as 'cooties'. The soldiers' opinion of these little creatures expressed mathematically was 'They added to the soldiers' troubles, subtracted from his pleasures, divided his attention, and multiplied like Hell.'"[16]

In other letters Storey went on to describe "hot bunking" in the cramped dugouts built into the trench walls. "We have to take turns sleeping in this place, for we haven't enough places to sleep to accommodate all of us at once. One of the fellows is getting up now, so I think I'll go back to sleep for a little while before supper."[17]

Rats always profit from war, and the unburied or hastily buried dead, as well as scraps of food, led to a population explosion. Corporal Storey: "I don't know whether I have ever mentioned the rats which infest the trenches or not, but I know you have read of them in different places. Never in my life have I seen rats of such size as these are here. They don't run from us, either, like any ordinary rat does. They will fight like a good fellow when you fool with them. Where we are now there are several cats, and in the daytime they come into the dugouts and around where we are, but at night they stay out in No Man's Land. One of the fellows remarked the other night that this is the first time in his life that he had seen cats run away from home by the rats."[18]

James Rendinell was more graphic: "We can't lay down without them starting in to nibble at our legs. They are nice & fat from eating dead Frenchmen & Germans. Now they want American meat."[19]

Frederick Wise: "One of my men was bitten through the lips by a rat that started to make a meal off his face as the man slept. Those rats swarmed like cockroaches around our galleys. They didn't mind the men at all." Indeed, the rats seemed confident enough to utilize the Marines to their own ends. "I was walking down the trench one day when a rat on one side saw me come along. He waited until I got opposite him, leaped onto my shoulder and before I could knock him off, leaped to the other side of the trench. He had used me deliberately as a stepping-stone, to save him the trouble of crawling down to the bottom of that trench and climbing the other side."[20]

Numerous Marines wrote of how the aggressive rats willingly faced off to fight humans, bit sleeping men, scampered across their face while sleeping, noisily fought and mated in the walls, and often snuggled under their blankets on cold nights.

March 31 was Easter Sunday, and Rendinell's company was back in the reserve trenches after a "rest" period. He recorded in his diary that the officers received turkeys for dinner. But "Sweeny gets the cook by the name of John away from the kitchen to give him a drink of vin & I reached into the oven & grabbed one of those fine turkeys. Gee, it was hot. It burnt my fingers but I kept a hold of it & ran. So we boys had turkey too.

"The first real meal I've had since Christmas, where I really had enough to eat. Only wish now that I had a bed to sleep & a chance to take my clothes off for a real rest but no such luck. Mud & water & man-eating rats & cooties in a dugout—that is our hotel at the front."

In early April Rendinell's company was rotated back for another reserve period, but each night from April 2 through April 5 they hiked several miles back to the front lines to dig trenches and string barbed wire. Each day "my feet are all sore and when we get to our dugouts we fall down in the mud & sleep & wake up as stiff as a board. Our eyes are swollen & red from the cold and damp."

April 4 was a banner day: "Got 24 packs of cigarettes from home. I wonder how they got through the S.O.S. [Service of Supply] without being opened. I shared up with the boys. We have been smoking dry leaves off of the trees ..."[21]

In the cramped and unhealthy conditions, hygiene assumed a crucial role, not always appreciated by men who had always left the cleaning to wives and mothers—or just lived in squalor. Storey noted that one "Irishman" had not washed his mess kit in over a week, and his exasperated sergeant ordered him and others to wash their kit in a nearby stream—itself undoubtedly of dubious cleanliness. The stream was clearly visible to the enemy, and "while in the midst of their job, about a six- or eight-inch shell dropped beside them, about thirty yards away. They forgot their mess kits and everything else in their hurry to get away from that particular spot." The men returned for their gear after dark. "Pat says he isn't going to wash his mess gear again soon, if he is going to cause anything like that again."[22]

In the lines training consisted of a monotonous series of small actions that could still get a man killed or maimed. Most of these raids were petty things designed to capture prisoners or gain intelligence, sometimes only for general harassment. On the night of April 19/20 in a typical German raid directed at the 2/5's positions, "They were discovered coming through the wire and fired upon by rifles and machine guns. This fire was not heavy enough to cause them to stop. They came on until close enough to our lines to throw hand grenades, by this time our fire was thicker and more effective, some of them reached our line and then the whole party withdrew. Fire with rifles, auto-rifles, pistols, and machine guns were kept up until all were out of range. Machine gun barrage was continued for several minutes." The fracas evolved into the usual exchange of artillery fire, and "A French observation post to the north reported that a number [of Germans] were seen carried across no man's land by their comrades." Two German officers and a corporal were found dead, and a dying private captured. "Our casualties in this encounter are Company L (45th) two killed and ten wounded, all enlisted men. One man was killed and two wounded by shell fire in Company I (16th)."

On the same night a patrol of a lieutenant and thirty men from Company E (28th Company) 2/5 was sent out with the battalion intelligence officer, Lieutenant August L. Sundvall, to establish an ambush in an area where Germans had been observed moving about. The patrol somehow separated into two groups and both got lost. One blundered into contact with a large German work party repairing a trench. In Sundvall's group "A member of the group Sergeant Parks who speaks German warned the others that they were near a German working party as he heard the language being spoken and noises made by tools. They kept on and suddenly came upon the enemy and were challenged." The patrol dropped to the ground and both sides waited it out. Finally Sundvall gave the order to withdraw. "As soon as this movement was started fire from machine guns was opened and grenades were thrown." Lieutenant Sundall [spelling discrepancy in original document] and a private were wounded, a gunnery sergeant and a private wounded and missing. With the gunny and the officer in charge wounded or missing, the indefatigable Parks was sent to find and bring up Lieutenant Fred H. Becker, the company officer. The reunified patrol encountered a friendly patrol from Company F (43rd) and returned with them.[23]

This incident illustrates the difficulty of unraveling old events. This was the only such incident recorded in the battalion records and by Wise, and there are discrepancies. Wise later recalled that the Marine patrol was to break up German efforts to dam a small stream, thereby creating an additional obstacle along their front, and to take prisoners. When the patrol was detected by the Germans, the German-speaking sergeant "reported that the Germans had been ordered to drop their tools and go get their guns. Instead of attacking at that moment, the officer attempted to withdraw the patrol. The Germans, about a hundred strong, came back with their guns and opened fire. The officer was shot. Under the sergeant's commands, those twenty men held their ground and shot it out with the Germans. The Germans beat it. The sergeant picked up his officer and ordered the patrol to return to our trenches."[24]

The increasingly aggressive actions of the Americans invited retaliation, making the *bon secteur* increasingly hazardous. Wendell Westover described how one night a visiting general just had to see the front lines. "When he finally reached an advanced observation post he addressed the sentry on duty with a bellow that must have startled the Boche in his reserve positions.

"AND WHAT IS THIS?"

"The reply was a low whisper. 'Listening post number eight, Sir.'

"'WELL, WHERE ARE THE BOCHES?'

"The sentry pointed. 'Right over there, Sir.'

"'AND HOW FAR AWAY ARE THEY?'

"Again a whisper. 'About twenty meters, Sir.'

"'-----ooooooh.' The voice was well subdued now, and the General withdrew to visit the supply trains in rear of the artillery."[25]

The Marines were also finding that lack of such simple devices as a way to warn of gas attacks was resulting in major casualties. Photographic evidence indicates sirens (mostly in base or headquarters areas) with units in the line forced to use such improvisations as salvaged church bells. The regimental chemical officer of the Sixth Marines reported that "Several men were gassed due to the fact that the enemy were force [*sic*] to keep on their contaminated clothing. It was impossible to get even a change of under clothes. It is strongly recommended that at least 5% additional clothing be kept in the Aid Station. Insufficient alarm devices thought to be the cause of men not getting respirators on in time .... Impossible to clean contaminated clothing due to lack of chemicals, or apparatus."[26]

Units were periodically rotated out of the lines, and when in rest areas whiled away their time building or improving the muddy roads, digging reserve trenches, and other duties.

Despite the raids and chemical attacks, the time spent in the Toul sector was primarily one of monotony. On April 7 the War Diary of the Sixth Machine Gun Battalion recorded an unusually active night. "Front line trenches. Ammunition: M.Gun 57713, pistol 10505. Ammunition expended 972 rds. at moving forms in front of wire at M.G. position #12 at 1:45 A.M. Enemy artillery active. Private Claude E. Brinker 108389 wounded in action by enemy shells about 6:30 A.M. 4-6-18. Sent to Battalion Headquarters for further transfer to Hospital."[27]

Rendinell went on at some length to describe front-line economics. He lost his last nine packs of cigarettes gambling, borrowed some money, and by a series of machinations amassed a small fortune of 2,300 francs. With no way to spend it and no way to send it home, he eventually arranged to get a pass and hiked nine miles to a rear area where he bought out the contents of a French store. He lugged the booty back to the front lines and shared the largesse with his friends: candy, cakes, and a crate of unidentifiable canned goods that turned out to be fish roe. "Awful salty but tasted fine. A guy that eats them should stick around a pump for a couple of days."[28]

John Rendinell: "*May 5*—We got a green lieutenant here, first time up. Say, he sure was nervous first night. At every little noise we was ordered to fire. We liked that, so last night we tied cans on our bobbed wire with a rope leading back to the trench and when he come by we pulled the rope. Well, he listened a minute then he yells 'The Germans are coming, Fire at will' & he ran and lit a flare. It was the wrong flare. It called for the artillery to increase its range when they was not even firing. The enemies opened up on us with machine guns then. I wonder what they thought of us crazy Americans."[29]

A few days later Rendinell volunteered for a scouting party to infiltrate German ground, described in a letter: "The funny part of it was, before I left they asked me if I had made out a will.... Some of the boys said, 'Joe, I'll take your razor and toilet kit.'"

All day the men studied their route from an observation post. "I was armed to the teeth with a trench knife, a .45 with 28 rounds, two hand grenades. At a certain hour over we went, the boys wishing us good luck. We got through our wire by crawling over and under it. Some places we cut through. While I was cutting through one wire I made a little noise & Gee, it seemed to me it sounded clear to Berlin. We crawled on our hands & knees & stomack, so finely we got to where we were going and laid there.

"We listened to what the Fritzies were doing. Everything quiet, so we started back & on our way back Fritz cut loose with a machine gun. Oh boy, I stretched out on the ground and tried to look like a piece of sheet iron. Some of those bullets did not miss us a foot & had me talking to myself for a minute."

The party returned safely. "So next morning I got a big fruit cake from Sister Mary. One of the boys said, 'Too bad you came back, Joe, I could have eat that cake myself.' Well, anyhow, I gave all the boys a piece. I believe I crawled on my hands and knees just over 900 yards. Well Dom old boy I had my experience. I would not take a thousand dollars for it."[30]

Following the front-line training, on May 6 the brigade moved to a training area near Vitry-le-Francois for training in open warfare. Marine Corps Brigadier General Doyen was relieved due to poor health on May 6 and invalided back to America. Army Brigadier James G. Harbord replaced Doyen because there was as yet no Marine officer of suitable rank in France, but Harbord proved to be an advocate for the Marines.

Back in the training areas the troops were billeted in whatever shelter survived, and there was inevitable fraternization with French civilians. First Lieutenant Gordon L. McLellan, attached to Camp Hospital 26: "Most of us are beginning to be able to speak some French. Opportunities are good when you are quartered in billets. Billets are either homes, barns, lofts etc. No men are quartered in tents. Officers draw real rooms. Swell beds of feathers but minus the bird. Fireplaces and all conveniences except baths, running water, etc. The enlisted men have ticks furnished them with straw, and with their own blankets, form a very comfortable bed. They are in attics, lofts, sheds, caves, etc. Dry and protected. Our quarters at the present are in the hospital, but I am talking about the army."[31]

Sunday, May 12 was Mother's Day and a nostalgic 17-year-old Lewis A. Holmes wrote home that "I did not appreciate, at least to a certain extent, my beautiful home, and most of all you, Mother. But for the last year, I have experienced the greatest part of my life, and have learned one of life's lessons, and that is the value of a home and a mother."[32]

On May 14 the brigade began the move to another training area near Gisors-Chaumont-en-Vixen; champagne was four francs a bottle, and the men had their first bath in weeks. Rendinell: "our company took its much needed baths, washed clothes & had the run of the town....

"We went into the village wash house where they wash all their clothes & took a bath. Along came some French women to wash their clothes.

"'Hand me my pants. Gimme that shirt quick.'

"Not necessary. They didn't pay us no attention. We are supposed to be shock troops & we didn't shock them at all."[33]

The Marines were marched through a series of towns, and in one Rendinell and others "paid four (4) franc for a feather bed. Sgt. Crow, Joe Rumbler and myself got supper, four bottles of wine for three franc & we all slept in the feather bed & could not sleep at all, not being use to it."[34]

Individuals also profited from relations struck up with the local civilians. Private W. H. Coughlin wrote home reassuringly that "Every morning I get a pint of milk at 8 o'clock from a French woman, right fresh from the cow and still warm, and also I drink two fresh raw eggs each day to aid in my strength. You can imagine how strong I am when I stick a 42-mile hike out without dropping out, as some of the men did nearly twice as big as I am." (This unfinished letter was found on the body of Coughlin, killed in action at Belleau Wood.)[35]

The occupation of the *bon secteur* was to be short. Hasty orders came for the division to move quickly to the Château-Thierry area. The Germans had broken through the Anglo-French armies in one of five massive summer offensives, and every formation—regardless of readiness—was urgently needed to plug the gaps.[36]

In Les Eparges the brigade's single motor vehicle, a Model-T truck donated by civilians, was used relentlessly and seemed ready for the scrap heap. Major Frank Evans: "And the Ford which Mrs. Pearce gave us will go down in Marine Corps history, at any rate. That 'Elizabeth Ford,' as the Regiment knows her, has had a unique career. Not only in Quantico, where I drove her, but in Bordeaux, and later up in our training area, she carried everything from sick men to hardtack. Then we had two months in the trenches near Verdun, and at the end of it it seemed as though she would have to go to the scrap heap. Her top was entirely gone, and we made a mail wagon of her. In some way the men, who have an affection for her that you can hardly comprehend, patched her together and we brought her down to our rest billets. A week later we had to go to another area [Belleau Wood], forty kilometers north of Paris, and in the long line of motor cars that made the trip the Elizabeth Ford sailed along without mishap and was the talk of the Division."[37]

CHAPTER 5

Belleau Wood

... we had the whole history of the Corps behind us, and what a Marine has he holds; he kills or gets killed; he does not surrender; he does not retreat.

ALBERTUS CATLIN, SIXTH MARINES

In the spring of 1918 the Germans began their *Kaiserschlacht* (Kaiser's battle), sometimes called the Ludendorff Offensive, a series of offensives designed to end the war before the full weight of American resources could make itself felt, striking in Arras (March 21) and Flanders (April 9). The third of these offensives, Operation Blucher-Yorck, was tardy and commenced on May 27.

The Germans were also introducing their new *sturmtaktik*, emphasizing close support by artillery, rapid movement, and fluid attacks that bypassed centers of resistance.

The Allied front was held by six battered British and several French divisions. The worst miscalculation was the decision by the commander of the French Sixième Armée, General Denis Auguste Duchêne, to defend forward positions without reserves in the case of an attack. A massive bombardment and two reinforced German armies pushed the French, outnumbered four to one, off a sector of the Chemin des Dames Ridge. Parts of the French and British armies withdrew in good order, but by May 29 the Germans had driven more than 40 km through five lines of defense, captured the transport nexus at Soissons, and were driving rapidly south. French resistance and counterattacks managed to save the crucial road nexus at Reims, but the divisions were too spent to exploit even that local success.

The German advance was slowing only because their very successes had created enormous logistical problems, but higher French commands estimated that it would take two weeks to assemble a force capable of halting the enemy. All in all, the Germans were on the verge of winning a stunning victory, capped by the probable capture of Paris.

The next logical place to halt the German advance was the small town of Château-Thierry where several bridges crossed the Marne River, at that point channelized between high masonry walls. With few organized units to throw into the path of the enemy, General Pétain requested the use of the untested American Second and Third divisions. (By a peculiar agreement signed on April 9 by each of the contentious Allied leaders—including Pershing—French Marshal Ferdinand Foch was in overall direction of Allied strategy. But each senior commander reserved the right to appeal to his own government if the Allies took measures that, in his opinion, jeopardized the safety of his command.)

Given the rapid German advance and uncertainty as to where the axis of the offensive actually lay, considerable confusion reigned in the Allied command structure as to where the American divisions were to be committed. The only thing that was known was that logically the Third Division was approaching from the east, the Second from the vicinity of Paris. Thus the Second Division was originally to deploy to the western face of the German salient that now pointed directly at the area between Château-Thierry and the Orcq River.

The looming battle would play a pivotal role in the history of the Corps, and is often referred to as "the birth of the modern Marine Corps". The battle would be fought out in a complex terrain of jumbled rocky hills, grain fields interspersed with dense woodlands, and villages. Units, both American and German, were thrown piecemeal into battle and stumbled into each other, often with no clear front. As a result the battle was both spatially and temporally complex, and numerous books have been written on the struggle.[1]

The orders committing the Fourth Brigade found men scattered all about the countryside. Sergeant Thomas had been returned to the 75th Company, 1/6, when the intelligence sections were "stupidly" disbanded. Some of his old comrades were billeted a few miles away. "Taking a couple of the boys in the platoon that I was fond of, original members, we walked over there. We found some chow at noon and went to the memorial service and then started back down the road. On the road a messenger caught up with us. He said, 'We're getting ready to move, and they want everybody to come back immediately.' I beat it on back, and I went to see Redford. He said, 'We're moving out tonight, and I want you to be sure that everybody has a hundred rounds of ammunition and that they have their reserve rations and that they draw enough food to last them a day for travel.'"[2]

Even as the Second Division marched forward, breasting a tide of refugees and broken French units, orders from General Duchêne, a rigid martinet who was now in over his head, kept changing. Units marched and counter-marched, and the worst confusion lay in the highway through Meaux. Even regimental commanders like Colonel Albertus Catlin searched for their troops who had been hastily rerouted along unfamiliar roadways.

Frederick Wise had managed to receive several liberties to visit his wife at her apartment in Paris, where she was working for an aid agency. They were dining with friends when the phone rang. "That call is for me," said Wise, perhaps joking. On the other end was his adjutant: "We've been ordered up to the front at once. The camions will be waiting here at five o'clock in the morning."

Wise was in a hell of a fix. He had sent his colonel's borrowed car back to Courcelles, north of Paris. Fortunately his interpreter, a Private Coutra of the French Marines,[3] had been brought along and was at his home in Paris. At the hospital where his wife worked, Wise, with Coutra's help, was able to borrow an ambulance. Driving through an air raid, the small party arrived at Courcelles with minutes to spare and found the battalion lined up and waiting for the trucks. Once in motion, "I learned from the French transport officer that we were not going up to relieve the First Division on the Somme [as planned]. He didn't know what our final destination was. All he knew was that we were to report at Meaux for final orders. I had heard back in Paris rumors of a new break in the Allied lines, and a report that the German drive was headed for a place called Chateau Thierry." Sergeant William Rogers vividly recalled that General Preston Brown, division Chief of Staff, "was standing at the crossroads in this little town directing traffic. So we stayed there that night, [amid] much pandemonium."[4]

On May 30 Joseph Rendinell was transferred to the Intelligence Section of 3/6, and at 1800 h on the same day the brigade received orders to march toward the front. The troops slept in the open that night and early on the morning of May 31 the first *camions* picked them up for a grueling road march of up to 33 hours.

Eventually the Marines would come to realize that a truck ride was a bad sign. "The long caravan of camions took a route that brought us close to Paris. The people in these small villages ran out & yelled 'The Americans are coming.' Most of these people never seen American marines & soldiers in great numbers as there were now, miles & miles of camions all loaded with American soldiers. We were kidding & joking with them as if we were on a picnic. Children were yelling '*Vive l'Amerique.*'

"On the edge of Meaux we seen refugees. The roads were crowded with them. A steady stream of carts with the few belongings they could take along. Some of the peasants pulled their carts themselves because they did not have any cattle. Old women & young women with babies at their breasts. Children hung on to their skirts & they all looked tired & were crying. Hundreds of them knelt on the side of the road when they seen us go by & prayed for us. It sure was a pathetic scene. We were not laughing now like we were before. This was the saddest procession I ever seen."[5]

"Nobody knew where the Germans were," said Alfred Noble. "The French would just say '*En bas*' ["below"—poor grammar, and perhaps a false memory] and so forth and shake their hands … and away they would go. You couldn't get any of them to talk. So we marched down there for quite a while and came to a place called Triangle Farm. Where we turned to the left …."[6]

Major Frank E. Evans was the adjutant of the Sixth Marines: "Then, as we neared Meaux, we saw our first fugitives on a road that was a living stream of troops in camions, guns, and trains hurrying to the front. And the refugees went straight to the heart of us. When you saw old farm wagons lumbering along with the chickens and geese swung beneath in coops, laden down with what they could salvage, cattle driven by boys of nine or ten years, little tots trotting along at their mothers' skirts, tired out, but never a tear or whimper, saw other groups camping out on the road for the night, there was the other side, the side that I think fired the men to do what they did later. I saw one wagon coming along towering to the top with boxes and mattresses, and on the top mattress was a white-haired old lady who would have graced any home, dressed in her best, and with a dignity that blotted out the crude load and made you think of nothing but a silver-haired old lady, who was the spirit of a brave people that met disaster with dignity." Evans consoled himself with the thought that the *camions* would pick up refugees on the return trip.

Evans went on to describe "troops on foot and in the lumbering camions. French dragoons trotting by them with their lances at rest and the officers as trim as though they had just stepped out of barracks; trains, ambulances, guns from the 75's to the 210's, staff cars whizzed by, and a trail of dust that coated the men in the camions until they looked like mummies."[7]

Fritz Wise of 2/5 was amazed to see "a couple of steam road rollers marked 'Soissons', so I knew the Germans had broken through there."[8]

The march was marred by incidents when the exhausted drivers fell asleep at the wheel and the *camions* veered off the road or into ditches. The situation was chaotic, orders changed constantly, and units were redirected hither and yon. Colonel Albertus Catlin, CO of the Sixth Marines, considered himself "a lost Colonel, hunting around in the dark for his command, and hunting with an anxiety that, in this crisis, approached panic."[9]

The Marines were directed onward, but there was no information, no plan. Wise encountered his brigade commander, General James G. Harbord, who told him "The French are not able to hold them. The Second Division is to be thrown in to back up the French, but when and just where I don't know now. We'll be out of here in the morning."[10]

Walter Gaspar had been told he could apply for a commission after 2 years' service back in 1912, but it never came to pass. Free of his training duties, in the midst of the confusion, he somehow located his 76th Company of Johnny "The Hard" Hughes's 1/6. Catching up with his company at midnight, the next morning the company CO

"Captain Stowell looked at me and said, 'You're supposed to be a second lieutenant!'

"Captain, it's news to me!" With that he was assigned as a platoon leader, though a gunnery sergeant.[11]

June 1

Around midnight the first troops disembarked from the *camions* and tried to get some rest, but other units were still wandering the roads until well into the next afternoon. At the headquarters of General Degoutte, the French XXI Corps commander, General Harbord was advised that the Fourth Brigade should get some rest, but be ready to go into action on a moment's notice.

At Degouette's headquarters the familiar row was renewed, with the French general eager to throw the American battalions into action piecemeal (a practice which had squandered his own reserves), and the Americans who planned to wait until the divisions could fight as a whole. In truth, there was as yet no coherent plan as to how the Americans were to be used except to act as a reserve for French troops. Sergeant Thomas, 75th Company 1/6: "My platoon commander told me as much as he knew, that we were moving toward the front. We were near the village of Montreuil-Aux-Lions. We moved several miles … on either side in squad columns. We kept on moving forward, and in all we moved about five miles. We came to a village, and were moved over into an assembly area. My platoon was kept together. I don't know where the rest of the company was. There was shooting. There was action. We saw the French falling back.

"For the next three days we shuffled around in that area."[12]

Out on the roads the Marines could hear the grumble of artillery, and German planes overhead dropping the occasional bomb. Rendinell: "The French were retreating. Thousands of them passed us & only the French rear guards were checking the Germans till the main body could beat it. As they went by they shook their heads & said Good bye to dear Paree. They felt sure it was all over now. The situation was mighty bad, at that. A few more miles and the Boches could shell Paris. We were ordered to move & support position in back of the French."[13]

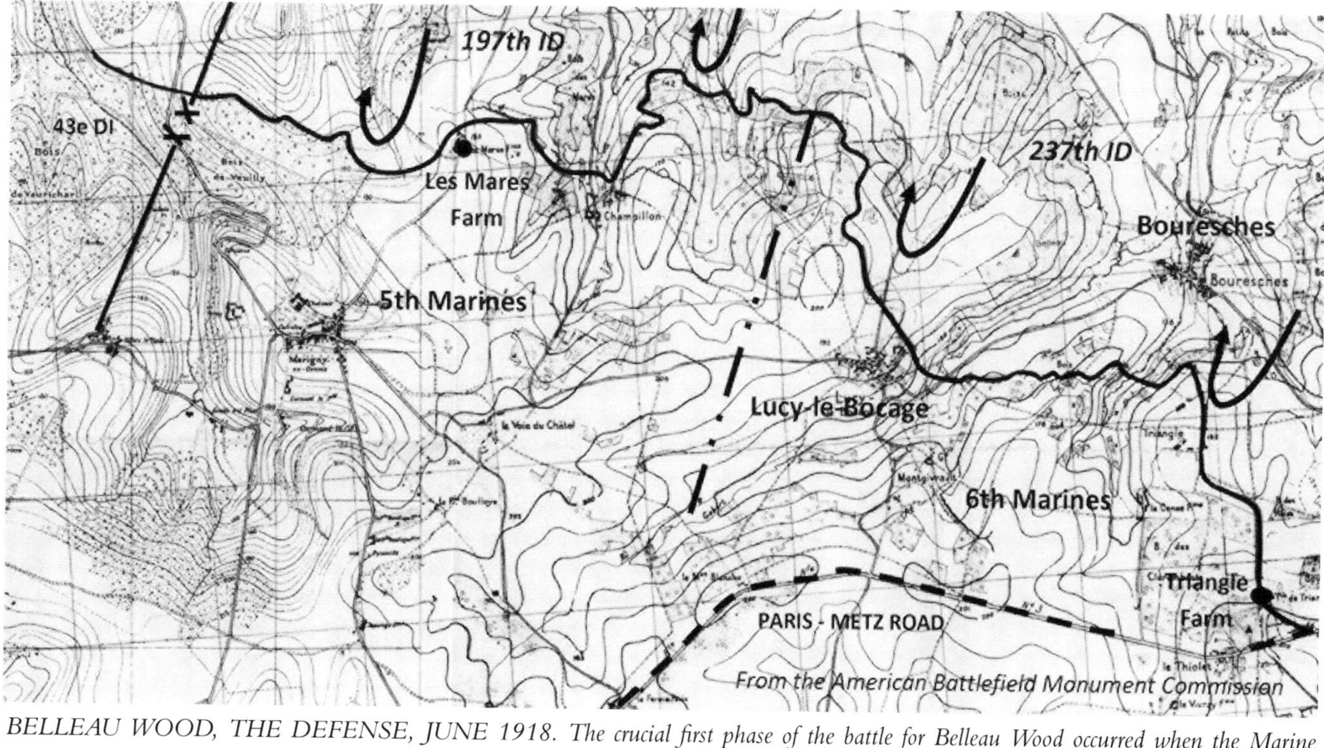

BELLEAU WOOD, THE DEFENSE, JUNE 1918. The crucial first phase of the battle for Belleau Wood occurred when the Marine Brigade, although rushed into action and poorly organized, halted the advance of two German divisions and elements of a third just short of the critical Paris–Metz highway.

Roland McDonald's view was more charitable. "I saw the French coming through with their 75s with six horses, like the chariot race of *Ben Hur*, racing across the field; and a couple of horses would get shot and they'd cut the horse off and they'd continue on with what they had. There was a lot of courage in the French people even those who were retiring.... And those who were going back, I'm sure, had just as much as we had, only they were a little bit weary of the whole setup...."[14]

Major Frank Evans: "the French told us, the Boche guns had got up in small numbers and that in their fights the Boche had fought with machine guns, a prodigious quantity of them, and grenades."[15]

The French were wary of the untested Americans, but General Harbord said, "Let us fight in our own way and we'll stop them." The Fifth Marines had one battalion in the reserve line, the Sixth Marines on their right with two battalions on line and the French to their right of the Sixth Marines. The men were thrown in incompletely equipped, digging fighting positions with their bayonets, with mess kits for shovels.[16]

The Germans were flush with success, and attacked the battered French with renewed energy. The French were tired of retreat, and remnants of four French regiments put up a stubborn resistance in the woods. General Joseph Degoutte held the Americans in reserve to defend last-ditch positions blocking the Germans from cutting the Paris–Metz highway. The French 43e Division d'Infanterie was ordered to counterattack, and "The American troops will maintain AT ALL COSTS the line of support they occupy .... They will not participate in the counter-attack which will be made to retake the positions of the French."[17]

Instead the Germans pre-empted the French attack, shoving them back. Yet the French counterattack had bought precious time.

Corporal Rendinell, 97th Company, 3/6: "The Germans made another attack on the French, who were forced back through our lines." In fact the French withdrawal was a rearguard action, and the Marine positions were to become the new front line. The withdrawal did necessitate an extension of the Marine lines: the Sixth Marines put three additional companies on line to hold a seven-kilometer front, with only one company as a reserve.[18]

In fact, the confusion was a much worse problem than the extended frontage. Frederick Wise's 2/5—directly in the path of the oncoming enemy—was strung out along a four-kilometer front from the Bois de Leiully, past Les Mares Farm to near Hill 142, with both flanks in the air. The poor maps were of little help and added to the confusion, and even with modern maps the positions are often indecipherable from the period communications. On the left 2/5 was not in contact with anyone. The battalion line ran about four kilometers to a point "about 1 km north of Champillon" that would place it opposite Hill 142. Yet Major Maurice Shearer of 1/6 reported that although he was not in contact with 2/5's right, his line ran from Hill 142, in an L-shaped line to the village of Lucy-le-Bocage. Most likely Shearer's scouts had mistaken the northern extension of Hill 176 for Hill 142; whatever the reason, there was a dangerous 1-km gap opposite Germans advancing through the Bois St. Martin west of Belleau Wood. From there 2/6 held a thin line through Triangle Farm, thence back to the highway. The brigade's Sixth Machine Gun Battalion was spread out all along the line. In the pre-dawn hours two companies from the Army's Second Engineers arrived to help construct positions. The 3/6, 1/5 and 3/5 were in support positions two kilometers south of Lucy-le-Bocage.

Another major issue was that deployment of the Sixth Machine Gun Battalion—a crucial factor in holding any defensive line—was flawed. A and B companies were positioned from south of Hill 142 to Lucy-le-Bocage; like Wise's and Shearer's battalions, the machine guns had left the gap undefended, and Wise was completely unsupported. On the east, C and D companies were spread along a line from the Paris–Metz road, through Triangle Farm to a point west of Lucy-le-Bocage, supporting both the 2/6 and the Army's 2/23 on the east.[19]

On the far right in the Army's 9th Infantry sector men were actually preoccupied with foraging, but units were subjected to German artillery fire. The commander of the 79th Company was wounded in the throat and evacuated.[20]

The new troops were eager to fight, and from their position south of the main highway aggressively sniped at the Germans south of Bouresches. Cates: "the railroad embankment was about six hundred yards away and there was a woods up behind that and they'd send men all day long up this railway embankment out to the woods evidently for supplies. We soon stopped that. We'd pick them off at six or eight hundred yards there. In fact, I got so I had three other good shots and we'd lie down and we'd fire every time we saw one man.[21]

June 2

On May 30 elements of the German 36th Division had crossed the Marne at Château-Thierry. On June 2 the French and the American Third Division drove the enemy back across the river, and in heavy fighting stalled the German offensive. The Germans would continue to batter at Château-Thierry, but thwarted at the bridges they gradually shifted their main attack 13 km to the west, threatening the Paris–Reims highway (the modern French A4 motorway though it has been partially rerouted) south of Bouresches and Lucy-le-Bocage. From there it would be 82 km along a major highway to the Eiffel Tower. The Germans were halfway to their goal of knocking France out of the war. There was a growing, mad scramble to find troops to throw into the German path.

Units of the Third Brigade, supported by French artillery, were by now moving into positions to back up the crumbling French line. The arrival was in the nick of time: the German Korps Contra launched a major three-division attack (the 10., 37., and 197. Infanterie Divisions)[22] across a broad front extending from Château-Thierry west to the village of Gandelu, then west of the town of Belleau. As the Germans advanced, they everywhere met surprising resistance from disorganized French units. Enemy penetration threatened the rear of the 164e Division d'Infanterie, forcing its retreat from Belleau Wood.

The Germans continued to push south and west and the battered French formations could stand no more; French stragglers were beginning to filter through the brigade positions. Little mention is made of the tentative German attacks, though the Report of Operations of the Sixth Machine Gun Battalion reported being engaged in both the Bouresches and Hill 142 sectors.[23]

At about 1100 h Colonel Wendell Neville arrived at the 2/5 headquarters position, and briefed Wise from a map: "The French are holding from the railroad on your front, but we don't expect them to stick. If you don't hurry up, the Germans will get there before you do. When you get there, you stick. Never mind how many French come through you."[24]

This was actually one of the moments of greatest peril for the Allies. The defense on the west was poorly organized, and an attack that breached the Les Mares Farm line would carry the Germans past Marigny (the modern village of Marigny-en-Orxois) and onto the main highway some three and a half kilometers west of Lucy-le-Bocage. The 2/5 would anchor the brigade's western flank, an extended position from near Hill 142 northwest to the Bois de Veuilly. The battalion would be spread thin along a four-kilometer front. Fortunately the problem with the machine-gun deployment was realized. C Company thinned and extended its line to the east, freeing up six guns from D Company to assist Wise.[25]

Battalion CO, Frederick Wise: "I established my P.C. [Post of Command] in the open, on the edge of the town [Marigny], against the cemetery wall. Company by company the battalion spread out .... Over to the left and out in front was Les Mares Farm, rising ground, dotted with clumps of woods, with grain fields and here and there, tall hedges. The ridge in front of my P.C. fell away on either side into level fields ...."

At about 1700 h the enemy launched a final push against French positions north of Les Mares Farm, and probed the 2/5 positions.

Orders were vague. Lieutenant Lemuel Shepherd of Wise's 55th Company pushed part of the company out onto a topographic nose that had a commanding view of the terrain over which the enemy must advance, with orders to withdraw in the face of an attack. Shepherd grew uneasy about the outpost, and with his runner moved through the German barrage to check on them. There he also found a composite group of *chasseurs* still holding. He found his own outpost was fighting off a local attack. "There were several trees on top of the knoll and I leaned against one of them where I could look over the top of the little knoll and could direct the fire of the men on the outpost on the advancing Germans. All of a sudden, something hit me in the neck and swung me around, completely around. My first thought was, my God, a bullet's gone through my gullet. I was gulping like this, you see. Funny what you do. I spit in my hand to see if I was spitting blood but I wasn't spitting blood, so then I felt relieved. We remained in this position till just about dusk when we could safely withdraw as we'd accomplished our mission. We'd held the Germans up and caused several casualties by our well-aimed fire. By nightfall, the Germans were working around our position within a couple of hundred yards of us and we weren't strong enough to hold out there by ourselves all that night, so we withdrew and brought back a couple of the men who had been wounded. We brought them safely back to our lines. I put a dressing on my wound in the neck and that night I went back to the dressing station and had my wound dressed. They wanted to evacuate me but I said, 'Hell no, it isn't bad.' It just cut a groove through my neck. It just missed my jugular vein by a quarter of an inch."

When orders arrived to withdraw back to the main line, the French commander implored Shepherd not to withdraw, but orders were orders.[26]

Now the French were retreating in a growing flood. Captain Lloyd Williams's 51st Company was the extreme right of 2/5's line. He sent a runner to Wise with an ominous message: "All French troops on our right have fallen back, leaving a gap." Williams had sent scouts to establish contact with the Sixth Marines, but the scouts reported going a mile without establishing contact.

To the south the Sixth Marines were still trying to locate Williams's company. Both battalions had been instructed to occupy Hill 142. The Marines were utilizing a few older French maps, and between that and the difficulty of identifying one low hill among many, *neither* had actually occupied Hill 142. The position of Sixth Marines was actually stepped back westward from the right of the 2/5 line.

On the left Captain Lester Wass's company could not locate the 23rd Infantry. The only help Wise could find were the remnants of the Bataillons de Chasseurs à Pied on each flank, and two French 75 mm field gun batteries still blasting away.

No rations came forward, the men had eaten their emergency rations, and refused to eat the rancid French canned "monkey meat" (corned beef hash).[27]

What happened next is a fundamental part of Marine Corps lore, but the precise circumstances are confused. An exhausted French major encountered Williams's second in command, and after a brief argument scribbled down a written order to retreat. When Williams was given the message he retorted, "Retreat, hell! We just got here!" Others would later claim credit for the famous words, but at 0310 the next morning Williams dispatched a message to Colonel Wise: "The French Major gave Captain Corbin written orders to fall back—I have countermanded the order. [28]

June 3

At dawn Wise made his way to his far left flank in the Bois de Veuilly and quizzed Captain Wass. "While we were standing there the Germans began to shell the Bois de Veuilly. Right over my head a shell burst. I saw a Marine a few feet away crumple up. A shell fragment had torn away his thigh. The shells kept coming. One struck a big tree that flew in splinters. Those splinters were as deadly as the shell fragments themselves. They killed and wounded several men." Wise made his way back to Les Mares Farm to find the French major commanding the survivors of the 1e and 31e Bataillons de Chasseurs à Pied. "'It looks blue,' he told me. 'The whole German army has broken through. I don't think we will be able to stop them. What are you going to do?'

"'Our orders are to stick,' I told him."

"He shrugged his shoulders."[29]

No continuation of the feared German attack materialized. For the remainder of the day the Germans contented themselves with shelling the Marine positions with heavy artillery, setting the village of Marigny ablaze. The Germans were also industriously fortifying the rocky, forested hills, while the Marines reorganized their defense and brought up the Second Division artillery, food, ammunition, and precious water.

The Germans maintained air superiority, and their reconnaissance and observation planes operated with confidence and near impunity. Private John A. Hughes, Battery C, 15th Field Artillery, was in a convoy moving into position. "A German aviator was circling over our heads. We stopped, expecting every moment to hear something drop. He kept flying around and I suppose he had seen the column coming up the hill. Finally he flew away but in about twenty minutes he was back again. By this time the battery was pulling into the courtyard where there was a big chateau. The aviator kept flying around. There were several French soldiers in the village, and I guess most everyone was firing his rifle at the plane and he was flying very low; in fact, we could see the Iron Cross painted on his plane. I kind of admired his nerve with all the bullets whizzing around him. Someone made a lucky shot as he flew over the chateau. We could see the observer looking over the side of the plane. I thought that he was going to take a 'Brodie' but they managed to land in a field close by."[30]

The French 3e Bn, 152e RI, 164e DI, commanded by Commandant Jenoudet launched a final assault in Belleau Wood on June 3.[31] They were the last French unit to attack in the wood, but it was no use. Their formations were too broken and disorganized. In the afternoon a counterattack was finally organized, but was driven back with heavy losses.

In the evening Major Berton Sibley's 3/6 was put into the line. After convalescing from being gassed, Louis Jones was reassigned to the 97th Company (Robert Voth's company) of Berton Sibley's 3/6. Sibley was an older experienced officer, and a calming influence on his men. "In Belleau Woods he would come up to the front line and turn and say; 'There is nothing to worry about, just take it easy.' A very quiet spoken old gentleman."[32]

Even as the Marines suffered under the heavy German shelling, the military bureaucracy continued to churn. An emissary from General Headquarters arrived at Wise's P.C.: "Are you holding the line in depth?"

"'No, in width,' I told him."

"Major Willard Straight was along with this G.H.Q. individual. Major Straight was in charge of War Risk Insurance. 'Have all your men had insurance taken out?' he asked.

"'They have, with one exception,' I informed him. 'And from present indications, you're going to have quite a lot to pay out in the near future.'"[33]

By day's end the Marines constituted the only organized defense along most of the front, although the disorganized remnants of French units continued to resist in the woods proper.[34]

June 4

At 0400 h the badly bruised French formations commenced a final withdrawal through the Marine lines.[35]

With a new day the Germans began fresh and heavier shelling with explosive and poisonous gas, concentrating on the Marine rear areas, and everybody was forced to dig in. At dawn Wise was out again, and found Gunner Gallivan on a stretcher, shot in the leg. "The old boy looked white; it was a bad wound. I thought that if I could get him mad enough, he'd have a better fighting chance to recover.

"'Gallivan,' I said, 'I never thought I'd see the day when an old soldier like you would shoot himself to get out of this mess.'"

"Gallivan rose up on one elbow and shook his fist at me. His voice was quivering with anger. 'The only thing that saves ye from a batin' is me inability to rise!' he howled."[36]

By some reports during the night the French took over the front line as far south as Hill 142 on the west, but Wise wrote otherwise. He phoned the regimental headquarters and inquired about the expected Sixth Marines and the Twenty-third Infantry.

"They ignored that detail.

"'The General is here and he wants to know if you can hold,' they told me."

The expected reinforcements "were getting to be a very sore subject with them."[37]

The American Ninth Infantry closed up on Triangle Farm south of Bourseches, and the brigade was able to shorten its overextended line.

During the day some elements of the Sixth Marines moved into the line, with 1/6 on the left of the regiment's line across the Paris–Metz highway. In the late afternoon the enemy launched their first onslaught.

At Les Mares Farm, Lieutenant Lemuel Shepherd, now in command of the 55th Company "placed snipers on top of a haystack where they could pick off individual Germans as they advanced. The Germans began their attack about 2 o'clock in the afternoon. Instead of jumping off in the morning they attacked in the afternoon."[38]

As the Germans began their attack their observation balloons were able to partially scope out the more obvious Allied positions, and German artillery drove the French batteries out from positions supporting 2/5. The Marines had no time to dig proper defensive positions, just shallow scrapes. Wise felt an overwhelming urge to look again at his front lines. "The German attack was coming. A long way off over those grain fields I could see thin lines of infantry advancing." Germans of what Wise identified as the veteran 26. Infanterie Division advanced in linear waves in extended order, each man separated from the next by several meters to minimize targets.

As in many battles, from this point onward senior leadership did not matter. It was now up to the enlisted men and platoon leaders. "I realized that I couldn't give an order that would be of any help. Everything to be done had been done. I stood there and watched them come....

"I was frozen but fascinated.

"The first thing that flashed across my mind was: 'Does this damned line extend beyond our unprotected flanks?' If it did, we were gone."

The battalion was indeed fortunate. German tactical doctrine emphasized finding a weak spot in the enemy line, and concentrating forces for a *schwerpunkt* (literally heavy point, the heaviest tactical blow). Without adequate reconnaissance, the enemy had completely missed several large gaps in the American lines.

Up and down the 2/5 line the Marines lay still in their scrapes, bound by hard discipline to hold their fire. "Suddenly when the German front line was about a hundred yards from us, we opened up. Up and down the line I could see my men working their rifle bolts. I looked for the front line of the Germans. There wasn't any! Killed and wounded, they had crumpled and vanished in the grain.

"Their second line moved steadily forward. Their rifles were at their shoulders. They were shooting as they came. Suddenly they too, crumpled and vanished.

"Had those German troops, outnumbering us more than two to one, pushed that attack home, we were goners. It sounds fine in fiction for a little band of men to knock them down as fast as they come. It doesn't happen in real war very often. But that deadly rifle fire seemed to take the heart out of the Germans who were still on their feet.

"Suddenly they broke ranks and ran."

Wise held no illusions that luck had not played a role. Had the enemy struck either open flank instead of the center of his line, they would have been on the road to Paris. As it was, the bloody field would be the closest the Germans ever got to Paris.[39]

From the Sixth Marines forward command post, Frank Evans had a "box seat. They were driving at Hill 165 from the north and northeast, and they came out, on a wonderfully clear day, in two columns across a wheat field. From our distance it looked flat and green as a baseball field, set between a row of woods on the farther side, and woods and a ravine on the near side." Unlike the situation at Les Mares Farm the Germans were advancing blissfully unaware of the American positions. "We could see the two thin brown columns advancing in perfect order until two thirds of the columns, we judged, were in view. The rifle and machine-fire were incessant and overhead the shrapnel was bursting. Then the shrapnel came on the target at each shot. It broke just over and just ahead of those columns and then the next burst sprayed over the very green in which we could see the columns moving. It seemed for all the world that the green field had burst out in patches of white daisies where those columns were doggedly moving. And it did again and again, no barrage, but with the skill and accuracy of a cat playing with two brown mice that she could reach and mutilate at will and without any hurry. The white patches would roll away, and we could see that some of the columns were still there, slowed up, and it seemed perfect suicide for them to try.

"You couldn't begrudge a tribute to their pluck at that!"[40]

Sergeant Thomas had a succinct but far less romantic assessment: "they didn't really have a chance. We killed a hell of a lot of them. They never got really close to our lines."[41]

In the forward positions "Make every shot count, men," Rendinell's leaders told the troops. "Pass the word on down the line. Do not waste ammunition.

"It was machine gun and rifle fire. How we raked the German ranks. We all took careful aim before every shot. My gun got so hot I could not touch it, so I crawled over & took one of my buddies' rifles for he was done for and I used both guns, alternating as they got too hot.

"The Germans kept a-coming though. Then they would stop and seemed wondering what kind of fighting is this, anyhow? At last they broke and started to beat it. A French observer reported he had never seen such accurate shooting as what we did."[42]

In his memoir Colonel Catlin wrote of "a Toledo boy", a machine gunner, who said, "Oh, it was just too easy; just like a bunch of cattle coming to the slaughter.

"I always thought it would rather a fearful thing to take a human life, but I felt a savage thrill of joy and I could hardly wait for the Germans to get close enough. And they came arrogant, confident in their power, to within 300 yards.

"Curiously the infantry, which had been steady up to this time, paused as though waiting for us of the 'devil's snare drums' to take up the great work. And we did! Rat-tat-tat-tat full into them, and low down, oh! But it was good to jam down on the trigger, to feel her kick, and look out ahead, hand on the [traverse] controlling wheel, and see the Heinies fall like wheat under the mower. They were brave enough, but they didn't stand a chance."[43]

Roland McDonald of the 23rd Machine Gun Company was not nearly so poetic about the carnage. "You didn't see anybody and all of a sudden they'd come in swarms, and all you could do was just mow them down, that's all. It was just a case—you stood there, you didn't move, you just stood there and you raised your barrel, just raised the barrel and just chopped away. I never did much thinking about it."[44]

On the left the Sixth Marines "raked the woods and ravines to stop the Boche at his favorite trick of infiltrating through. An aeroplane was overhead checking up on our artillery's fire, and when the shrapnel lay down on those columns just as an elephant would lay down on a ton of hay, the French aviator signaled back to our lines 'Bravo!'"[45]

Private Eugene M. Abbott was probably referring to the carnage in this area when on September 22 he wrote to his mother from Casual Company 5, probably after being wounded at St. Mihiel. (A casual company is a holding unit, where the wounded Abbott was awaiting either transfer back to the US or return to his unit.) The context of his comments suggests he was more seriously wounded than he implied.

"The French didn't understand our setting our sights, and taking good aim, and then shooting, at all … And we piled the dead up on them in great shape. And then a few days later we fought over that same field and had to lie down among them, as it was impossible to bury them, as the field was continually being raked with machine gun fire. But that is nothing. You don't mind it at all; after you once get used to it, one could sit on one of them and eat a meal. Ha! Ha!"[46]

After the main attack faltered, the Germans began to move forward artillery and *minenwerfers*, heavy wheeled mortars manned by the Foot Artillery. The big, slow *minenwerfer* shells exploded with earth-shaking concussion. The guns deluged the Marines with shells: high-explosive, shrapnel, and gas. Catlin's "Toledo boy" had carried a wounded man to the dressing station and was returning when "I heard it [the shell] whistle and I knew it was going to hit close.

"I jumped into a hole and the shell hit it at the same time. A blinding, deafening roar, and a sensation of hurtling through space, and then oblivion—until several days ago. I have one faint recollection of bleeding terribly at the nose and ears …"[47]

The wounded were already flowing into the battalion aid stations, but Assistant Division Surgeon Richard Derby was deeply concerned that owing to the fluid situation the French had not allowed the division's hospitals any closer to the front than Bézu-le-Guéry (modern Épaux-Bézu), 60 km to the rear.[48]

The situation along the thin line of Marines was chaotic. The 1/6 commander, Major John A. "Johnny the Hard" Hughes, remembered Sergeant Gerald Thomas's experience with the intelligence section, and summoned him to the P.C. "Hughes said to me, 'This front line is in a hell of a mess. I can't make heads or tails out of it. Colonel Catlin [CO 6th Marines] is coming up, and I am going with him over to the Fifth Marines on the left. I want you to go to the right of our battalion and plot in every one of our units, and then someplace in our battalion front we'll meet.'

"There were two brothers by the name of Krause, who were in the Seventy-Sixth Company. Both were very artistic and excellent sketchers. I had a so-called map. They sent our unit people in on these lousy, fifty-year-old maps, you know. That was all we had to go on, and the front was truly in a mess. It didn't take me long to get the Krause brothers, and we shoved off and went over to what we thought was the right of our battalion. Just to be sure, we moved over a little further; and bumped into the company commander, now dead, by the name of Bobby Vogt. He was commanding the Ninety-Seventh Company of the Sixth Marines. He said, 'I'm the left flank company of Sibley's battalion, the Third Battalion. There's a gap of a thousand yards between me and Burns on your right.' Burns was in command of our Seventy-Fourth Company. (He was killed a week or so later.)

"We went then and found Burns's right, and sketched his company in. By that time we were walking up along the line and sketching things on the map. We came near the edge of a woods, and I head this voice say, 'You people get down. You'll just draw artillery fire.' I looked over there. Standing there at the edge of the woods, there was Catlin. Hughes then stepped up beside him and said, 'Thomas, go on back to battalion headquarters; and I'll be there shortly.' We turned around and made our way back to battalion headquarters. He came in. We turned in our work. He then told me, 'Nothing can be done to rectify our present position. We're going to drop back two miles tonight.' He put a line in on the map. 'We're going to form a unified line. As I said before, this thing is in a hell of a mess. We'll move at midnight.'

"About 8:30 at night … I heard a commotion; and I went outside. There was Johnny Hughes talking to Major Ben Berry, the commander of the Third Battalion, 5th Marines. He said, 'Deadoe, I'm going to relieve you tonight; and we're going to attack tomorrow morning.' Hughes said, 'Berry, you're a goddamn fool. I don't believe a word that you said.' [Berry replied,] 'Well, we are.' It ended, and that's what happened. Ben Berry's outfit came in and relieved us about midnight and we pulled out. We moved back into Corps reserve about four or five miles to the rear." [49]

The flow of retreating French troops, intermixed with Germans in the forest, continued well into the night.

The enemy was as yet not holding the woods with a coherent defense, and that night small parties crept out to reconnoiter the German lines.

Corporal Joe Rendinell, a Lieutenant Marshall, and a Private Moore "reached their lines & started to crawl snake fashion down into a small ravine when Marshall signalled to me & I crawled up close to him. My heart was going mighty fast—what we saw there was hundreds of Germans. It looked like they were going to attack & were just waiting for orders, so we crawled away from there to go back to our own lines & we encountered [a] German patrol scouting our own lines like we were in theirs. They never got back to their lines. We killed them all in hand to hand fighting."[50]

Sibley then sent Lieutenant Marshall and his scouts into Lucy-le-Bocage, but the Germans were still shelling the village. Rendinell: "A shell come along & hit a wall & knocked me into a Frenchman. I lit right on top of the frog and knocked him ten feet. It knocked Marshall down too. I got up & shook myself to see if I was all there and the lieut says, 'You don't need to worry no more. You wrote home & told your mother the Germans did not make a shell with your address on it, didn't you?' I says 'Yes, but they are sure knocking next door.'"[51]

A three-man patrol, led by Lieutenant William A. Eddy of the Sixth Marines intelligence section, moved north along the road from Lucy-le-Bocage. By midnight the patrol probed as far as the outskirts of Torcy and returned safely.[52]

June 5

The next day the Germans held back and contented themselves with heavy shelling of the 2/5 positions along the western margin of the Bois St. Martin, around Marigny, and the Les Mares Farm. Invisible to the soldiers and Marines in the front lines, the division artillery was now giving as good as it got.

Sergeant Joseph J. Gleason, Battery D, 12th Field Artillery: "June 4th. Up at 2.30 and opened fire at 3.00 A.M. until 9.00A.M; rested for a few hours and started again. Opened up on Boche in P.M. at different intervals. Boche plane dropped; also balloon.

"June 5th. Fired all night. Hundreds of guns were firing and such a war! Undesirable! Boche trying to break through but we mow them down. Rested all A.M. French plane burned. Big advance by Marines. Fired all night."[53]

Artillery fire was coming against 3/5 on the Marines' left, but at 0300 h an attack by the French and the Marines of the 49th and 67th companies from Major Julius Turrill's 1/5 pushed the enemy back and captured many of the irksome enemy guns. Captain George Hamilton's 49th Company overshot their objective, Hill 142, and moved into the next wooded area. This company was forced to pull back to the hill. Later in the day companies D and E of the Army's Second Engineers moved in to help consolidate positions.

Sibley ordered his battalion to dig in and, and that night he and the intelligence section toured the front-line positions. Rendinell, 97th Company 3/6: "Some of the boys was using dead marines for breast works. At another place there was a pile of them, arms and legs lying around. The Major ordered them buried. The boy he gave the order to says, 'Major, they were buried once, sir, but the Germans blowed them out again.'"

Late in the day General Harbord issued orders for a nocturnal realignment of brigade units. Berry's 3/5 would hold the entire sector from roughly Triangle Farm west to the Lucy–Torcy Road (exclusive), and the Sixth Marines would take over the extended sector from that road to Champillon (inclusive), with the 167e Division d'Infanterie to the west, and specified a June 6 attack. Wise's 2/5, having suffered amazingly light casualties, was pulled out of the Les Mares Farm line and shifted east to support an attack on Belleau Wood proper. Sibley's 3/6 was relieved, and moved to a reserve position on the Paris–Metz road. Additional orders instructed 1/5 to move to a reserve position.[54]

That night the intelligence sections sent small patrols to infiltrate the edges of the Bois St. Martin, and the southern margin of the Bois de Belleau.[55]

June 6

The Marines had blunted the German offensive, but the overall situation was that German possession of the hill complexes placed them in a tactically advantageous position. The terrain to the south was lower, mostly open farmland. The hills and their forest cover were advantageous to the defense, overlooked the Allied-held positions to the south, and screened German operations from Allied observation. Now it was thought necessary to roll the enemy back from the fortress they had created in the hills. The forested hills were just too good a position as a jumping-off point for a renewed drive on Paris.[56]

The trees concealed a rough topography of rock outcrops and shallow ravines. The wooded areas were not wild forest, but carefully managed woodlands with tall trees set close together. The margins of the woods were more densely overgrown with shrubs and smaller trees, providing excellent concealment for troops positioned inside the margins of the woods. Attackers would have to cross open, undulating fields of waist-high summer wheat and oats. All in all, the woodlands were natural fortresses surrounded by excellent fields of fire.

The American artillery was now pounding the enemy without letup. Joseph Gleason: "No sleep for third night; fired about 1,000 rounds. A beauty of a day but too tired to enjoy it. Sleep by relays. When it comes to having it rough, this can't be beat! Most of the boys deaf from noise of guns."[57]

Apparently some considerable confusion prevailed on both sides. All day the Marines along the southern margin of the woods waited for a resumption of the German attacks. None came.

At 0035 h the Fifth Marines issued preliminary orders for an attack on the western margin of the woods. At 0345 h 1/5, supported by machine guns from the 15th Machine Gun Company, pushed toward the Lucy–Torcy Road.[58]

Brigadier Harbord (diary entry dated June 23) wrote of the attack: "The eternal waiting, waiting, waiting which seems to characterize a Brigade Commander's duties, gives time for reflection but makes great demands on one's patience. You decide to try and straighten out a small reentrant in your lines, perhaps, or the Boche decides to do something to you, and for about 1 min of thought followed by a decision delivered perhaps in ten seconds you sit through hours of waiting. You wait for the necessary preliminary reconnaissance; for some artillery preparation;

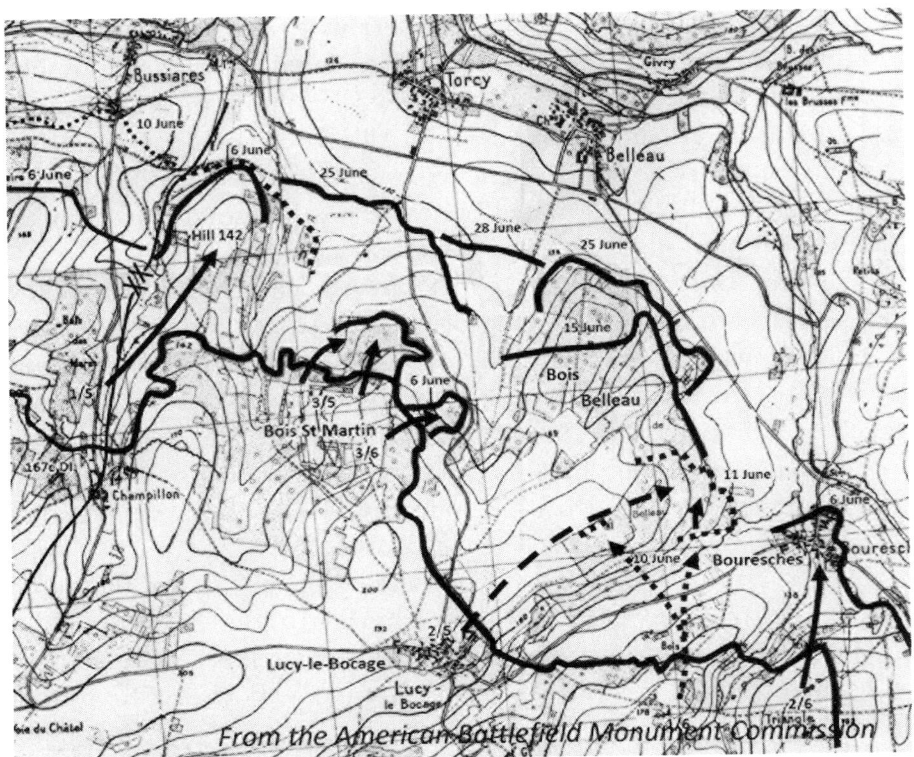

BELLEAU WOOD, THE COUNTERATTACKS, JUNE 1918. Poor coordination marred the hasty Marine counterattacks commencing on 6 June against enemy positions on Hill 142, the Bois St. Martin, and the village of Bouresches. The Brigade conducted a confused and bloody series of attacks in the dense woodlands, until on 26 June Major Maurice Shearer, of 3/5, was able to dispatch the message "Woods now U.S. Marine Corps entirely."

perhaps for the approval of some superior whose mind does not seem to you to function quickly; for the reconnaissance you must await the report before you can make up your mind what it is you wish your action to be; the artillerymen must get some data to tell you whether he can do what you ask; the necessary matters of ammunition for rifle, Chauchat, V.B. [rifle grenades], 37 mm, or machine gun, all of which now form part of your armament must be considered; also the weather, the interval to nightfall as compared with the time it will take to make your operation; what the enemy is liable to do; what your own people on either side of you can do or will do, etc., etc., etc. Finally all these preliminaries are gone through, and your orders are made, and your attack is launched in the Bois de Belleau or wherever it is going to be. Then comes the hard waiting.

"You know your people have started forward, and the outcome is on the knees of the gods. You can do nothing more, but you wish you could, and it is sometimes hours before you know what is happening. The telephone wires are cut; runners are killed; your men are out of sight and hearing ....

"Meanwhile one waits and walks the floor, or smokes (some play solitaire), or worry over whether you have left anything undone or not."[59]

Captain Lloyd Williams's 51st Company from 2/5 had been attached to Julius Turrill's 1/5 for the assault on the wood, and the balance of Wise's battalion moved into a reserve position south of the wooded hills, near the junction where the road south out of Champillon met the road west out of Lucy-le-Bocage. After dawn Wise could hear artillery, machine-gun, and small-arms fire. "After a bit the walking wounded began to come down the road. They came in every conceivable way: individuals, little groups, arms in rough slings, bandaged heads, men hobbling along with rifles for crutches. They brought the damndest cargo of rumors any man ever listened to. According to them, everything looked black. They said things hadn't gone well. The Germans were holding the woods in heavy force. Every attack against them had been thrown back." This grim parade was followed by slower stretcher cases borne by German prisoners.[60]

Richard Derby had gone on to visit the grim aid station of the Fifth Marines, and ventured by motorcycle sidecar up the Champillon road. There he found Wise's battalion aid station with a surgeon, Captain Shea, operating alone, with only prisoners to carry the wounded away. The aid station in a small house and nearby shed was under constant sniper fire: Shea showed Derby a bullet hole through his blouse pocket from when he ventured outside for a breath of air.

From there Derby headed along the brigade front, but his motorcycle stalled under German observation. The driver, "a rosy-cheeked boy, very deliberate of manner, and studying for holy orders when the war overtook and interfered with his career, much to his credit and to the relief of my rather strained feelings, gave vent to language not taught in theological schools. During the few moments that it took Goodyear to coax the car to run again I admired the view and abjured the makers of motorcycles."[61]

As always in combat, there was confusion over who ordered what. In another version, about midday a group of ambulances established an evacuation point near Wise's position, but "Knowing the country, I suggested to the doctors that it was all damned foolishness to have the wounded carried two miles down from Champillon when there was a perfectly good road up which the ambulances could run and get them."

A company from the Second Engineers headed north toward Champillon, but quickly returned. Their obviously distraught captain reported that "'The attack has failed in every way.... The Marines are cut to pieces.'

"Just at that minute some ambulances came rolling up the road toward Champillon. He stepped out into the road and tried to stop them. I stepped out into the road, too.

"'You're a damned liar,' I told him. 'Get out of the road and leave those ambulances alone or I'll shoot you.'" The captain headed on down the road west, toward the Marigny–Paris Farm Road.

Shortly afterward a runner came with orders to move east, into the southern edge of the Bois St. Martin northwest of Lucy. By 1400 the three companies were headed across the open fields south of Hill 176. "High in the air I saw several German sausages. I knew those woods were going to catch hell shortly."[62]

Turrill's 1/5 objective was Hill 142, with the 49th and 67th companies to lead the attack. The enemy was stubbornly holding onto the margin of the wood, and raked the Marines with machine-gun fire. Equally stubborn, the Marines pressed on and the fighting became hand to hand. As a result of this action Gunnery Sergeant Charles F. Hoffman became the first Marine to be awarded the Medal of Honor in France. "Immediately after the company to which he belonged had reached its objective on Hill 142, several hostile counterattacks were launched against the line before the new position had been consolidated. Gunnery

Sergeant Hoffman was attempting to organize a position on the north slope of the hill when he saw 12 of the enemy, armed with five light machineguns, crawling toward his group. Giving the alarm, he rushed the hostile detachment, bayoneted the two leaders, and forced the others to flee, abandoning their guns. His quick action, initiative, and courage drove the enemy from a position from which they could have swept the hill with machinegun fire and forced the withdrawal of our troops." The assault companies had suffered crippling casualties, yet managed to hold on to the edge of the wood against furious counterattacks.[63]

The Marines had little sympathy for German subterfuges during the fighting for the hill. "There was poor Sergt. Jerry Finnegan, one of my pals, who haggled a precious can of salmon open with his bayonet and had been told by a lieutenant to 'damn well fix that bayonet and get on with the war.' Two hours later Jerry lay dead across a Maxim gun, his bayonet thru the body of the gunner. There was Hill 142 there and the Germans wanted it desperately. They sent wave after wave over and their dead were piled all about it. We ourselves, the 49th, lost 62% of our company. We let Red Cross workers among the Germans pick up their dead and wounded until the wind lifted the cover on one stretcher and showed the snout of a machine gun. Then we let them have it. As one German wrote, 'The Americans are savages. They kill everything that moves.'"[64]

Brigade orders were not issued to the regiments until 1545 h for an attack on the southern margin of the Bois St. Martin and the Bois de Belleau at 1700 h. The commanders knew this hastily organized attack would be poorly—perhaps fatally—uncoordinated.[65]

The order was nothing if not ambitious: clear the Bois St. Martin, and take the Bois de Belleau and the small railway station at Bouresches. Albertus Catlin, Sixth Marines, would have operational control of 3/5 (less one company) and 3/6 for the attack on the wood. To the far right, 2/6 would conform to the advances made in the main attack. The order went on to optimistically specify a second-phase attack. Orders specified that one platoon from each company would be held back to form the nucleus of a new company; such were the expectation of casualties, and it did wonders for morale.[66]

The 3/6 with Cates's 96th Company from 2/6: "We had just gotten back in reserve and gotten cleaned up when Major Holcomb got an order to attack at five—it was then twenty minutes to five—and we were a good kilometer from our jumping off place. So we double-timed part of the way and got into position. Actually we didn't know our objective or where we were deployed across this wheat field ... taking very heavy fire—my platoon was."[67]

Not until 1600 h was Sibley's 3/6 actually ordered back into the line. Rendinell: "There was 7 enemy observation balloons directing their artillery fire at us. Their range was good too."

The lieutenant pointed out a very shallow ravine—really just a ditch—on his map, and instructed Rendinell to take three men and reconnoiter the German machine-gun positions in advance of the attack, sending runners back with any information he gleaned. "I said a little prayer. It didn't look to me like there was any chance of coming back at all.

"We hunched along with our heads down. I spotted a bunch of Heinies around the bend of the ravine. I signalled back to Pvt Moore, he rushed back to headquarters, & then the attack started."[68]

American machine guns began to beat Belleau Wood with suppressive fire. Major Evans, Sixth Marines headquarters: "At 5 P.M. we started out for our new objectives, on a wonderful day, and the twilight is so long here that it was practically broad daylight. The eastern edge of the Bois de Belleau and Bouresches were our main objectives, with Torcy and other parts of the Belleau the Fifth's. The colonel [Albertus Catlin] and Captain Laspierre, our French military adviser, went out to Lucy, the central point behind the advance, Sibley's moved out in perfect order, and poor Cole told me the night before they got him that when Holcomb's Ninety-sixth Company moved out later and came through the woods and into the wheat-fields in four waves, it was the most beautiful sight he had ever seen."[69]

In the attack wave William Rogers was pinned down and not so impressed by the artistry of battle. "We got up so far until we hit this enemy resistance and we were held up there until dark, and finally we pulled back a little piece. I was lying down behind a rock shooting at

Germans down where I could see one down a little pathway through the woods. I had a light marching order [pack] on my back."[70]

(One of the outmoded tactics used was the company attack in four waves. A line of riflemen and grenadiers was followed at a 75-yard interval by a wave of riflemen and rifle-grenadiers. Waves three and four duplicated the first two.)

Sibley's faltering charge went down in Marine Corps lore for the actions of one man more than any other. First Sergeant Dan Daly of the regimental 73rd Machine Gun Company supporting the 3/6 was a long-service Marine who had already won two Medals of Honor, one for his single-handed stand atop a high stone wall in Peking during the Boxer Rebellion. Correspondent Floyd Gibbons (who was actually with Berry's 2/5 at the time) wrote that an anonymous gunnery sergeant "arose from the trees first and jumped out onto the exposed of that field that ran with lead, across which he and his men were to charge. Then he turned to give the charge order to the men of his platoon—his mates—the men he loved. He said: 'COME ON YOU SONS-O'BITCHES! DO YOU WANT TO LIVE FOREVER?'"[71]

Rendinell's scouting party laid low until other Marines had cleared the German machine-gun position. Then "I heard some shooting about 15 feet [from behind] a tree & I could not see this Heinie, so I crawled out of the ravine and walked on the side, stooping real low, & then I saw him in the bushes so I took careful aim & fired & I got me another belt buckle."[72]

Behind Rendinell that main attack was coming. "I looked across the wheat field & there were our buddies still coming along through the machine-gun bullets. As fast as they would drop, another marine would take his place." In his own party "Pvt. Howe didn't keep down and was hit."[73]

The regimental commander, Colonel Albertus Catlin, had gone forward to observe the attack, and his liaison officer, Captain Tribot-Laspierre, implored him to take cover. Instead, Catlin was hit in the chest by a bullet fired from long range; he spun around and fell. Laspierre dragged the bigger Catlin back to a nearby trench. Catlin wrote that he felt no pain, remained conscious, only annoyed that he was *hors de combat.*

Catlin lay in the trench for about 90 min until the regimental surgeon arrived, but heavy artillery fire kept the party pinned in place. The Germans began to drop gas shells. His companions strapped his gas mask over his face, and Catlin struggled to breathe with a lung filled with blood inside the stifling mask. When the shelling slackened he was carried to a dressing station, shot full of the usual tetanus anti-toxin, and sent on a priority eight-hour ambulance ride to a base hospital in Paris.[74]

Rendinell crawled forward until he spotted about 20 German pickets running for their own lines, and he "helped them along with the old rifle." Lieutenant Marshall instructed the scouts to form an outpost line, and not retreat in the face of an expected counterattack. Behind him the surviving Marines were frantically digging in under a rain of artillery fire. The lieutenant returned and "stayed with us a while & said, 'Guess we've got them going today all right.' He asked me how I felt and I said, 'Nervous, and this waiting for a counter-attack is enough to drive a man crazy.' I asked him, 'Where the hell is our artillery? We sure could use those babies today.'"[75]

Frank Evans: "Out in the thick Bois de Belleau liaison was extremely difficult. The woods were alive with machine guns, and at times where our lines and those of the Fifth had passed through, they soon found Boches and machine guns in their rear."[76]

The 96th Company, 2/6, was tasked to take Bouresches, the small village east of the wood and at the extreme right of the brigade's line. "Captain Duncan … had gone two hundred yards in advance, raced forward on the double quick with the 96th Marine Company, and was met by a terrific machine gun barrage from both sides of Bouresches.

"Lieutenant Robertson, looking back, saw Duncan and the rest of his company going down like flies as they charged through the barrage. He saw Lieutenant Bowling get up from the ground, his face white with pain, and go stumbling ahead with a bullet in his shoulder. Duncan, carrying a stick and with his pipe in his mouth, was mowed down in the rain of lead. Robertson saw Dental Surgeon Osborne pick Duncan up.

With the aid of a Hospital Corps man, they had just gained the shelter of some trees when a shell wiped all three of them out."[77]

Cates: "We received word that Captain Duncan had been killed—the company commander. So with that I yelled to this Lieutenant Robertson, I said, 'Come on, Robertson, let's go.' And with that we jumped up and swarmed across a wheat field toward Bouresches. About two-thirds of the way I caught a machine gun bullet flush on the helmet. It put a great big dent in my helmet and knocked me unconscious. So Robertson, with the remainder of my platoon, entered the western part of Bouresches. Evidently I must have been out for five or ten minutes. When I came to, I remember trying to put my helmet on and the doggone thing wouldn't go on. There was a great big dent in it as big as your fist. The machine gun bullets were hitting around and it looked like hail. My first thought was to run to the rear. I hate to admit it, but that was it. Then I looked over to the right of the ravine and I saw four Marines in this ravine. So I went staggering over there—I fell two or three times, so they told me—and ran in and got these four Marines. Then about that time I saw Lieutenant Robertson who, with the remainder of my platoon, was leaving the western end of the town. By that time we were right on the edge of the center of town. So then I yelled at him and I blew my whistle and he came over and he said, 'All right, you take your platoon in and clean out the town and I'll get reinforcements,' which I thought was a hell of a thing. Well, anyway he did. We went on in and after getting into that town, we took heavy fire going down the streets. In fact one clipped through my helmet again and another hit me in the shoulder. We cleaned out most of the town but by that time I had, I think it was twenty-one men left. So I just posted them in four posts around the town and set up a kind of Cossack post [a four-man outpost with one man on watch]."[78]

Despite Cates's original doubts, Robertson's instincts had proven good. "Within an hour, though, the 79th Company [2/6] came in with Captain Zane. From then on, there wasn't any question about holding the town. I mean, in two or three hours we had enough men in there to hold half a dozen towns."[79] Zane's arrival was fortunate because the attack was poorly coordinated with the Fifth Marines' attack.

The 79th Company, 2/6, was to execute a near suicidal attack across 900 yards of open fields. Graves Erskine, Second Platoon leader described the wheat as about waist high. The men could see the machine-gun bullets clipping the wheat, "But the crack is what we'd listen to. If you heard it didn't hit you … [and] after they'd passed you there'd be this feeling of the vacuum at high speed" The enemy fire was heavy and accurate. "In my company we got a hell of a lot of machine gun fire after we started out, and it just cut us to pieces. I remember very clearly there was one young fellow—I think he was in the 4th Platoon—name of Nelson, a very fine looking kid, one you'd never forget. [It was 4th Platoon that was actually left behind as a cadre.] He was crawling back to get evacuated and he was shot right straight through the nose and he was such a bloody mess. And I took his first aid kit and bound up his face and told him to tell the captain that we were pinned down. And that I could not advance. Nelson crawled back, about twenty minutes later, and said, 'I told the Captain what you said and he said, get going goddammit.'

"Anyway we got into the town around 8 or 9 o'clock and we captured one machine gun getting in. This fellow was still firing; I walked up behind him and kicked him on a shoe; he fired a few more bursts and he finally got up, slung his gun over his shoulder. I was holding my pistol on him—a great big husky German, and my hand was going [shaking] just like that.

"Before I knew it he had turned me around and was drinking out of my canteen. They only had about five or six men left at that time out of 58." Erskine picked one of his men: "You come here and take this prisoner back to battalion headquarters." The prisoner still had his machine gun, but had unloaded it.

"He was back, I thought in much less time than he should have been back, and I said, 'Slattery, you shot that prisoner.' He said, 'How did you know?' I said, 'You didn't have time to take him back to battalion headquarters. Don't you know you are not supposed to kill prisoners?' He said, 'Yes, but I haven't had a chance to kill one of the bastards all day, all they are doing is killing us, and I can't go back to Minnesota and tell them I didn't kill a German.' That's how cold-blooded he was."[80]

In actuality killing prisoners was not that uncommon. From World War I numerous accounts exist of the cold-blooded murder of prisoners. German machine gunners in particular were much hated for their tactics of firing at knee level and then firing on the wounded, and for firing until the last moment before throwing up their hands in surrender.[81]

Erskine and his survivors made their way into Bouresches, where they were to meet up with Captain Zane at the town fountain, "which wasn't selected too wisely because naturally the Germans would look for a water hole that's where most people would go to get water." Zane interrogated Erskine about his platoon's strength. "I said, 'I have five, I think.' I might have had a couple more. And I checked them off, and cool as a cucumber he said, 'I want you to go out and locate the Germans.' I said, 'Captain, I know where the Germans are.' He said, 'Where are they?' I said 'They seem to me to be all over the goddamn world.'" Unamused, Zane repeated the order, oriented Erskine using the railway station as a reference point, and sent him on his way.[82]

Resupply of the exposed, partially surrounded position was precarious at best, but resupply was critical. Again the Model-T truck Elizabeth Ford came through. Resupply was crucial and Brigadier General Harbord later wrote that "One of my youngsters, Lieutenant Moore, with the veteran Sergeant Quick,[83] a medal-of-honor man, volunteered to run an ammunition truck [the famed Elizabeth Ford] down a shell-swept road into the town of Bouresches the night we captured it, and did it. Instances of men rushing out and carrying in wounded comrades which in other days called for the Medal of Honor have been so frequent as to be almost common in this brigade."[84]

The perilous supply shuttle would continue for days. Major Frank Evans: "The night we took Bouresches with twenty-odd men, and news came through that others had filtered in and the town was ours, we shot out a truck load of ammunition over the road. The road was under heavy shell and machine-gun fire. Later in the night we sent the Ford out with rations. For the next five days she made that trip night and day, and for one period ran almost every hour for thirty-six hours. She not only carried ammunition out to the men who were less than two hundred yards from the Boches, but rations and pyrotechnics, and then, to the battalion on the left of the road, in those evil Belleau Woods, she carried the same, and water, which was scarce there. For these trips she had to stop on the road and the stores were then carried by hand into a ravine. I saw her just after her first trip and counted twelve holes made by machine-gun bullets and shrapnel. At one time the driver, Private Fleitz, and his two understudies, Haller and Bonneville, had to stop to make minor repairs, and another time, when they had a blowout, how she and the men escaped being annihilated is a mystery. The last time I saw her she was resting against a stone wall in the little square of Lucy-le-Bocage, a shell-wrecked town, and she was the most battered object in the town. One tire had been shot off, another wheel hit, her radiator hit, and there were not less than forty hits on her. We are trying every possible way to find new parts and make a new Ford of her. She is our Joan of Arc, and if it takes six old cars to make her run again we'll get those six and rob them. The men have a positive and deep-seated affection for her that is touching. The service she did us just when it was vital to get out to the fighting men ammunition, food and water can never be estimated." [85] (Today the truck is restored, and sits in the National Museum of the Marine Corps in Triangle, Virginia.)

In the wood the situation was too chaotic for anyone to keep track of as the Marines fought from one rock outcrop fortress to another. "Lieutenant Overton, commanding the 76th Company [1/6] made a brilliant charge against a strong German position at the top of a rocky hill. He and his men captured all of the guns and all of their crews. Overton was hit later when the Germans retaliated by a concentration of fire against the captured position for forty-eight hours.

"Lieutenant Robertson, according to the report brought back by a regimental runner, was last seen flat on a rock not twenty yards away from the enemy gun, at which he kept shooting with an automatic in each hand. He was hit three times before he consented to let his men carry him to the rear."

Some companies had lost all their officers. Junior enlisted men stepped up to fill the voids, but even senior officers, who had no business in the front line, were forced by circumstance to intervene directly. Frank Evans, the Sixth Marines Adjutant wrote to correspondent Floyd Gibbons that at one point "some one said: 'Major Sibley ordered that' and another man said: 'Where in hell is Sibley?'" Sibley was twenty yards away at that time and a hush went down the line when they saw him step out to lead the charge.

"And when the word got around through that dead-tired, crippled outfit that 'the Old Man' was on the line, all hell could not have stopped that rush."[86]

The Germans were not about to tolerate an American foothold in Bouresches or the wood. About an hour later the anticipated counter-attack came, with high-explosive and gas shells, and German machine guns beating the ground. Rendinell "thought Hell had broke loose." Again the Germans faltered in the face of aimed rifle fire, but "My gun was good & hot from firing it so much & my ammunition was running low. Lt. Marshall sent back for hand grenades and rifle ammunition." The rest of the night the enemy contented themselves with very heavy shelling of the Marine positions. "Lt. Marshall stood guard while we laid down trying to get some rest."[87]

The situation was still confused, and higher level commands had no realistic picture of what was transpiring. About 2200 h the 2/5 in the southern margin of the Bois St. Martin received the expected heavy shelling. "They gave those woods hell. For half an hour all you could hear was the whistle of those shells, the deafening crash as they exploded, and the sound of splintering trees." Casualties were few, and the shelling ceased as abruptly as it began. Then about midnight a runner arrived, and "That was the damnedest order I ever got in my life—or anyone else ever got." Wise was to take his battalion north up the Lucy-Torcy road, right into the heart of the hill complex, but also locate Lieutenant Colonel Feland somewhere around Champillon and receive new orders from him. To simplify coordination, Feland—the Execuive Officer of the Fifth Marines—had been given operational control of all units in the woods. "It was pitch black. Finding Feland would be a miracle" but Wise sent out runners, none of whom returned.[88]

As the fighting settled into a night-time lull, the Germans began terrific artillery barrages on the American rear areas. Derby had taken an emergency convoy of ambulances to a Sixth Marines battalion aid station at the Petit Mongivault Farm: "as I stepped from the car and turned up a hedge-lined lane leading to the dressing station, I felt the combined rush and explosion of a shell, which toppled me over against the hedge, and on top of me a mule drawing a machine-gun cart. The orderly of a Ford ambulance was killed and the driver of another wounded by the same shell. The mule was between them and me. In the dust caused by the explosion and the pitch darkness, I groped my way to the wounded driver, guided by his groans. With the assistance of the ambulance driver, who turned up out of the darkness, I got the wounded man on a stretcher, and together we stumbled with him to the aid station."

Inside, Derby found the battalion surgeon laboring over the seriously wounded, and he told Derby that he had attended to Colonel Catlin. "Having exhausted their strength they worked on their nerves, automatically doing what instinct dictated. These were days in which men worked until they dropped and then rose to work again."[89]

June 7

At 0200 h Wise began his ill-advised march north into the hills. The first stretch was in a topographic bottleneck between high ground, a sort of sunken road between the Bois St. Martin on the left and Hill 169/ Belleau Wood on the right. Beyond, the terrain opened out into more fields. Wise's instincts warned him that it was "too damned peaceful."

Wise halted his battalion and "Taking [Second] Lieutenant [James Hennen] Legendre and a couple of squads of men, I went down the road to reconnoiter. It was still pitch black .... Suddenly rifle fire broke out on our left. We could see the flashes in the dark. A couple of my men dropped.

"I knew by the sound those rifles were Springfields. I yelled over there, 'What in the hell do you mean by shooting into us! We're Americans!'"

The firing stopped and the ambushers from 3/5 warned Wise that the woods east of the road were full of Germans. The patrol headed back south, but "We hadn't gone twenty yards before the Germans opened up. A sudden burst of machine gun fire came out of the blackness of the Bois de Belleau. Sparks began to fly around our feet. It was a metal [paved] road—chunks of rock in it. Wherever those machine gun bullets hit, sparks flew.

"All the bullets didn't hit the road. Most of my men went down. Those of us still on our feet sprinted for the shelter of the bottle-neck.

"My mind was racing. There were orders to be given the minute I got back to the battalion. I couldn't give them if I was all out of breath. I slowed down. All the way back the Germans smoked us up.

"Less than half of us got back safe. If that battalion had been out in that open road, instead of those two squads, we would have been cut to pieces."

Snipers were now firing into the Marine column. "Captain John Blanchfield, second in command of the rear company, was a few feet from me. I saw him grab at his groin. Then he doubled up and fell. A sniper had got him. A couple of men picked him up and carried him. He was dead before we reached the top of the ridge." Dawn was breaking and Wise ordered his battalion up into the protection of the Bois St. Martin under sniper fire that then grew into "a perfect hell of machine gun and rifle fire." Groups of Germans were by now spilling out into the open to fire down upon the Marines.

Taking steady casualties in the road, Wise ordered the battalion up into the woods west of the road, where they were able to re-form behind the shelter of a low ridge. "The Germans were pouring everything they had into that ridge," and the Marines began to dig in with no prompting. Patrols soon established that the Germans held "everything east of the road." At 0330 h the enemy began to probe the Second Battalion lines but were easily driven off.

"I went down past my left flank to find out about that remnant of the Third Battalion. I found about fifty men there—the remains of a company—with some youngster in command." Wise reported to regimental headquarters that "Their positions were lightly held and the enemy were making attempts to get through this point and am convinced that if we had not been there at this critical moment that the line would have been broken." Wise incorporated the group into his command, and settled in under a rain of artillery and machine-gun fire.

Soon the Germans added heavy *minenwerfer* trench mortars. "Those aerial torpedoes, nearly four feet long, packed with T.N.T., would come sailing through the air and land on the ridge. That whole ridge literally shook every time one of them exploded." The shelling continued all day.

Wise had given orders that any remaining wounded from the ill-fated patrol were to be left behind. "It may sound heartless. But it was war and it looked to me like throwing men away at a time when we needed every man we had." The next day, unknown to Wise, Legendre took three men and in broad daylight under heavy fire retrieved two wounded from the ambush site. Legendre was awarded the Distinguished Service Cross.[90]

With no grenades left, Erskine's patrol crept through the darkness toward Bouresches, and "where we heard a noise and threw a rock, and if anybody fired back we figured there was a German.

"So we got back in about 3 o'clock in the morning. It was wet, the wheat was wet from dew, and it was cold." As the patrol approached Bouresches by a small gully, someone dislodged a rock, and "when this rock rolled down I heard a voice that I recognized right away: it was that of Sgt. Mazareu." The Irishman "had the vilest mouth, I think, of any man that I have run into in a long time. When this rock rolled down there he came out with this string of oaths, 'You goddamn bastards, if you'd stayed with me, you would have been in Berlin.'" The sergeant had been shot through the leg, was repeating himself and simply would not be silenced.

"He started talking again and I said, 'Shut up!' He said, 'You goddamn bastards if you had stayed with me we would have been in Berlin in the morning.' And I said, 'You can't even walk, now one more word and I am going to crack you one.' And he said, 'I'll be goddamned if you will.' With that I wacked him one."

They dragged the wounded man along, but "I couldn't sacrifice the whole patrol to listen to his profanity." Erskine reported back and was given about 20 newly arrived men from the Army's Second Engineers. With his small force of 30 or so men, he was assigned a northeastern sector of the small perimeter to defend. The junior officers had been taught never to dig in behind a hedgerow because it was such an easy artillery registration point, but the sector was behind a seven-foot-high hedgerow since "the German artillery had the same thought, and unless you had movement to give away your position they'd never know you were there."[91]

In the early morning hours the 3/6 repulsed another counterattack in two hours of fighting. Sibley instructed his intelligence section to make contact with 2/6 in the village of Bouresches. Worming their way across the open fields, Lieutenant Marshall, Rendinell, and two privates found Lieutenant Robertson and about 20 men, the remnants of a company. The 97th Company moved into the village.[92]

The 84th Company of 3/6 was pulled back to the margin of the wood, and was able to secure a rare prize: food. "I don't know if you know what the French bread was like. They shoveled it around like coal. And some molasses.* So I got out my mess gear to get some molasses and bread, and I had a bullet hole right through the middle of my mess gear, the mess pan. I carried that thing for months."[93]

All that day the Sixth Marines and the enemy were engaged in small, violent struggles in the margins of the woods.

At 0200 h the 2/5 began to move up into the front line. Lemuel Shepherd's 55th Company came under artillery fire. The company commander was a former sergeant major whose duties had been primarily clerical, but he was promoted to warrant officer and then captain upon assuming command of the company. He had a premonition that he would die, took leave to visit family in Ireland, and was uneasy about going into combat. That morning "on the Lucy–Torcy road. I got a message, 'Blanchfield has been killed and you take command.' Poor old fellow. Modern warfare was just too fast for him. He was an older man and had spent most of his Marine Corps service in an office with paperwork .... Poor fellow, he was severely wounded on the morning of June 7th and died a few hours later in route to a hospital."[94]

In the late afternoon the 45th and 16th companies of 3/5, with units of the Second Engineers, launched one last attack and seized a small patch of woodland southwest of Torcy. *Chicago Tribune* correspondent Floyd Gibbons had hurried up from Paris to accompany the attack. Gibbons, a crime reporter, had often wondered what it was like to be shot, but was never successful in satisfying this morbid curiosity by interviewing victims.

---

*An inexpensive, non-perishable, easily transportable byproduct of refining sugar, molasses was repeatedly fed to troops from at least the eighteenth century. Its primary tactical drawback is that it is a natural laxative.

Incredulous that Gibbons was looking for the "big story", a lieutenant warned him that "If I were you I'd be about forty miles south of this place...."

Lieutenant Oscar Hartzell, a reporter in civilian life, was assigned to act as an escort. When the attack commenced, "There are really no heroics about it. There is no bugle call, no sword waving, no dramatic enunciation of catchy commands—it's just plain get up and go over."

The Marines advanced in open order, in platoon rushes, one platoon moving forward as others lay prone to provide suppressive fire. Once in the wood, the Marines contended with snipers, and having to cross small grain fields that broke up the forest. Gibbons and others followed Major Benjamin Berry across one such field when an enemy machine gun opened fire from the flank. Berry shouted for everyone to get down.

"I was busily engaged in flattening myself on the ground. Then I heard a shout in front of me. It came from Major Berry. I lifted my head cautiously and looked forward. The Major was making an effort to get to his feet. His right hand was savagely grasping his left wrist.

"'My hand's gone,' he shouted." A bullet had entered his left wrist, and torn down the bone into his left hand. Gibbons shouted to him to get back down, but Berry replied that "We've got to get out of here .... We've got to get forward. They'll start shelling this open field in a few minutes."

Gibbons started out in a low crawl to help the major. "And then it happened. The lighted end of a cigarette touched me in the fleshy part of my left arm, that is, no feeling as to ache or pain." Feeling no real pain and seeing no noticeable blood, Gibbons continued onward, feeling "that the pain in no way approached that sensation which the dentist provides when he drills into a tooth with a live nerve in it."

Gibbons continued onward, crawling with his left cheek in the dirt and helmet pushed to one side. "Then there came a crash. It sounded to me like some one had dropped a glass bottle into a porcelain bathtub. A barrel of whitewash tipped over and it seemed that everything in the world turned white. This was the sensation. I did not recognize it because I have often heard it said that when one receives a blow on the head everything turns black."

The impact had thrown his head up and back, and he recalled putting his head back down into the safety of the dirt. His reporter's mind was working hard to record events; he tested himself to see if he were still alive, moving one limb and another. "Then I brought my right hand up toward my face and placed it to the left of my nose. My fingers rested on something soft and wet. I withdrew the hand and looked at it. As I looked at it, I was not aware that my entire vision was confined to my right eye, although there was considerable pain in the entire left side of my face." Gibbons was able to see the wounded Berry stagger to his feet and run to the shelter of the trees.

He had thought that the place he fell was low ground, but now he felt exposed as if on the top of a hill, with no shelter anywhere, afraid that American artillery would lay a barrage on the German machine guns. He found that he could no longer move his left arm to see his wristwatch. He called out to Hartzell lying nearby to ask the time.

"'Are you hit badly?' he asked in reply.

"'No, I don't think so,' I said. 'I think I'm all right.'

"'Where are you hit?' he asked.

"'In the head,' I said. 'I think something hit my eye.'

"'In the head, you damn fool,' he shouted louder with just a bit of anger and surprise in his voice. 'How the hell can you be all right if you are hit in the head? Are you bleeding much?'"

Gibbons assured him he was not, and dissuaded Hartzell from coming to his aid for fear of attracting more machine-gun fire. The Marines had observed that German machine gunners were trained to deliver a grazing fire that cut men's legs from under them, and then fired at any who continued to move. They decided to try and remain immobile until darkness came, in three hours.

"During my year or more along the fronts I had been through many hospitals and from my observations in those institutions I had cultivated a keen distaste for one thing—gas gangrene." The bacteria that caused it throve in the soil of fields fertilized by manure.

Gibbons struggled to get his box respirator gas mask under his face to minimize contact with the soil. Twenty feet to his left lay a wounded Marine. He unconsciously struggled to roll onto his back, prevented from doing so by his pack. Every motion brought a hail of machine-gun fire that flew a few inches over Gibbons's head. "I could see the buttons fly from his tunic and one of the shoulder straps of the back pack part as the bullets struck him. He would limply roll off the pack over on his side. I found myself wishing that he would lie still, as every movement brought those streams of bullets closer and closer to my head." He painfully brought his thinner French gas mask case up and replaced the thicker one, lowering his head about an inch; anything to gain better shelter from the incessant fire.

For three hours Gibbons and Hartzell carried on a desultory conversation, with Gibbons struggling to make Hartzell memorize his wife's mailing address. Finally Hartzell laboriously gave Gibbons directions to turn and crawl back toward the trees.

Once in the trees "In an upright position of walking the pains in my head seemed to increase. We stopped for a minute, and neither of us having first aid kits with us, I resurrected a somewhat soiled silken handkerchief with which Hartzell bound up my head in a manner that applied supporting pressure over my left eye and brought a degree of relief."

About a mile back of the line they came upon a dressing station where a medical corpsman loosely bandaged the wounds, but there was no water even to rinse away the dirt. Another half-mile and they came across a number of men on stretchers awaiting evacuation. Under enemy shelling the surgeon there decided he could do nothing for Gibbons, who thought he could walk further and the doctor gave instructions to Hartzell to accompany him.

On the trail the two men were stumbled upon by a loaded ambulance, its attendant feeling the path with a stick to locate shell holes in the darkness. Gibbons was put in the front seat, upset by the groans of wounded in the rear as broken leg bones were ground against each other in the jolting truck. One of the men in the rear began bleeding heavily from a chest would, coughing up copious blood.

"The driver considered. He knew we were 10 miles from the closest doctor." Then he addressed himself to other three stretcher cases—the men with the torture-torn legs. "'If I go fast, you guys are going to suffer the agonies of hell,' he said, 'and if I go slow this guy with the hemorrhage will croak before we get there. How do you want me to drive?'

"There was not a minute's silence. The three broken-leg cases responded almost in unison: 'Go as fast as you can ….'"[95]

The 2/5 entered the line between the First and Third battalions, and spread out as the mangled 3/5 left the line.[96]

Rendinell: "When we got into the town we scouted around for German snippers. We were hiding any place for shelter. They were up on roofs, in trees, every point of vantage. We located a few and silenced them & while we was scouting around, we found a hog that the Germans had butchered, so being very hungry Lt. Marshall sent the other boys to find some cooking utensils & salt in order to have a meal. I was the chief chef & fried the whole hog before we'd had enough. The remains was put in our pockets for an emergency."[97]

As dusk fell Lieutenant Marshall's scout section was ordered back to the outpost positions in the forest. Rendinell recorded that the men "ran across from the town through the wheat fields, zizzagging, to this little ravine. The German snippers cracked down on us but they missed all their shots at us."[98]

Once back in the wood, the scouts were sent to see how the attack was progressing. Rendinell found that "The woods was trackless jungle and there was Germans in trees, behind woodpiles, in ravines, hid in piles of stone. We had to advance from tree to tree, looking all around to see where those shots were coming from. It was like playing Hide & Seek, only if you lost you were out for keeps."[99]

Lieutenant Marshall went out with another scouting party in the dark, leaving the enlisted men to try and get some sleep. After midnight the Germans again launched a heavy barrage, and Rendinell, groggy and disoriented, "couldn't keep my gas mask on manoeuvering around in those bushes & the next thing I knew I woke up in a Field Hospital. I was gassed and hit in the head with a chunk of shrapnel."

During the night the Germans launched counterattacks against beleaguered Bouresches, a pattern that would continue for two more nights.

Erskine found that his hedge "was the best protection I could have" since it prevented the enemy from throwing grenades over the obstacle.[100]

By now the French Sixième Armée had been granted some breathing space, and was realigning units to push the Germans back. But the wooded hills still formed a salient and were the linchpin of any German defense.

June 8

Two men destined to be among the most influential in the history of the Corps arrived unheralded aboard the *Henderson*. Brigadier General and future Commandant John A. Lejeune had created the Quantico base. One of his most trusted subordinates, Major Earl H. "Pete" Ellis also played a major role in development of Quantico, and the first Officer Candidate School. He would go on to serve as a senior staff officer in planning the major offensives in the final months of the war. But his greatest achievement would be the formulation of the amphibious assault doctrine that played such a major role in defeating the Axis Powers in World War II.

When Lejeune landed at Brest, the Allied cause still seemed bleak. He was greeted by aides to the Navy and Army port commanders, who painted a dark picture. The senior American naval officer in France, Rear Admiral H. B. Wilson, was even more pessimistic. He closed his office door and told Lejeune that "It is worse than it has been at any time during the twelve months that I have been in France. The defeat of the Allied forces on the Chemin des Dames was a disaster of far greater proportions than the general public has any idea of, and the French officers at Brest are more pessimistic in regard to the outcome of the war than at any time since it began." He went on to advise Lejeune that the only bright spot was the action at Belleau Wood.

Lejeune might be bearing a message from the Commandant, the Allies in the midst of a terrible crisis, and officers desperately needed, but the AEF bureaucracy was still in control. Despite his efforts, Lejeune was told to report to the Officer Reclassification Camp. "Blois was a good place to stay away from, I had been told, as officers sent there frequently awaited orders for weeks, and when the orders did come, they were almost always what one did not want."

Frustrated, Lejeune would have to content himself with visiting the wounded in hospitals.[101]

Zane's small command was resolutely holding on to Bouresches, and at 0015 h the enemy launched, and failed in, an attack on the town. Cates: "We were pretty badly chewed up and we took terrible fire while in Bouresches. I mean the Germans layed it on us. In fact we had a mystery there that has never been cleared up. It was a twelve or fourteen inch gun that fired once every twelve minutes into the town. And the people in the rear swore and be-damned it was a German gun but there wasn't any question about it. I went way back down the ravine and I could hear the damned shell coming from the south and I'd watch it and hear it go right over and hit in the town. We understood it was one of the big railway guns—naval gun …."

The gun was at least extremely accurate. "Luckily the thing was hitting right in the center of the town and practically ninety percent of our men were out on the perimeter. So it didn't do much damage except to morale.… It kept up for thirteen hours."

Decades later Cates remained uncertain about the timing or dates of events, but one incident stuck in his mind. The Germans did not launch a major counterattack but contented themselves with exchanges of artillery fire. "I was behind this stone wall at night and all hell was going on. They thought we were attacking and we thought they were attacking, you see. A great big shell hit in a manure pile about twenty or thirty feet behind me and you can imagine the mess it made. It knocked everybody down. In fact it killed my orderly, [illegible], standing beside me. He was standing there and the concussion got him." [102]

In contrast, Erskine remembered that the enemy continually probed at the village. "On one night attack they got down their machine gun in the street over there. It wasn't covered evidently. They were enfilading our line, but they didn't shoot close to the hedge. They thought we were further back. We stayed there till we pulled out."[103]

At 0500 h the 3/6, reinforced by the 80th Company of 2/5 and Company B, Second Engineers, attacked the margin of Belleau Wood, but were driven back from a gain of only 200 yards. The infantry pulled back to allow an intense barrage directed against the margin of the wood.[104]

Sibley's 3/6 continued to struggle against enemy positions in the southern margin of the Bois de Belleau, until withdrawn during the night to absorb much-needed replacements and recuperate.

The Marines were taking heavy casualties particularly among junior officers. Walter Gaspar was ordered to report to his regimental commander with two other men. "And Colonel Lee said, 'Hold up your hand!' And we spoke the oath and he said, 'You're a second lieutenant. Where do you want to go?'

I said, 'My company needs a second lieutenant.'

"Report to your company!"

"That night we went back into Belleau Wood."[105]

Wise's 2/5 and the attached bits of the 3/5 were strung out along the western side of the Lucy–Torcy road, but held out under a continuous rain of shells. About 0900 h "Colonel Feland came up behind the ridge on foot. He told me the First Battalion was just a little on my left. But the Third, he said, had been badly cut up and the rest of it was around Lucy-le-Bocage.

"'It's a damned lucky thing you happened to be where you were,' he said. 'You stick here until further orders.'"[106]

The struggle for the patches of rocks and forest had quickly evolved into a struggle of wills. On this day the German VII. Armee issued an order that:

> Should the Americans on our front even temporarily gain the upper hand, it would have a most unfavorable effect for us as regards the morale of the Allies and the duration of the war. In the fighting that now confronts us, we are not concerned about the occupation or nonoccupation of this or that unimportant wood or village, but rather with the question as to whether Anglo-American propaganda, that the American Army is equal to or even superior to the German, will be successful.[107]

As a consequence of the two adversaries' plans, even more savage fighting would take place within the small patches of forest.

June 9

The operations of both sides were grinding to a stop because of heavy casualties, and the failure of either side to make headway inside the wrecked, gas-saturated forest.

On the afternoon of June 8 Johnny Hughes had summoned Gerald Thomas back to the 1/6 battalion P.C. to again make use of his scouting skills in the absence of useful maps. The battalion was to move back into the line for an attack the next day. "'The battalion has got to move to an assembly position, and I want you to reconnoiter a route from here to a sunken trail, which is right along side the La Ferme Paris.' He gave me an idea of how to get there. I got one of my scouts, and I just loped for about two and a half or three miles; and I found this place. Then we turned around and went back.

"Hughes didn't come back so the march devolved on the commander of the Seventy-sixth company, Captain George Stowell. Hughes said to me .... By this time Waggy Burr was gone. He had been hit lightly. Etheridge ... was acting as intelligence officer. Hughes said, 'You lead the battalion to the sunken trail, and Etheridge will know the route from there on.'

"We came back and got ready to move. I was out in the lead. We had some trouble because the connecting file was broken where we crossed a road. The rear units turned instead of going straight across. It was well after midnight before we closed up again, and we got down to this sunken trail and had turned into the trail. We went for awhile. The trail was not very distinct, and it was dark. The adjutant said to me, 'Do you know where you are going?' I said, 'No, sir, but Lieutenant Etheridge does. Major Hughes told me that Lieutenant Etheridge would know the way from here.' And Etheridge said, 'I don't know a damned thing about it.'

"Well, we kept going. Daylight caught us, and we moved off to the left to a woods. There we were under German observation. We couldn't move during the daylight. There was a hell of a mess about it. George Stowell got relieved and sent to the rear. But anyway, we were supposed to make an attack that afternoon; we were in no position to do it. We were supposed to have continued on down, past Lucy, on this sunken trail.

"That night they moved us. We moved back to the sunken trail, went on down it, went to the proper assembly position, and they delayed the attack until the morning of the tenth, when we jumped off it."[108]

June 10

Even as the Marine Brigade was fighting desperately at Belleau Wood, Lejeune was still trying to get into the fight. Pulling strings with his contacts from Army schools, he was "burning up the road" en route to an appointment at the AEF Headquarters at Chaumont, where he found the outlook of both the Americans and the French far brighter.[109]

In the east, Zane's isolated command was finally withdrawn from Bouresches.

Wise's 2/5 had suffered under an intermittent rain of artillery and mortar fire for 3 days, and at 2200 h received orders for another attack on Belleau Wood proper.[110]

Sibley's 3/6 had suffered heavy losses in attempting to force a path into Belleau Wood, and it was decided to withdraw the battalion, shell the area heavily, and commit Hughes's 1/6 to the attack. In the morning "we passed a lot of dead men from Sibley's battalion, we didn't see any Germans until we got up in the Woods and we hit strong machine gun nests. There we had one hell of a fight. We held our own; but after we hit the nests, we didn't make much progress."[111]

June 11

Sibley's mauled battalion (3/6) moved into a reserve position. Wise's 2/5 was ordered into another almost suicidal attack northeast from the vicinity of Lucy-le-Bocage. The 3/6 would support the attack by advancing its own left flank.

Gerald Thomas: "it was just barely light but of course light came early there, 4:30, in that northern latitude, Hughes sent for me. He said, 'The Second Battalion, Fifth Marines is supposed to come up on our left and make an attack this morning. I don't hear anything. I don't trust that damned fellow Wise, and I want you to go up there and find out what's going on.' I took a runner; I didn't want to go straight west because I knew that might not be healthy, so I swung back south towards the edge of the Woods. We were climbing up a hill, maybe twenty minutes after we left Hughes; and we could hear a lot of shooting. Before long I saw a group. It was obviously a command group. They were walking along. I went up, and found it was Wise. I reported to him; and I said 'I'm Sgt. Thomas. I'm from Major Hughes, who sent me up here to get in touch with you and find out what was going on.'"

By this time Wise's battalion had cut into the enemy flank and rear amid vicious hand-to-hand combat.

"In the meantime, his people were fighting like hell. We could see the shooting and the fighting going on down at the edge of the Woods. He had moved along sort of at the side of his battalion. While we were talking, a runner came up; and he said, 'Colonel Wise, they say that our men are being overcome in the Woods. They would like some reinforcements.' Wise turned to the runner; and said, 'Go back to that Eighteenth Company and tell them to move forward into the Woods.' They were in his reserve. Then Wise turned toward the first lad and he said, 'Where did you get that word?' The boy said, 'From the wounded.' He said, 'God damn you, don't you know that the wounded are very poor witnesses.' Then he turned to another runner; and he said, 'Tell the Eighteenth Company to go back to Lucy.' Then he said to me, 'What you can do, one of your companies is supposed to attack alongside of me, and I haven't seen them. I want you to find that company, and tell them to move forward.'

"I went. I knew who he was talking about. He was talking about a lieutenant in command of the Seventy-Sixth Company by the name of Overton. I had a good idea of where I could find him. I went off through the Woods, and I came up to Overton. He was moving and had just hit some machine gun nests and was having a hell of a fight. It was over before long because they killed all of the Germans. I told him what Wise had said. He said, 'Well, they expected me to go out and deploy in that wheat field, and I would have lost half of my men. If he had come into the Woods along with me, he wouldn't have lost all of those men.'"[112]

Wise's summary report: "Attacks started as ordered and found quite a few machine gun nests inside of the barrage which gave a great deal of trouble. The whole line received flanking machine gun fire from both sides, but strongest on the right [south], which had been reported clear, the men naturally drifted toward it and by 1:00 a.m. [P. M?] all opposition had ceased." Once into the margin of the wood, Germans began to infiltrate into 2/5's left flank. Wise was ordered to refuse his left flank, and after dark he received 150 replacements and the support of two companies of the Second Engineers to improve his position.[113]

The German artillery continued to probe at the American positions, and no place was safe. Navy Assistant Surgeon Lester L. Pratt of the Fifth Marines "attended to and evacuated the wounded under the most harassing circumstances. His aid post was completely destroyed, his dugout wrecked, and surgical dressings destroyed and the air laden with gas fumes, which nearly blinded him. Although wounded under the left eye, he refused to leave his post until all the wounded had been safely evacuated.[114]

June 12

The last parts of Holcomb's 2/6 were relieved and moved out of the Bouresches–Triangle line. Sibley's 3/6 returned to front lines southwest of Torcy.

The 2/5 received orders for an afternoon attack to drive the enemy out to forestall any more attacks, and at first the attack succeeded in clearing the northern part of the wood. An irregular advance had left the companies in the northern margin of the wood exposed, and at about 1900 h these disorganized units fell back to connect with the units that had driven up through the eastern edge of the wood.

The 2/5 was now faced with two open flanks, and the enemy soon found them. The Germans counterattacked as the Marines were withdrawing, and recaptured most of the lost ground. Enemy infiltration continued through the night.[115]

In the nearly continuous reshuffling caused by heavy casualties and the need to give units even temporary respites, 3/6 relieved the 1/5 in the sector southeast of Bussiares.

June 13

Prisoners taken the previous day revealed that yet another enemy push would attempt the recapture of Bouresches during the night. The attack, at 0315, gained a temporary foothold in the town, but was driven back.

The confused fighting in and around the wood was beginning to take a toll on the commanders' tactical grasp of the battle—and the troops. Holcombe's 2/6 was ordered back into the eastern and northeastern part of the Bois de Belleau, apparently on a rumor that the Germans were to mount an attack near Lucy-le-Bocage. Cates: "About that time, Major Holcombe received word that the Germans had retaken Bouresches. So he called me—I don't know where Robinson was at that time. Anyway he said, 'Cates, can you take Bouresches again?' And I gulped and said, 'Yes.' And he said, 'All right, take your company, and the 79th, Zane's company, and recapture it.'" The companies moved out "at a dead run. The rumor turned out to be false, but that did not much console the weary men."[116]

The previous evening Holcomb's 2/6 was ordered to move through the center of the wood, toward the hunting lodge, one of the few surviving landmarks, to relieve Wise's 2/5. Lieutenant Cates, 96th Company: "So we started out and we were just south of Lucy. The Germans had about four observation balloons—sausages—and we knew they were watching us. Just when we got to Lucy, we received word that the retaking of Bouresches was false. So then we went into a kind of bivouac in a woods ravine near Lucy and stayed there all day long. In fact, I got out and spent the day going over the battle fields trying to find a friend of mine who was missing—Lieutenant Brailsford."

At about 2000 h 2/6 received word to stand by to relieve units in Belleau Wood. Cates: "So again Robertson left and went into the woods and left the company with me and said, 'you bring the company in at midnight—leave at midnight.' So about five minutes to midnight, I passed the word along to everybody to saddle up, put on their equipment and stand by to head for the [illegible] out in the wheat field."[117]

June 14

The division command ordered the Third Brigade to shift westward during the night and assume responsibility for Bouresches to shorten the Marine Brigade lines, and ordered a general reshuffling of Marine units in the line. The Fifth Marines would shift to the east, and 2/6 (under Fifth Marines control) would move into Belleau Wood.[118]

The 4th Machine Gun Battalion was in support of the Third Brigade, and Captain Westover recorded that the enemy had changed from impact-detonating fuses or his big long-range guns, no longer allowing the Americans to shelter underground. "The 'two-twenties' (220 mm shells) set to explode two seconds after impact, tore through walls, ceilings, and far into earth before going off like a charge of well-tamped dynamite," collapsing bunkers and wine cellars where troops sheltered.[119]

The German sausages had not called down artillery fire upon 2/6 in its rest position, but waited until after midnight to begin a general bombardment of the middle and southern part of the wood. The 2/6 began its night march just after midnight. Cates: "Well, it was dark as pitch and I hadn't gotten fifteen feet from my hole when I heard a salvo of shells coming. I realized that they were no ordinary shells—the gas makes a different whine to it. So they hit and there was no detonation so I knew it was gas, but I waited to smell. By that time there were more salvos coming in. So I got the first whiff of gas and I yelled gas and everybody passed it along. And I reached for my gas mask and no gas mask. I had left it up at this hole about fifteen feet from where I was. I evidently became excited and tried to find my hole and couldn't. By that time we were getting plenty of shells. I remembered seeing a red-headed kid named Hall who had picked up a German gas mask in Bouresches, and I yelled for him. I heard his voice way down underneath the hill in a hole saying 'Here I am. Here I am.' So I stumbled down there and said, 'Hall, where's that gas mask, the German gas mask?' So he gave it to me and I put it on and wore that thing for five hours. It was so small I couldn't get it on entirely. We made the mistake of staying there and taking that gas. We were not only getting gas, we were getting everything—shrapnel and high explosives—and we took terrific casualties."[120]

Erskine: "On the way in we went over what was called Suicide Lane [north of Lucy-le-Bocage]: we were going in 5 yards apart, almost 200 men, and it was quite a long column. The German artillery cut our company headquarters, and that was one of the most intense bombardments that I think we had."[121]

Erskine had acquired a new platoon sergeant, Bernard L. Fritz. Fritz was tall, German-born, had graduated from Heidelberg University and a seminary in the United States. Viewed with some suspicion because of his German origins, he was never considered for a commission though he dominated the drill field by force of personality. Erskine considered Fritz the single biggest influence on his career, and like any good NCO he was circumspect, at least with Erskine. "Fritz took a liking to me, and many times I was stumped when I was out on the drill field, and he would sneak over and he would—he always spoke in the third person—he would say, 'Maybe the Lieutenant would consider doing this or that or something else.' Which I found later was pretty good [advice]." Captain Zane did not care for Fritz at all, perhaps because "if he thought something was wrong, he would tell the Captain in no uncertain terms, and he knew his business."

Fritz had been away—Erskine speculated because of a wound— and in his absence another NCO had taken his place as Company First Sergeant: Erskine asked Zane to assign Fritz as his platoon sergeant. So "in the midst of this bombardment I'll never forget the picture I saw, Fritz standing up saluting, 'Sir, you are in command, what are your orders?'

"And my orders were, 'Lie down, goddammit, just as fast as you can.' He finally took cover, but I had to tell him at least three times. When this bombardment was over we collected our people, went on and made the relief."[122]

Writing immediately after the war, surgeon Derby described the aftermath of one of that day's gas attacks somewhat more grimly. "The battalion aid station was situated beneath a culvert on the Bouresches–Lucy road. The main avenue of approach to the Bois-de-Belleau led up the ravine from the culvert, along a dry stream bed. Down this natural communicating trench passed the gassed men, each receiving at the culvert station a gauze compress wrung out of bicarbonate of soda to place over his badly inflamed eyes. The Battalion commander, Major Hughes, was among the last to come out." Both the battalion surgeons were evacuated as gas casualties from exposure caused by treating the men.[123]

The anticipated relief that was to provide sufficient force for 2/5 and 2/6 to attack northward did not actually materialize. Instead of a full battalion (2/6) of nearly 800 men, "only 325 effectives arrived, so the attack could not be delivered, and I [Wise] did not consider that they were sufficient to relieve me and remained in position. I had received orders to stay in the sector with Major Holcomb until the enemy were cleared out but Major Holcomb brought the word that I could be relieved, but did not consider it safe to do so." Lieutenant Colonel Feland arrived to take command of 2/5, 1/6, and 2/6 now in that sector of the wood.[124]

A probe into the margin of Belleau Wood from the west by the 17th Company, 1/5, was in insufficient force to deal with the enemy facing the gap on the western side of the forest. The company retreated.[125]

The one consolation was that the mess wagons had caught up, and hot chow was beginning to appear, mostly steak and mashed potatoes—the abundant French *patates* were to become a familiar staple of the diet. One night the carrying parties inexplicably appeared with bags of charcoal. Cates: "I don't know why they brought charcoal in—I guess it must have been to heat emergency rations on—and a shell hit this charcoal—about four bags of charcoal, and we thought the worse gas attack in the world was coming off because it was just all this cloud of dust. And I must say it blew up that great big can of steak they had."[126]

One reason for the issue of charcoal was that uncooked food was being supplied. Walter Gaspar, 76th Company: "the first ten days I had one can of tomatoes; and how was I going to divide one can of tomatoes among the platoon? We got raw meat; the beef was raw. We had to cook it ourselves. All of us were issued these little cans of something, canned heat [jellied alcohol]; put your mess pan right over it and that's the way we did. We did the best we could. And the French bread—great big round loaves of bread. Potatoes. It was sufficient, if one meal a day you could call sufficient."[127]

The famished Marines were sometimes fortunate if they could cook such rations. Louis Jones (97th Company, 3/6) said that "At one time for several days we hadn't gotten any rations, and finally they brought us up a cold shoulder of pork, and you couldn't cook it, you had to eat the thing raw, because the Germans were within 50 yards."[128]

June 15

Sibley's battered 3/6 was again withdrawn to a reserve position, since the Marines had taken a terrible beating.

Cates: "Finally, though, it got daylight. So I moved them out and went on into the Belleau Woods. The first thing you should do after a gas attack, of course, is to get rid of your clothing. We got into the Woods and it seems that one of the battalions from the Fifth Regiment had attacked that night and taken severe casualties. So they took my company to carry the wounded out.

"You can imagine what happened. Inside of an hour there wasn't a man left. The gas was in the clothing—the ones that didn't get it in the lungs up on the hill [181], got it from the clothing." The first step in treating a mustard-gas casualty was a thorough shower with lye soap at special gas casualty clearing stations just behind the line. "I must admit I stripped off my clothes and soaped up but it turned out I was pretty badly burned around my legs and underneath my arms and my forehead—around these places.

"Any place it was wet from perspiration—your feet and underneath your arms and particularly between your legs." Cates was the only man from the company fit for duty, so he was moved to the 80th Company, 2/6.[129]

Despite a constant flow of replacements, many of them fresh from training in the United States and with no advanced training in France, the Fourth Brigade had been seriously depleted by two weeks of fighting. Army units began to flow into Belleau Wood to relieve the most battered units. The units along the western side of the wood were relieved by the Seventh Infantry and moved into a rest position. From official records: "We were continually fighting for two weeks and during that time the men did not have even a hot cup of coffee and lived entirely on cold food, and at times water was scarce, and from June 11th were without packs. I have never seen such a spirit as existed in the men in regard to every task that was given them and their losses seem to inspire fresh courage …."[130]

June 17

By this time both sides were almost totally depleted. Division officers were pressing the German regional commander to withdraw and form a new defensive line north of the forest. But both sides were too persistent.

June 18

The 3/6 strength report for this date depicts the cost of the fighting. Thanks to replacements the battalion was at nearly nominal strength, with 25 officers and 980 enlisted, as opposed to 29 officers and 981 enlisted on May 31. But in 2 weeks of fighting the battalion had suffered 14 officer and 400 enlisted casualties, and it was junior officers who were not being replaced in adequate numbers. Casualties were heaviest in the 83rd Company, which had suffered 63% losses. The official report went on to note that "37mm. guns and Stokes mortars were taken forward by the battalion but little opportunity was found for their use." The men were, however, being trained to use captured German machine guns. Holcomb's 2/6 was even more badly savaged, with 21 officer and 836 enlisted casualties. The battalion had suffered a staggering 88% casualties.[131]

June 21

When his short convalescence was completed, Rendinell was issued new gear to replace that abandoned on the battlefield, and sent back to his battalion. His timing was impeccable. After he found Lieutenant Marshall, "He said, 'you are just in time, we go back in again tomorrow.'"

Passing through Lucy-le-Bocage, he described the difference in the quaint village: "Not a house left standing. Ammunition dump under a big tree in the center of the town was blown to pieces. The tree was only a stump now. A water cart was full of holes. No wonder we never got any drinking water. Supply wagons with dead mules alongside the road. There was bread, hardtack, canned Billy scattered everywhere. Dead horses & cows laying out in the fields. So this is the price of war."[132]

The Marines went back to locate all the Army companies. The Sixth Marines were to relieve the Army's 7th Infantry, 3rd Division so the 3/6 Intelligence Section went with Major Sibley to locate the Army units. On the way "we saw a bunch of our dead Marines just as they had fallen. The stench from the unburied bodies was terrible. Lt. Marshall asked their commander why he hadn't buried the dead. He answered that the casualties had been so heavy it would take weeks to bury them all."[133]

June 22

At 0300 the Marines began to move back into the front lines. Over the next few days the brigade aligned its units with battalions intermixed. In Belleau Wood the Fifth Marines had tactical control of the 3/5 and the 3/6 in its front line. To the west the Sixth Marines front line consisted of the 2/5.[134]

Rendinell was assigned as a runner to carry messages to company positions. Runner was one of the most dangerous assignments, with a high mortality rate. "Today two runners were sent out … by the name of Reynolds & self. We both started out with a message apiece to same commander, 2 different routes. I delivered my message & on the way back I came across Reynolds. He had no head. We did not have anything to eat. I rolled him over & looked in his pack for bacon & found only a set of barber tools." He scavenged the barber tools.[135]

After constructing a dugout for the battalion command post, Rendinell went to work on his own shelter. "We had plenty of picks & shovels now. It wasn't like before, when we were told to dig in & had to use baynotes for picks & hands for shovels. We looked more like a labor gang on a railroad than soldiers. They could borrow my rifle, but not my shovel. Was offered fifty franc for it."

Rendinell and a Sergeant Bill Barnett constructed a shelter with "a large limb of a tree in the middle for center support and a lot of branches, two German overcoats & four feet of earth on top. It was 3 feet deep & 4 feet wide. Bill said we could use it for a grave easy." It was so cramped that the men had to coordinate rolling over in their sleep, and their legs stuck out one end. "It would be nice to get hit in the legs, a nice trip to the hospital. But to be hit above the waist, it might mean pushing up daisies."[136]

A few days later the men were singing and frying bacon and potatoes when a German plane dropped a random bomb. The bomb struck about twenty feet away and everybody dove for shelter, Rendinell colliding with Barnett.

"He was sore. He says to me, 'Joe, you ought to let me go first.'"

"Why?"

"Don't you know I am married?"

"I can't help that."

"After the shelling was over I crawled out & told him to come out, his potatoes were burning."

"'Hand them down,' he says."

"I says, 'No, come out and get them.'

"He did not come out, so I ate every-thing & the sgt reported me to the lieut. Marshall gave him the laugh."[137]

June 23

The day was relatively quiet save for exchanges of artillery fire. Erskine said "the artillery got us and hit me, it bruised my [left] hip and I got a fragment in my leg. But I could still walk."[138]

During the shelling Rendinell spotted "Pvt. Byington, a Tennessee mule skinner who drives a ration cart, was trying to get food up to the line. Up on a ridge one of his mules balked when the Germans was shelling the road. There he was in plain view. He busted the General Order [not to beat draft animals] and beat them up a while. They would not move. He left those mules & carried some of the rations on his back. 'All right, you bastards, stay there & get killed. I don't aim to.'"[139]

Rendinell used the barber tools, and "I gave a few of the boys up in line a haircut."

The front line, in the northern part of Belleau Wood, was held by the 2/5 from Hill 142 to the Lucy–Torcy road, with the 3/5 line extending from the road to through ill-defined positions in the northern part of Belleau Wood, and tied into Sibley's 3/6 northwest of Bouresches.

At 1900 h 3/5, with a few attached units, began an attack with its companies, from left to right, the 45th, 16th, 20th and 47th. Small groups from the two middle companies preceded the attack, but only the 16th Company was able to make headway, feeling out German positions, grenading advanced enemy machine-gun positions, until German resistance stiffened. The 20th Company was able to advance only 20 yards to the crest of a low rock outcrop before being driven to ground by heavy machine-gun fire.

Battalion commander Major Maurice Shearer reported that "The enemy seems to have unlimited alternate gun positions and many guns. Each gun position covered by others. I know of no other way of attacking these positions with chance of success other than one attempted and am of the opinion that infantry alone cannot dislodge enemy guns."[140]

June 24

Both sides were now at the point of collapse, and spent the day licking their wounds, shelling and being shelled. The issue would now be decided by Ulysses Grant's dictum that "In every battle there comes a time when both sides consider themselves beaten, then he who continues the attack wins."

Rendinell: "Four of our snippers went out. Three came back. Two Germans did not go back. The Germans are using whiz-bang on us. You hear the whizz of the shell, the bang, and the report of the shell all at once & it is impossible to duck them.

"Our artillery is sending plenty of shells over. They sound like freight trains going over. One of our planes brought down a German plane about 200 yards from us. Aviators taken prisoner."

In his diary Rendinell expressed his gratitude that "No scouting party tonight. The hard part of scouting is waiting until zero hour. It is nerve-wrecking. Your whole life is a motion-picture in front of you. No wonder my hair is gray at twenty-three years old."[141]

June 25

From 0300 until 1700 h the reinforced division artillery shelled German positions in the north of the wood without letup.

For the attack it was crucial to coordinate the actions of the Sixth Marines with the Fifth Marines to the left." Rendinell: "Five of us were given the same message to First Battalion, 5th Marine Hdqrs, and each took a different route. I put the note in my mouth, got over & back again on the run all out of breath.

"'I wish I had a good drink of water,' I says."

"Try and get it here, ha ha."[142]

The climactic attack began at 1830 h and Lieutenant Marshall sent Rendinell and another runner to determine 1/5's progress. "We started out on a run but didn't get very far. I heard a noise, a sort of moaning & crying. We listened to hear where it come from. There, out in a shell hole, was one of our buglers acting as a runner, with a leg shot off. I put a tournet [tourniquet] on his leg to stop the flow of blood, gave him my canteen of water & left him to carry out my orders."

His duties completed, "I told Trindad to get first-aid men up to that wounded bugler and I would meet him at our Hdqrs.

"There was hundreds of prisoners going back. Gee, they were scared, for their own artillery was sending over a small barrage. I met a sgt who had two prisoners.

"Here, corp, take them, I'm in an awful hurry."

"'So am I, Sarge,' I says."

"I saw him a few minutes later. I asked him who took those prisoners back. He said, 'Oh, they had the dropsey disease, they both died of heart failure.'"[143]

June 26

Holcomb's 2/6 was now in a reserve position in the southern margin of the Bois St. Martin, northwest of Lucy-le-Bocage, but the area was still crawling with Germans. The ground farther into the wood was littered with German dead. Men were given a punishment detail to prop the bodies up along a low crest and put American helmets on them, and the Marines dug in at the edge of the trees. Occupying the edge of a wood was strictly forbidden, since it was an obvious artillery target.

Erskine and Fritz were sitting on the edge of a foxhole "when a gentleman in a French helmet and a green armband came up … very neatly dressed, and he said, 'Who is in charge here?' I was sitting beside my foxhole and I said, 'Who the hell wants to know?' I was company commander, and I was just about 21." Erskine assumed he was a civilian war correspondent, a breed he did not particularly care for. 'He said, 'I am your brigade commander.' I said, 'Don't give me that. I know my brigade commander and it's not you.'"

The ever-wary Fritz took a closer look, and motioned for Erskine to get up. "I got up and looked on the other side of his shoulder—brigadier general. 'I don't know what goddamn army you are in, but you'd better pull out of here pretty goddamn quick. We don't tolerate any goddamn strangers up here.' The man just smiled. "It turned out to be Harbord." Erskine demanded some identification, and then took Harbord on a tour of his positions. After Erskine explained the logic behind his regulation-defying position, Harbord said, "If anybody ever relieves you, you just communicate with me and you will get it back."

That evening the Marines were finally able to construct a defensive line all the way across northern Belleau Wood.

June 27

Corporal Rendinell's diary: "Everything quiet. My uniform is all tore."

"Some funny things come off. Pvt. Humler & Kerr were ordered to take 28 prisoners back to regimental headquarters. When they got there they had 43. It sure did surprise them. They could not figure it out &

nobody else could. Some of the German dead they passed must of come to life & joined the parade."[144]

The front had stabilized, but the runners continued on their hazardous missions. Rendinell was carrying a message and kept diving for cover from artillery fire. "Once I fell right on top of a dead German. He was fat and ripe and his face came away under my hand." [145]

June 28

The Allied units on either flank were now advancing against minimal opposition, while repulsing minor German counterattacks.

Harbord toured the 3/6 lines and Rendinell was assigned as his guide. "I was wishing the Germans would send over a few shells just to see if he would duck them. No such luck." But "He talked to the boys from the 97th Co., sat right down among them. He's a real fellow."

At 2200 h the Army's 26th Division relieved the Marines and "we ran practically the whole way back."[146]

When the fighting was over, "The only thing left alive in Lucy was a chicken. We took it and kept it for the 3rd Batt. [6th Marines] pet." But by July 5, "Some sucker has gone and ate it. We sure were fond of that bird too."

June 29–30

Over a period of days the Marine battalions were shuffled about, and Third Brigade moved into the line. Ultimately the Twenty-sixth Division relieved the last of the Second Division units on the night of July 4/5.

In the rest area the men had to sleep on leaves with no blankets, but the YMCA, Red Cross, and Knights of Columbus passed out tobacco and candy. Rendinell: "After dinner we had a shirt reading contest to see who had the most cooties."[147]

In total, the Fourth Brigade had suffered 665 killed and 3,533 wounded.[148]

Rightly or wrongly, the Marines were celebrated as the troops who had saved Paris. Cates recalled that about July 2: "We received orders to select twenty men from each company—to go to Paris to parade on the Fourth of July. They drew lots to see who would get these—one Lieutenant from each battalion. And they drew lots and it turned out to be Johnny Overton .... He had just come into the battalion though. Our Major Holcomb said that wasn't fair so he appointed me. So I took these eighty men to Paris and we paraded there."

July 4

Cates: "I might say that I have been in as many parades as anybody in this country. But this was the most wonderful one I've ever seen. You see, we had been under fire for approximately a month then—no bath, no nothing—so we got to Paris and the men were given an hour to clean up.... The next morning we formed for the parade and had this wonderful parade. And later they took the whole bunch out to a great big ammunition depot where they employed 10,000 girls. You can imagine the time these Marines had with these girls."

Another thing the men had not seen for months was a paymaster—they were dead-broke in Paris. Cates: "at that time, I remember I had ninety-six hundred francs left." (About $16,000 in 2017 value; Cates did not elaborate on the source of all this cash). Cates called for his Gunnery Sergeant and said, "Ben, I know the men haven't got any money and we are going to give them liberty this afternoon and night .... Here's fifty francs for each man," about $150. "Well, my reputation was made from then on ...."[149]

Back at the front, the fighting had only paused for a while. At 2145 hours Lieutenant Colonel "Hiking Hiram" Bearss led a large patrol from both the Fifth and Sixth Marines into the area south of Torcy. The patrol captured several prisoners, and interrogation determined that Torcy was held by "about a battalion."[150]

Joseph Rendinell: "Lt. Marshall was decorated with D.S.C. [Distinguished Service Cross]. He sure deserved it .... He is a man that would not let you do anything he would not do himself." [151]

July 7

Corporal Rendinell: "Our kitchen has not showed up yet. It must of got lost. I turned cook, got some potatoes, beans & peas from a garden, cooked them all together. Potatoes were cooked, peas & beans were not, but we were hungry & it did not matter.

"Borrowed a razor and got shaved today. First shave since leaving the hospital June 20th."[152]

July 8

Even after the field kitchen arrived the food was lousy, but Rendinell and others scavenged a cow, butchered it, and gorged themselves.

July 10

The Marines continued to scavenge for food. Rendinell and others got wind of a calf some ambulance drivers had hidden in a shed. They fabricated a story of an animal with a broken leg, and were granted permission to put it out of its misery. "It was funny, the calf did not want to go. We pulled & pushed & twisted its tail & finely had to carry it to our camp." En route the animal repeatedly balked, so they killed and skinned the calf, and posted guards around the carcass at the camp. "Major Sibley & his staff got away with the whole hind quarter & we finished the rest. It certainly was a meal. Too bad we didn't get their wine too."[153]

That afternoon 3/6 was moved to a rest camp at Nanteul on the River Marne. For several days they fished with grenades, ate food cooked by civilian women, and generally screwed around. For Rendinell and his friends, the period was marred only by being sent on a mapping mission on July 11. Instead they skylarked about, riding horses, scrounging food from the Army, shooting at trees, and anything else they could think of. Back at camp they fabricated a report and "reported to Marshall & got Hell. It didn't correspond with the map."[154]

The liberty detachments had returned from the Paris parade, and Holcomb's badly mauled 2/6 returned to a reserve position near Belleau Wood. This rest area was still within range of enemy artillery.

It was standard in the AEF not to wear uniform devices other than the division patch on the left sleeve and service stripes, et cetera. The Marines had often attached the distinctive metal eagle, globe, and anchor collar badge to the front of the helmet, and transferred such distinctive items as buttons, rank stripes and such to the despised Army uniform. The order was not always obeyed. Even General Harbord habitually wore a French Adrian helmet rather than the standard American helmet. Some of the Marines contrived to get hold of Harbord's helmet, and "they took a big pick and they drive a nail through it and put a Marine emblem that says, 'You were in that.' And I don't think if you'd given him a Medal of Honor he'd have been prouder." Thereafter there was no question of the Marines retaining their unique uniform items.[155]

On June 18 Fritz Wise had compiled an exhaustive list of lessons learned in the Belleau Wood fighting. A few of his observations were that the Germans had no stomach for bayonet fighting, tended to be disorganized if no officers were present, and were very docile and cooperative when captured. They were masters of camouflage and tenacious in defense. Machine guns were positioned such that if a gun was captured or put out of action, several other positions opened fire on the lost position. (He recommended the ruthless but simple expedient of placing a few prisoners in front of a captured machine-gun position, since "they would not shoot on their own men.") Other recommendations were that all Marines should be trained to use German machine guns (since invariably there were a lot of them lying around), but that any not so utilized should be disabled since the Germans had a tendency to hide until attacking troops had passed, and then use machine guns to fire into the rear of American units. Pragmatic recommendations were that inexperienced and unfamiliar replacements should not be fed in while a unit was in the front lines, and that "a great many officers are casualties, and you don't get correct reports from the inexperienced ones left...."[156]

A proud Brigadier General Harbord summed up the accomplishments of his brigade. "The effect on the French has been many times out of all proportion to the size of our brigade or the front on which it has operated. Its firm stand brought the Germans to a halt in their farther advance on Meaux, which was the road to Paris. It heartened the French up immensely. It has caused the enemy, we know positively, to divert fresh divisions against us that were intended for other parts of his lines, and it has used up four of his divisions so that they have had to be withdrawn....

"They say a Marine can't venture down the boulevards of Paris without risk of being kissed by some casual passerby or *boulevardière*. Frenchmen say that the stand of the Marine Brigade in its far-reaching effects marks one of the great crises of history, and there is no doubt they feel it. In another way it has given their High Command a confidence in American troops that will contribute powerfully to the early establishment of an American sector in the Western Front where our troops shall operate under their own staff and no longer be step-mothered by the French or British."[157]

Cates recalled that on July 17 the battalion "got orders to prepare to move out, and when we woke up there were a lot of French camions. We knew the minute we saw those that it was bad news. You never ride to the rest area. So we loaded into these camions and had this forced march you might call it, up west of Soissons.... The camions finally left us and we put on what you might call the Aisne-Marne offensive."[158]

CHAPTER 6

Replacements

> It takes 15,000 casualties to train a major general.
>
> FERDINAND FOCH

Heavy losses at Château-Thierry and Belleau Wood necessitated quick replacement of losses. The Army had a large pool of replacements, but given the Corps' struggles to train and transport men quickly enough, replacements were always a thorny issue. While he cooled his heels at Chaumont during the Belleau Wood fighting, Lejeune argued Barnett's case for a full Marine division in France.

Pershing was still vehemently opposed, telling Lejeune that "he could not approve the assignment of a Marine division to the theater of operations in France for the reason that its presence there would interfere with his plan for a homogeneous army and would add greatly to the many complications incident to providing replacements.... He pointed out that it was scarcely possible to always provide the 4th Brigade with Marine replacements, and a division would require such a large variety of marine replacements as to make the problem almost or altogether insoluble." Pershing went on to say that he would be glad to absorb individual officers into the National Army.

Barnett's plan had been to incorporate additional Marines, along with the Corps' own light field artillery, to form the nucleus of a Marine division. Perhaps unknowingly, Lejeune was caught up in the jaws of a bigger struggle being waged at the level of President Wilson's Cabinet. Pershing had grown increasingly annoyed at the intrusion of Commandant Barnett and Secretary of the Navy Daniels into AEF policies, and particularly Barnett's continuous barrage of letters and cables about the use of his Marines. The uproar over the publicity from Belleau Wood was the last straw. Exasperated, Pershing cabled Secretary of War Baker that "the formation of such a unit is not desirable from a military standpoint. Our land forces must be homogeneous.... While the marines are splendid troops, their use as a separate division is inadvisable."[1]

Commandant Barnett had already authorized establishment of the Fifth Brigade, consisting of the Eleventh and Thirteenth Marines, and the Fifth Brigade Machine Gun Battalion under Brigadier General Eli K. Cole. This brigade arrived in France between September 24 and November 9, too late to see action.[2]

It was absolutely clear that the Marines would remain a tiny component of the AEF. Any Marines other than the existing brigade would essentially become a replacement pool.

Marine replacements were shipped over as battalions, but were assigned, as individuals, to existing units in France. DeWitt Peck was an officer in one such battalion, and recalled that by this time the influx of highly educated recruits was being felt. "I would say that a very high percentage of those men should have been commissioned, and undoubtedly many of them were subsequently commissioned. They were potentially too valuable to serve long in the ranks. Wonderful foundation training for them, but they were a superb bunch of men. Every one of them outweighed me."

Peck said that most of the enlisted men were soon sent up to line units. Losses had been heaviest in the rifle companies, so many of Peck's trained machine-gun specialists were fed in as infantrymen. Many officer billets were being filled by combat veterans promoted from the ranks and the drafts ended up "leaving the officers and senior non-coms of this replacement training unit for a cadre of Army units coming over...." Eventually Peck was assigned to the Fifth Marines as a company commander.[3]

William Manchester was one of the replacements aboard the *Henderson* when a fire broke out in a cargo hold on July 2, 1918. The fire quickly grew, and filling with water used to fight the fire caused the ship to assume a 15° list. Two destroyers evacuated 1,600 troops to the *Von Steuben*. Although some sources say that the baggage was successfully offloaded, Manchester recalled losing his gear and personal belongings, a far more likely scenario. The fires were brought under control and the *Henderson* sailed back to the US. Refurbished, she put back to sea on the shuttle service to France in August 1918 on her endless task of ferrying more men to France.[4]

CHAPTER 7

The Sick, the Wounded, and the Dead

He was one of life's great helpers, for he cleaned up foul places and made them sweet.

THOMAS W. MARTIN, OF SURGEON GENERAL DOCTOR WILLIAM CRAWFORD GORGAS[1]

Many call it the 1,000 yard stare and can't realize the pain when PTSD takes us there.

STANLEY VICTOR PASKAVICH

As early as 1914 the new Surgeon General William Crawford Gorgas (who had seen field service in Cuba and Panama, both hotbeds of tropical diseases) advocated creation of a medical service support organization separate from the strictly medical, to eliminate the administrative responsibilities and workloads of medical staff. In 1917 the Army created the Sanitary Corps, "for want of a better name." The new service would assume responsibility for all functions that were strictly non-medical in nature.[2]

In previous wars deaths from communicable diseases had always outnumbered deaths from enemy action. In an era that pre-dated antibiotics, and many inoculations, Gorgas was among the first to advocate measures such as the eradication of disease vectors like flies and mosquitoes (his early work was with disease-carrying mosquitoes in Cuba and Panama), preventive quarantines, simple field sanitation to deal with waste, water purity, and prevention of food spoilage.

Among the communicable diseases that ravaged armies were measles, mumps, and meningitis, all of which could be dealt with by quarantine. Influenza was less well understood and highly contagious. A particularly virulent form—the Spanish influenza—would ravage armies and civilian populations in 1918, one of the worst epidemics in human history. The most senior American casualty of the Spanish Influenza epidemic was Commandant George Barnett. He arrived in France aboard the SS *Leviathan* on October 7, 1918 scheduled to review all Marine units serving in that country. Falling ill, he was returned to the US on the same ship, departing Brest on December 18.[3]

Tetanus had long been a major cause of death for wounded soldiers. The spores are present in the animal manure in agricultural areas, and in areas of military operations it was ubiquitous as a result of the animal transport. The disease is most commonly transmitted by any sort of anaerobic puncture wound, from bayonets to barbed wire. By the 1890s an anti-toxin had been developed for tetanus, but no preventative inoculation. A massive dose of the anti-toxin was administered as part of the standard protocol for treating all wounds.

The functions of the "Sanitaries" were unusually diverse: sanitation, food safety and nutrition, laboratory services, venereal disease prevention, psychology, finance, supply and medical logistics, reconstruction, pharmacy, optometry, X-ray services, and hospital administration. The functions most notable to the wounded were operation of gas decontamination stations, the establishment of evacuation hospitals near the front, and ambulance service operations.

Under field conditions a major task was to assure the safety of food and water supplies. Carl Brannen of the Sixth Marines wrote that in the advance through the Argonne Forest, "Before drinking from wells, which were nearly all poisoned we would wait until a doctor [a Sanitary] made an examination and in order to counteract the poison he would add another chemical which purified the water but left it with a taste about like the worst medicine." Brannen was probably writing of the standard use of sodium hypochlorite used to treat water for bacteria; it has a strong bleach-like taste and odor, and for some is a powerful throat irritant.[4]

Each division was typically assigned four ambulance companies, with three motorized companies allocated to the infantry regiments, and a horse-drawn company to the artillery. Surgeon Richard Derby wrote that "There were no braver or more devoted men in our forces, and I include in this category not only the men driving for the French and Italians and those who drove for the French before we entered the war. And I am speaking of the orderly who accompanied each driver as well as the driver himself. After dark it was possible to bring the ambulances much closer to the line than during the daylight, although shell-swept roads, under plain observation from enemy balloons, did not in the least daunt these men. Their one idea was to keep their cars rolling, and roll they did, in and out of shell holes, over and around fallen trees, around death corners sprayed by Austrian eighty-eights. The work of the ambulance drivers in the forward area required brave, cool, and daring men, and such men did the work."[5]

An important hygienic function of the Sanitaries was to operate the division's two Thresh-Fodden disinfestors that eliminated (at least temporarily) the omnipresent cooties—body lice that caused debilitating itching and transmitted typhus and relapsing fever. The massive trucks were powered by steam and looked much like a hybrid of a truck and a railway locomotive, with a coal-fired boiler in front, and two massive steam chambers mounted crosswise on the cargo deck. The blood-sucking body louse (*Pediculus humanus humanus*) and its eggs can survive only within a limited temperature range. The steam engine both propelled the truck and provided 220°F (104°C) steam to disinfect clothing. The disinfestors were so heavy that most bridges could not support them and, coupled with their slow speed (4 mph, or about 6 kph), they often wandered by devious routes to find the Sanitary Train.[6]

Carl Brannen described both a cootie infestation, and a visit to a delousing station after the Soissons fighting. "This was a boiler with a fire under it, in which your clothes were placed and steamed until the cooties were killed. While that was going on, we took a bath and put back on the same clothing." The clothing was not laundered to remove weeks of ground-in dirt, blood, urine, and other unpleasant things. Men like Brannen, whose trousers had been ripped off days before by barbed wire, were the most fortunate, as they were issued replacements. "In a few weeks conditions would be just as bad again, necessitating a new delousing. While you were in motion, you did not notice the cooties, but when you stopped, and especially when your body was wet with perspiration, their crawling around was most irritating."

The war against cooties was without truce, and when there was a bit of free time the troops launched their own offensives by running a lit cigarette along the seams of their clothing. At St. Miheil "I found a lull in the fighting and made an assault on my cooties by burning them with my cigarette. A cigarette was the best friend a fellow had."[7]

In addition to the usual bullet and shrapnel wounds, the Great War was the "chemist's war" and the medical services had to contend with poison gas casualties. The first steps were to separate mustard-gas casualties from those affected by chlorine or phosgene, and give the casualties a thorough shower or wash-down with lye soap. Mustard gas was primarily a harassment and area-denial weapon. It forced the victims to live and function in gas masks, and inflicted debilitating burns. It clung to low, wet areas for days or weeks until disturbed at which time it vaporized and attacked more victims.

Richard Derby, later the Division Surgeon, observed victims of a mustard-gas attack: "the eyelids had become so swollen that sight was shut off. Where actual closure of the lids had not occurred, light was so painful that the eyes were kept tightly closed. They sat there with their faces buried in their hands, rocking to and fro in an agony that was dreadful to watch."[8]

For mustard gas, which clung to and burned any moist area of skin (including the lungs if inhaled) the next treatment was an alkaline poultice to neutralize the liquid gas on the affected areas. Louis Jones was gassed at Les Eparges: "I remember I was in this French hospital, and a Frenchman put a bicarbonate of soda compress on the family jewels which were burned, and he forgot to take it off, and four days later it had dried on there so he took it off, and put his foot on me and pulled it off."[9]

By long tradition the Marine Corps had no medical or chaplaincy services of its own. The Headquarters Company of each battalion included a medical section staffed by two officer Navy surgeons, and 20 enlisted

Navy medical corpsmen. In action two to four of the corpsmen were attached to each company to operate a company aid station, while the balance assisted the surgeons.

Litter bearers were not specific specialists, but men from the company temporarily assigned to this duty. Both memoirs and period photographs indicate that the use of prisoners to carry the wounded to the rear was common.

The job of the battalion medical staff was not to treat the wounded beyond simple first aid and dressing wounds, but to perform a quick triage to determine who had minor wounds and could wait for evacuation, separate out and provide rapid evacuation for those who might be saved by prompt care, and those who were beyond hope. The criteria were of necessity flexible, controlled by the sheer number of casualties and capabilities of transporting wounded. Detailed surgery beyond simple removal of visible fragments, and anesthesia were not available at the battalion aid station.

In past wars the evacuation and treatment of wounded was haphazard at best. Ambulances picked up the wounded at the battalion aid station, or as close to the front as possible. Varieties of trucks, 12 per ambulance company, were fitted out as ambulances, typically a mixture of lighter and more mobile Ford Model Ts, and larger and more comfortable General Motors trucks. It was also fairly common for the floods of wounded to be loaded into cargo trucks that had brought ammunition and supplies forward. These cargo *camions* usually lacked springs, and the ride over rough terrain and rutted roads was agonizing for the badly wounded.

There were typically four field hospitals. One was assigned as a sorting station or triage hospital, where the wounded were sorted, gas-contaminated clothing removed, dressings and splints checked, a massive dose of anti-tetanus serum was administered and the patient marked by iodine with a T on the forehead, and men were treated for shock with hot food and drink. Two others were designated for short-term care of non-transportable wounded, while a fourth specialized in treating gas victims.[10]

The evacuation hospital was the first stop at which the wounded received any true medical care, with general anesthesia and detailed surgery to stabilize the wounded for the next stage of the journey. Surgery to remove bullets, shrapnel, and other debris often utilized fluoroscopy, a new sort of real-time X-ray. An X-ray source was placed beneath the surgery table, the X-rays passed through the patient and illuminated a chemically-coated glass screen that produced a low-quality image. (Leaning over the table into the X-ray beam was not particularly good for the surgeon.)[11]

Carl Brannen was wounded at Blanc Mont, and provided a rare description of what he saw. "They placed some sort of machine [over] my wound and were looking through it apparently. They seemed to have discovered a bullet inside of me when one of them found that they were looking at a [metal] button on the back of my pants."[12]

Lieutenant Colonel Richard Derby, Assistant Division Surgeon, and chief of the 2nd Sanitary Train, had first gone to France in 1914, where he had seen even relatively minor wounds prove fatal. "In those early days it as a distressing sight to see man after man come into the hospital at Neuilly, all with badly infected wounds. As rounds were made through the various wards, it seemed that every man was running a temperature, every man was reeking with pus. The hectic flush and pinched countenance of the men spelled sepsis. It was universal. One felt hopeless in the presence of an unvanquishable foe."

After joining the Army, in 1917 he had been detached early to study French medical practices based on their experiences in treating mass and serious casualties, and their innovations were many. In a day when abdominal wounds were almost inevitably fatal, the French had radically reduced the mortality rate. Other innovations ranged from wheeled litters, to the much safer use of local anesthesia as opposed to chloroform, the innovative new field of plastic surgery, and the use of the Carrel-Dakin Fluid (a chlorine solution flush) to prevent gangrene in an era before antibiotics.[13]

Derby described in detail Field Hospital Number One, set up in a village church and school near Belleau Wood: "The pews and desks had been removed and given place to litter racks, each with its blanket draped litter. A portion of the schoolroom had been partitioned off by means of blankets into a resuscitation ward where the heat from several primus stoves was conserved to the maximum. The remainder of the schoolroom was arranged as a dressing room for the seriously wounded. In the courtyard a tent had been erected in which men exposed to mustard gas could be undressed preparatory to their bath in a small concrete chamber adjoining. Here one of the portable showers baths always carried by the hospital, had been set up, and was supplied with water by pump from an adjacent well. Another small tent adjoining afforded a dressing room, and was kept well supplied with pyjamas, underclothing, socks, and towels. Under a shed in the corner was piled the men's discarded equipment, which was removed daily by a salvage truck. The church was used as a temporary refuge for the slightly gassed."[14]

It was here that Floyd Gibbons was brought after evacuation from Belleau Wood. After being examined by candlelight on a makeshift table—the altar—he was given the usual dose of anti-tetanus serum, some narcotics, and loaded into the straw-covered bed of an ammunition truck without springs. At the next stop Gibbons was briefly examined, and moved to what he later found was the moribund ward for the dying. Hartzell again rescued him for another ride to the Base Hospital on the outskirts of Paris.

Unlike Gibbons, for a wounded man this stage of the journey was more usually done by train, more because of the massive number of wounded than for any greater comfort of rail travel. The wounded were moved to base hospitals, typically in urban areas. There the wounded man received more intensive surgical care, long-term nursing care, reconstructive surgery if required, followed by a period of convalescence.

Gibbons was anesthetized with ether, all the time carrying on an argument about the anesthetist's detached attitude. His last conscious thought was to ask the time and where he was: the Base Hospital at Neuilly-sur-Seine, Friday, June 7.[15]

The base hospital wards were often equipped with recreational and reading materials, letter-writing materials, and the food was vastly better. A common complaint, however, was that the wounded man was usually separated from his personal belongings—his issue gear like packs—and as a result he lost his personal gear. A very common complaint was the loss of the toiletry kit. The kit was a privately purchased item from the

Marines' pay (not military issue), so the wounded man was required to purchase a replacement. Since a wounded man generally disappeared from the payroll system for a lengthy period of time, he usually had no money to purchase the replacement.

The details for Gibbons's most serious wound were that the heavy bullet had passed under the rim of his helmet, entered his left eye socket and smashed the eyeball, inflicted a compound fracture of the skull, and blown out through the left side of his steel helmet. Moved to a convalescent ward, he went on to describe in detail the visits of the "Agony Cart" that periodically rebandaged wounds. "Some of the men would grit their teeth and grunt, others would put their wrists in their teeth and bite themselves during the operation. Some others would try to keep talking to the doctor or the nurse while the ordeal was in progress and others would just simply shout. There was little satisfaction to be gained from these expressions of pain because while one man was yelling the other thirteen in the ward were shouting with glee and chafing him, and as soon as his wounds had been redressed he would join in the laughs at the expense of those who followed him." Gibbons went on to describe life in the wards in terms that would be familiar to any unfortunate resident of a military hospital: the black humor, nicknames like The Cyclopean, and the young man with a grenade fragment in the head who could only sing repeatedly a few lines from a melancholy song. "I frequently noticed my nurse standing there at the window listening to him. Then I would notice that her shoulders would shake convulsively, and she would walk out of the room, wet eyed but silent."[16]

Cecil Avery readily survived being shot in the chest at Blanc Mont to describe his journey. A light Ford ambulance picked him up as he was being carried by stretcher from the battalion aid station, and carried him to a dressing station "Where we were lined up again on the ground .... No medication, though. The KofC [Knights of Columbus, a Catholic charity] came along, lit a cigarette, stuck it in my mouth, and wished me well, and all that sort of thing." The next stage was by bigger GMC ambulance to an evacuation hospital (he referred to it as a base hospital), "just a bunch of tents." The medical orderlies picked his litter up and "They put me on the operating table, probed and went over me thoroughly. Still no medication." He was carried to a tent with a sawdust floor, and his litter placed on simple wooden saw-horses.

The tent—under supervision of a single nurse—filled up with wounded, and "That girl had one time that night. Men sweating, cussing, screaming, yelling in pain all night long. Every time she'd come back to her desk, she'd pat me on the head. I was awake all night; I couldn't sleep with pain, and chills, sort of shock had set in."

The next day the men in the ward tent were loaded into a boxcar. "They had chains hung from the floor to the ceiling, and they hooked the litters three high on these chains." The rail cars had no springs, and the trip to Paris lasted through the next night. Another ambulance ride to Red Cross Hospital Number One followed. There they finally cut away his filthy uniform, with the contents of his pockets stuck into a small bag, bathed him in cold water, and he was placed in a long line of litters to await his turn in the operating room. After surgery—and 52 hours on the dirty litter—he was placed in a clean bed and given a meal. "It was probably horse meat, but it was good."

Temporary paralysis in his legs eventually subsided, though "my left leg was dead."[17]

From an evacuation hospital near Blanc Mont William Rogers was sent by train to Paris, then to a base hospital in a suburb. "They looked me over down there, and they painted it with iodine, gave me a shot of anti-tetanus, and that's all they ever did for the wound, because it made a hole about as big as my thumb where it came out."[18]

Surgeon Derby was much impressed by the attitudes of wounded Marines. "Major Burton Lee, the Consulting Surgeon of the Division, was passing through a ward one day, hunting out the American wounded. He came upon a figure, swathed in blankets, from which protruded a smiling face.

"'Are you an American?' queried Major Lee."

"No, sir,' came the answer, quick as a shot. 'I'm a Marine."[19]

Rogers: "We had a pretty good time there. I had been there about four or five days and I was looking down through one of the other wards, and who was lying there on his tummy but [Lieutenant] Ralph Marshall .... He'd been sitting up outside of this telephone hole where we'd established ourselves, and a shell hit right close by and it just went right across his tail, and cut a slice, a gash in there about an inch deep. He laid on his tummy for almost a month.

"I finally got him up and I took him down, with a cane, down to the Follies Berger [Folies Bergère] … and we were down there the night the Kaiser abdicated…." Most men were returned to their units, but seriously wounded men like Marshall were placed on an emergency retired list for repatriation to America.[20]

Most men simply wanted to get out of the hospital and return to their units, for a complex variety of reasons. After being wounded in the leg Roland McDonald was unusually candid. "I began to become a little apprehensive about, if I went to a hospital about whether or not I'd get enough courage to come back, because the shelling was … it was night and day. You saw no enemy, and people being blown up. So I didn't know whether I'd have enough courage to come back, so I said I think I'll come back and either get killed or so badly mauled up that I won't be of any use to anybody. So later on I was concussed and gassed, and that was it."[21]

Officers seemed unusually adamant about returning to the fight, as John Lejeune found when he visited both enlisted men and officer friends in Paris hospitals. Of Albertus Catlin he observed that "Physically powerful, he chafed over the confinement to his bed and begged the nurse to let him sit up, insisting he was nearly well enough to return to his regiment. Poor fellow! He has never fully recovered from his wound."[22]

William Nice had received a minor wound while scouring the Blanc Mont battlefield for lost survivors, but was ordered to report to the aid station. "Hell, I didn't want to leave; I felt well enough to stay …. But I didn't want to face a military court and so I went to the hospital. There was a Captain Kelly there and the following night he said, 'To hell with a hospital discharge; let's leave anyhow and go back.' I felt the same way too and without a cent in our pockets we bummed our way to Paris. There the military police picked us up and as we had no traveling orders we were held as absent without leave. But we got out of it all right. The officer in charge of the provost guard was a prince. We told him our story and he not only gave us passes but railroad transportation back to our commands and loaned us 20 francs, for we didn't have a cent to our names."[23]

Similarly, Gerald Thomas had been gassed in the Meuse-Argonne. "They put us into a great big trench getting ready for the jump off. The day before the jump off, the Germans just showered this thing full of gas. I was evacuated. I went back to the field hospital, and they gave us soda baths and things for our eyes and things like that. The next morning, the first ambulances started to arrive, and I saw some wounded from my company. Among others was my own battalion commander, Major Freddie Barker, who was being evacuated … [Will K.] Bill [McNulty] and I were there in this hospital, gassed. We said, 'To hell with this.' We went out and crawled in an ambulance and went back to the front. For the first time my pal Jim [was in] the 10% [the cadre left in the rear to later constitute a new company]. He was with the M.P.s. We crossed the old front and came to a ruined village, and there were the M.P.s. So for the rest of the operation I rode the roads with the M.P.s.

"We joined our company the morning of the Armistice. It was cold, bitter, rain, ice, snow. God, it was a rough time. This of course was November 11. The company commander said to me, 'I want you to go back and get the baggage.' You see, we left our bedding rolls, which we never carried into action, and the officers left their sleeping rolls and baggage. So I rode back. It took us a day to go back and a day to return though the distance was not over 20 miles. The roads were in horrible shape."[24]

After being wounded and gassed at Belleau Wood, Joseph Rendinell was carried to the battalion aid station "in a little culvert under a road, four feet wide, eighteen feet long. That was where all the wounded were brought back & given first aid & they waited there for Ford ambulances that came there only at night, loaded up with wounded & drove without lights across fields to field hospital Bézu-le-Guéry about six miles in back of our lines." The wounded were transferred into larger ambulances for transport to base hospitals. "There were hundreds of ambulances taking wounded back. The French people ran alongside our ambulance & gave us cookies and some were crying. They were tears of happiness as well as sadness, for the Germans were checked and their beloved Paris was saved." From base hospitals the wounded were transported by hospital trains to the interior." [25]

Rendinell's injuries were not serious, and he spent little time in the base hospital. "Stayed there one week & was evacuated to Casual Company St. Argonne. I called it St. Agony. It was worse than being up at the front."[26]

During his stay in the hospital, Rendinell wrote to his sister about his observations on how low the proud German Army had fallen. "You ought to seen the prisoners we took. Why, they were scared to death. Most of them were kids, and I don't believe they ever took a bath. I seen some of the hard black bread they eat. Why, I would be ashamed to feed it to the hogs.[27]

Graves Erskine had been concussed at Soissons, but that proved to be the least of his problems with the medical services. "I was first put in a hospital behind the lines there, the name of which I don't remember. The Germans came over and bombed this little hospital, and we were all taken out and put outside of the hospital in the open, then put on a train and taken to Paris." Since he had no visible wound, the physicians decided he had an infection of the mastoid sinus. Before the days of antibiotics this dangerous condition was treated surgically by scraping out infected tissue. "The next thing I knew they had me on the operating table. I figured that this wasn't right, so I got up from the operating table and said, 'No operating on me until you find out what the hell is wrong with me.'" Erskine was transferred to another hospital at Nantes, where the process was repeated and "I didn't get much attention for about a day there. Finally a nurse came in and asked if she couldn't syringe out my ears, because it looked like I had a blood clot in there. And she did, and by golly that was all that was wrong with me."[28]

The government equipment issued to each man was salvaged when he was killed or wounded and evacuated. It has never been unusual, and in fact usually a common practice, for men to rummage through the personal belongings of casualties for anything useful. Cates: "And every time a person was killed, of course, they'd take his bedroll or his blanket roll. Or if he was an officer, his trunk locker .... I can remember that we got a report that an officer had been killed. In fact it was Edgar

Allen Poe. So I remember taking a camel's hair bathrobe and a brand new suit he had there. And after the war I found that Edgar Allen Poe was as well as I am. He had been wounded and so I didn't know what to do about it. I told the story so many times that finally after the war he wrote me a letter and said he'd like the bathrobe back.

"He wanted it back because his mother had given it to him."[29]

Graves Erskine's adventures with the Army medical service were by no means over. After he was badly wounded at St. Mihiel, he was sent to a special surgical hospital, where the surgeon simply said, "'I think I am going to have to take it off.' And there was a very nice nurse there, and she looked at him and she said—I remember this so clearly—'He is so young, try to do what you can, Doctor.' He said, 'We don't have time, we have so many thousands, we don't have the facilities.'" The nurse continued to implore the surgeon until he gave up and set Erskine's mangled leg. He was sent to a succession of hospitals in Paris and Brest, and eventually back to America.[30]

After being wounded at Blanc Mont, Wilburt Brown was sent to a Red Cross hospital near the Arc de Triomphe, then to Base Hospital Number 57, then to a casual company. He was finally well enough to ship home on Christmas Day, 1918, but it took a while to recover the full use of his right arm.[31]

Lance Corporal William Manchester had survived the fighting at Soissons and St. Mihiel unscathed, but on November 1 his luck ran out. In a letter dictated to his family, he rather clinically understated his grievous wounds. Struck by shrapnel from an artillery airburst, "The first I realized I had been hit was when my right arm grew numb and my shoulder began to ache. One piece went through the shoulder, just missing the shoulder blade. Another went in about 4 ½ inches below the other, but by some miracle missed my lung. The two wounds together are about eight inches long. The bones were missed but the cords and nerves were cut connecting with my hand." [32]

Lance Corporal Manchester was finally recovered and sent to the battalion aid station; there a harried surgeon took a brief look at his wounds and had the corporal sent to the moribund ward tent, a quiet place to die. Gangrene had started in his arm, and he lay in the dying place for five days. "Three civilians passed through the tent, representing the Knights of Columbus, the Red Cross, and the Salvation Army. The first, distributing cigarettes and candy, saw the Masonic ring on his left hand and skipped his cot. The Red Cross man tried to sell him—yes, *sell* him—a pack of cigarettes; Manchester had no money. So he got nothing."

The younger Manchester observed that such exploitation was "nothing short of criminal. It was the Salvation Army man who finally gave the penniless, suffering lance corporal two packs of Lucky Strikes and tried to cheer him up. As long as he lived, Manchester reached for coins when he passed a Salvation Army tambourine. But he never forgave the Red Cross.

Eventually a crew of corpsmen removing the dead found him inexplicably alive, and he was sent to a hospital.[33]

Not all the wounds were physical. The Great War was the first in which psychological injuries were acknowledged, from temporary "shell-shock" to the longer lasting post-traumatic stress disorder. Psychiatric issues were not generally acknowledged, and veterans of the war often did not speak of their problems. They usually just attempted to drown them in alcohol, or abused those close to them.

One of the few who wrote openly was Daniel E. Morgan, a pre-war regular who attempted to make a career of the Marines but was eventually discharged because of behavioral problems. Unable to find work, he eventually drifted back to the West Virginia coalfields. The steam whistles at the mines "nearly drove me mad and sent me seeking shelter. How I long to run anywhere to get away from the shrieking whistles that sounded so much like high explosive shells in flight, tearing their way through the atmosphere on their murderous missions."[34]

One of the aspects that set the Great War apart was the massive number of dead. American troops for the most part were not involved in the static trench warfare, where hundreds or even thousands of dead lay unburied for months, contributing to the rat population, general squalor, and rampant disease.

In war it is not uncommon for men to have premonitions of their own deaths, though in truth it is usually only the ones that come true which make it into the history books. At Blanc Mont William Nice was talking with another officer. "Before they went over the top [Lieutenant] Chuck

[Connor], one of the bravest Marines who ever marched beneath Uncle Sam's banner," turned to Nice and surprised him with the statement, "Nice, I guess I'm getting yellow. If the old man [Captain George W. Hamilton] sent me back now I'd go."

"Yellow hell, there isn't a better nor a braver soldier in the whole damned A.E.F. or any other army."

"Well, I've got a hunch I'm not coming back."

"Ah snap out of it. All you got is an empty belly."

"But poor Chuck was right," said Nice. "He had command of the first platoon and I had the second, about 40 paces away. There wasn't any cover on the slope we charged. The ground shook with the thunder of the guns and the hills were lousy with Germans. And then a one-pounder got him; tore him all up. I tried to give him first aid but there was nothing that anybody could have done for him. He just smiled, patted me on the arm and died. He had seen 30 years of service and he was a prince."[35]

Others remarked upon the scale of the killing. "The dead out in the wheat fields near Belleau Wood laid where they had fallen. We had no chance to bury them. There were Frenchmen, Marines & Germans laying together. One place, a marine corporal & three Germans laying together in a heap, a story untold. At another place, a Marine in a prone position with his rifle to his shoulder & finger on the trigger, just as he died. Another with his baynote still in a German and both dead. Such were the scenes they told at the hospital."[36]

As he lay in a Paris hospital bed, Rendinell reflected upon those who had not survived the carnage, how the families would be notified: "your boy was killed in action, died of wounds or missing in action like Alarm Clock Bill from Chi[cago], I forget his name, but a shell exploded under him & they found only his shoe."[37]

The Americans had come late to the fighting and in the more open warfare of the final months, did not as a rule adopt the often casual attitude toward the dead. Where possible recovery and burial of the dead, both Allied and German, was supervised by chaplains attached to units—in the case of Marines, Navy officers. The emphasis was on getting the dead below ground as quickly as possible. The chaplains supervised burial parties of enlisted men who, where possible, assembled the dead for burial in small makeshift cemeteries that dotted the countryside.

Lieutenant Marvin H. Taylor of the division's Twenty-third Infantry recorded his experience as a burial officer for a field hospital at a farm where "The roof was practically demolished as were the outbuildings, and dead cattle were lying in the farm yard in an advanced state of decay, and as the place was under constant observation it was as much as your life was worth to attempt to reach the station in daylight."

Still, the burial was unusually elaborate. "We established a little cemetery in the edge of the wood and made some crude railings about the graves and placed a large rustic cross in the center. A tiny cross on each grave bearing the identity disc of the soldier sleeping beneath completed the arrangement. The pioneers would dig the graves during the day, and as soon as darkness would fall we would we would hasten across the open area, get our burden, and hurry back to the shelter of the woods. After lowering the body into the grave, word would be sent to the Chaplain who would be waiting in the dugout and he would come and repeat the simple service; then the grave would be filled, the cross placed, and another patriot had paid the price."[38]

In most cases bodies were hastily buried, often in shallow graves, where they had fallen. Usually marked only with a makeshift marker, or none at all, within a relatively short time many of these isolated burials were forgotten, only to be rediscovered months or years later.

In only scattered instances were efforts made to locate specific dead or missing men, or at least determine their fate. At Belleau Wood Brigadier James Harbord had persuaded his youthful clerical sergeant major to accept a field promotion, without attending the normal training course. Harbord assented to his request to be sent forward to gain some combat experience. "He went but did not return. Three days afterward we had been able only to learn that he reported to Major Shearer, who sent him to the 16th Company, and that the company commander put him in charge of a platoon. No one remembered seeing him after that. The Bois de Belleau was a perfect mass of tangled growth of timber and almost tropical jungle. Eventually we found a regimental runner who said he was carrying a message that afternoon and remembered seeing a man with sergeant-major's chevrons fall as he was leading a platoon, and he believed he could find his way back to the same place again. I sent him out and he found the body, torn with high-explosive shall, dead four days."[39]

Almost as soon as the first Americans were killed in action, a debate arose as to how the bodies were to be dealt with. Pershing was adamantly opposed to repatriating the dead: there were inadequate time, resources, and shipping space, and he hesitated to send mangled bodies home to be viewed by relatives. The debate continued well into the 1920s, when a decision was made to recover and repatriate the bodies of any whose families wished it. Eventually about 60% of American dead would be shipped home for reburial.[40]

In May 1921 four unidentified bodies were exhumed from cemeteries in France, and one was selected at random to represent the unidentified dead. Graves Erskine was assigned to receive and help escort the body aboard Admiral Dewey's old flagship, the USS *Olympia*.

Erskine thought he once spoke French "pretty well", but he was rusty. "I found that when the body was turned over, I was supposed to translate. And I made a pretty poor job of that, but I think it got over all right." Aboard ship "the Captain [Henry Wyman] didn't want to put it down in the hold for fear that something might happen to it. He wanted it kept under surveillance the entire time, and as soon as we got out of the harbor in Brest we took this casket up to the signal bridge .... We lashed this fellow down with everything we could put on him; we had some very rough weather coming home, and there were times when we thought we might not make it home." The seas were so rough that it was almost impossible even to eat, and water was four inches deep in the wardroom.[41]

The body was reinterred at Arlington National Cemetery on November 11, 1921.

In 1923 the American Battle Monuments Commission was established to construct and maintain cemeteries and memorials for the dead that remained. In 1937 cemeteries were established at Aisne-Marne, Flanders, the Meuse-Argonne, Oise-Aisne, the Somme, St. Mihiel, and

Suresnes. As resources allowed, the scattered dead were disinterred and relocated to these cemeteries.

Despite these efforts, many men were listed as missing in action. Some were simply obliterated by artillery fire, and many of the dead from isolated burials remained unrecovered. A century later bodies are still being recovered as they are discovered by accident during construction projects, or as old trenches and bunkers are excavated as part of archeological studies.

CHAPTER 8

Soissons

Their fiery advance and great tenacity were well recognized by their opponents.

LIEUTENANT COLONEL ERNST OTTO, GERMAN ARMY

The recuperation period after Belleau Wood was absurdly brief, but it was imperative to begin rolling back the enemy gains. As a veteran division, and moreover one with a reputation for hard fighting, the Second was given even less rest than usual. When the Marines were pulled out of Belleau Wood, they briefly went to rest areas along the River Marne, as William Rogers recalled "for a swim and [the] boys threw in hand grenades and caught some fish. We stayed there a week or ten days."[1]

Advance intelligence and Allied preparedness thwarted the next German offensive in mid-July, and Marshal Foch decided the time was ripe to pinch off the German salient by attacking from the shoulders at Soissons in the west and Reims in the east. The Second Division was selected to attack eastward toward Soissons, another of the important railway centers that controlled the logistical fates of the opposing armies.

While the division was in rest camps, James G. Harbord was promoted to major general. He rushed back to assume command of the division. Colonel Wendell C. Neville was promoted to brigadier and assumed command of the Fourth Brigade, with Colonel Logan Feland taking over the Fifth Marines. Harbord's meeting with the Fourth Brigade officers was at least reassuring. "Colonel Neville said the motto of the

Marines was 'Semper Fidelis' and that I could depend on them. The other, Colonel, Catlin, was a classmate of mine in the War College in 1916–1917, and is a good man also."[2]

At the larger scale, Foch's planning was meticulous, establishing in complete secrecy massive supply dumps to support the attack. Unfortunately that planning did not extend to the last-minute forward movement of the fighting units. The Second Division was to be attached to the French Dixième Armée.

On July 16 the Marine infantry climbed aboard the *camions* that invariably meant that they were on their way to another battle. Considerable confusion existed in the deployment of the Second Division. "Not even the Division Staff knew their ultimate destination. The trucks were simply ordered to proceed to a certain point when they would be met by a French Staff Officer, who would direct them further, in some cases, the staff officer was late and this resulted in unnecessary delay and many misdirections by French officers who thought they knew the ultimate destination. However, the troops finally arrived during the morning of the July 17 in the vicinity of Taillefontaine, where they were unloaded from the trucks."[3]

Louis Jones provided a more personal view of the confusion: "all of a sudden one morning they took all our rations, baggage and carts away, they took all our water, and we were going to move. We stayed around until 10 o'clock at night, and finally these trucks came, driven by these Annamites [Vietnamese].... And we got aboard those and rode all night, and finally they dumped us out in an open field about noon the next day. Nobody knew where we were supposed to go. About three o'clock somebody came around and found us to issue orders, and we started to hike, and we had to hike all night and get ready to go into this fight the next morning at 5 o'clock." More than anything else veterans of Soissons remember the weather. "It was pouring down rain, we had to march in the gutters [roadside ditches] in the mud, because there were French artillery, there were tanks, there were trucks and so forth going up this highway." The usual congestion was made worse by the division reinforcements: an additional regiment of French artillery and six battalions of tanks.[4]

July 17

Like many senior officers, Harbord was frustrated by the French security measures which added greatly to the confusion. Orders were not promulgated downward: "the French never tell one where they are going. You are always told to proceed to some distant point where an officer will meet you with orders, and though every voluble Frenchman in lovely France may know where you are going it is a secret from the person most interested, the American commander."

After a frantic night of preparing orders and maps, "we left [headquarters at] Tellefontaine in my motor car to attempt to find the division, concentrate it, distribute the necessary orders, assure the supply of ammunition, rations, evacuation of the wounded, and to guarantee its assault at the prescribed hour. The artillery brigade was now in position near the Carrefour de Memours. General Bowley knew the location of his own and adjacent artillery, but had been unable to effect any personal reconnaissance to his front. As to the remainder of the division, the whereabouts of not a single man was known to me."

Harbord went on to describe the few roads useful to the division as "generally paved in the center, with the ordinary soil on either side. They are practically tunnels through the dense timber."[5]

Private Fitch L. MCord (6th Company, Sixth Marines) provided an unusually detailed account of the approach march to a massive World War I battle. "The highway leads straight into the forest. Many roads empty into it, and from every road debouches a stream of horses, men and guns. The sky clouds up. Suddenly it rains—a regular April shower. It is mid-afternoon of July 17th and as we are hot and sweaty the shower is a relief.

"The rain quits as suddenly as it commenced and the sun pops out as we enter the forest, our uniforms steaming—a regular Turkish bath, and thirst becomes a torture.

"The number of war-wheels multiplies; stupendous is a mild word. Every implement of modern war is moving up, and there are French soldiers everywhere.

"We are in the great Bois de Retz. Majestic trees tower to a height of ninety feet above the forest floor. In under the trees and clear back into the forest are picket lines of artillery and cavalry. Small arms ammunition is piled along the road and under the trees. There are rows upon rows of every caliber of shell, dumps of winged aerial bombs, hand grenades and pyrotechnics. French infantry with stacked rifles seem to be appraising us, smiling approvingly through wiry black beards and moustaches, as we plod along the right side of the road.

"The tanks are new to us. There are big tanks and little tanks, all with weird camouflage in colors of green, red and brown. They rattle and crunch and groan and snort along, and no one argues with them in the matter of right-of-way. Through the slit at the base of the coning tower of each small tank protrudes a machine gun. The larger tanks carry three-inch guns.

"On the right side of the road moving forward in a never-ending stream, plods a single file of drab colored infantry...."

"The center of the road is a jumble of the machinery of war, heavy howitzers propelled by squatty, low-built, powerful caterpillars; roan, black and sorrel horses, hitched in teams; the graceful French seventy-fives and their caissons drawn by six horses, with eight larger horses, tugging, struggling along, pulling the heavier hundred and fifty-fives.

"Occasionally a heavy gun or caisson slips into the ditch somewhere ahead, and the diversified column jams up, remaining in a solid, almost motionless pack, and amid a jamborie of sounds, squawks, horns, whistles and shouts, sways back and forth a few times and moves on, the crippled gun having been heaved over to the side of the road out of the line of traffic.

"A horse's leg is broken. He is dispassionately pistoled. Nothing is permitted to interfere with the forward movement of the troops, the transport, the machinery of war, the balance of power of the big drive in the offing.

"Interspersed with the heavier traffic are the rolling kitchens, water wagons and combat wagons, each drawn by a span of mules. Ever attempting to forge ahead are the despatch riders on motorcycles with officers in their side cars—and now and then some general officer's staff car in the van. There are never-ending trains of heavy ammunition trucks, loaded, rumbling, groaning and grinding, ever holding to the center of the road.

"On the left, winding through the trees, are the famous French horse, the Dragoons, picturesque indeed with plumes and lances, men and horses alike, big and well-conditioned. Just inside the trees in the ditch on the left of the road patiently plugs the French poilus in faded blue, now gray with dust, with the inevitable drooping moustache—his much-too-long rifle and enough paraphernalia, pots and pans, etc., on his back to start up light housekeeping....

"Between the guns, caissons, supply and ammunition trucks, in other words, between the heavy transport that ever holds command of the center of the road, and the single drab column of Americans on the right, is a Moroccan machine gun outfit, each individual a tall, dark, rangy cuss who moves along with the ease of the true sheik of the desert ... These represent the famous First Moroccan Division, by far the best colonial division in France. With them, we understand, is a regiment of the French Foreign Legion.

"A number of British troops are scattered through the unending line. Beside the Americans whom they pass, their uniforms look smart and tailored."[6]

Inevitably such a massive operation was bedeviled by disorganization. Gerald Thomas of the Sixth Marines: "In the morning of the seventeenth, my truck got lost. We were in an air attack, and a bomb landed at a crossroad right in front of us. Our driver turned right instead of left. After about two miles though, we had an artillery battery right along side of us. He knew damn well that he was going in the wrong direction so we turned around and went back and that got us straightened out."[7]

Because of the confusion and the storms the Twenty-third Infantry and the Sixth Marines were late getting into position, and none of the division's machine gun or 37 mm infantry gun units arrived in time.

Thomas also described the disorganized mass of men and matériel moving up the road, where "everybody was just told to move forward. I don't know whether there was any staff work done other than to say, 'Go (so-and-so).' Hughes knew where he was going, and I think that every battalion commander did. They were just told to make their way the best they could. It would have been impossible to regulate traffic on that road. We were pushed off of the road and we marched out on the edge of the woods. Here and there would be five solid lines of artillery going forward."

In the confusion and congestion, units were separated. "Finally, at seven o'clock at night, we pulled up. Hughes walked off the road and said, 'This is it.' I was right behind him. I don't think that we had 50 men with us." All night long groups of men straggled into the bivouac.

"It rained that night and I didn't know where we were. I knew we were close to the front because, at the end of our march, I could see this artillery along side the road all pointed out to the northeast."[8]

Thomas: "We joined the battalion about eight o'clock the next morning. Then we started to march. Moving forward was a mass of men, transport, munitions, and artillery. There were no tanks that day, but there were troops and artillery marching along this one great highway, the Maubeuge Route through the Villers-Cotterêts Woods—a big place. Hughes decided to stop and take his ten-minute break. Then those behind us started running over the top of us. He said, 'Well, we're just going to keep on marching.' We marched from about nine o'clock in the morning to about seven o'clock at night."[9]

Despite the massive stockpiles of supplies, the distribution system proved totally inadequate to supply even basic necessities as units moved through the countryside. Carl Brannen of the 80th Company, 2/6, remembered not only waiting for hours, muddy roads, and delays caused by ditched vehicles like tanks, but the usual absence of food. The men had not even been issued the unpalatable emergency rations. "Sometime during the day, I got about a spoonful of corned beef, which several of us divided. One of the men had gotten hold of a can somewhere and opened it with his bayonet." [10]

Harbord: "Different units began to arrive in the open edges of the forest by the middle of the forenoon, and only rain clouds screened them from the sight of Boche airplanes and balloons. All day they were arriving tired and worn out. A regiment was held up for two hours by a French major who demanded receipts or the transportation by trucks before they had arrived at destination, and which if given would have resulted in the troops being dumped out as soon as the receipt was signed."

July 18

In the massive confusion "The machine guns of the Marine Brigade had been dumped off near the old Château of Pierrefonds. The men had no transportation and no orders. When finally located and told the mission of the division, these men carried their guns by hand on the long march across fields and muddy roads, getting into position at the last moment. No one can understand exactly what this means unless he has tried to carry a machine gun twelve miles through a plowed field." In the end, only Herculean efforts by the division's Military Police unraveled the blockages and salvaged the situation. Even so, "At 3 A. M., the 5th Marines and the 9th Infantry were forcing their way through the forest and the most careful computation indicated that they would probably arrive in time to attack. At 4 A. M. it was almost a certainty that they would be up with perhaps five minutes to spare."[11]

None of the machine gun or tank units were able to fight their way through the congestion on the roads. The attack would commence without them at 0435 h. Harbord: "As a matter of fact, the regiments got to the point designated for the assault, at the double-time, and ran behind the artillery barrage. There had been no time for reconnaissance by proper officers. There were only the maps showing the approximate position our front lines should be in at the zero hour, with the broad red lines showing the lateral limits of our sector."

At this point the troops had not rested for two nights, had only reserve rations of hardtack and canned meat (many habitually ate these even before attacks). The region had few water sources, with each man carrying only one canteen of water.[12]

The Fourth Brigade was the left flank of the division line, where the attack was led by the Fifth Marines, with the Third Brigade to their right. The Sixth Marines followed as division reserve. The First Division was positioned on the Second Division's right flank. Flanking both divisions were French colonials, including the 1ère Division Marocaine, thought by many to be the best shock troops in the French Army.[13]

The 1/5 on the far left arrived piecemeal, with companies committed as they arrived after the attack began. The lack of adequate briefing on the tactical plan was to cause considerable confusion.

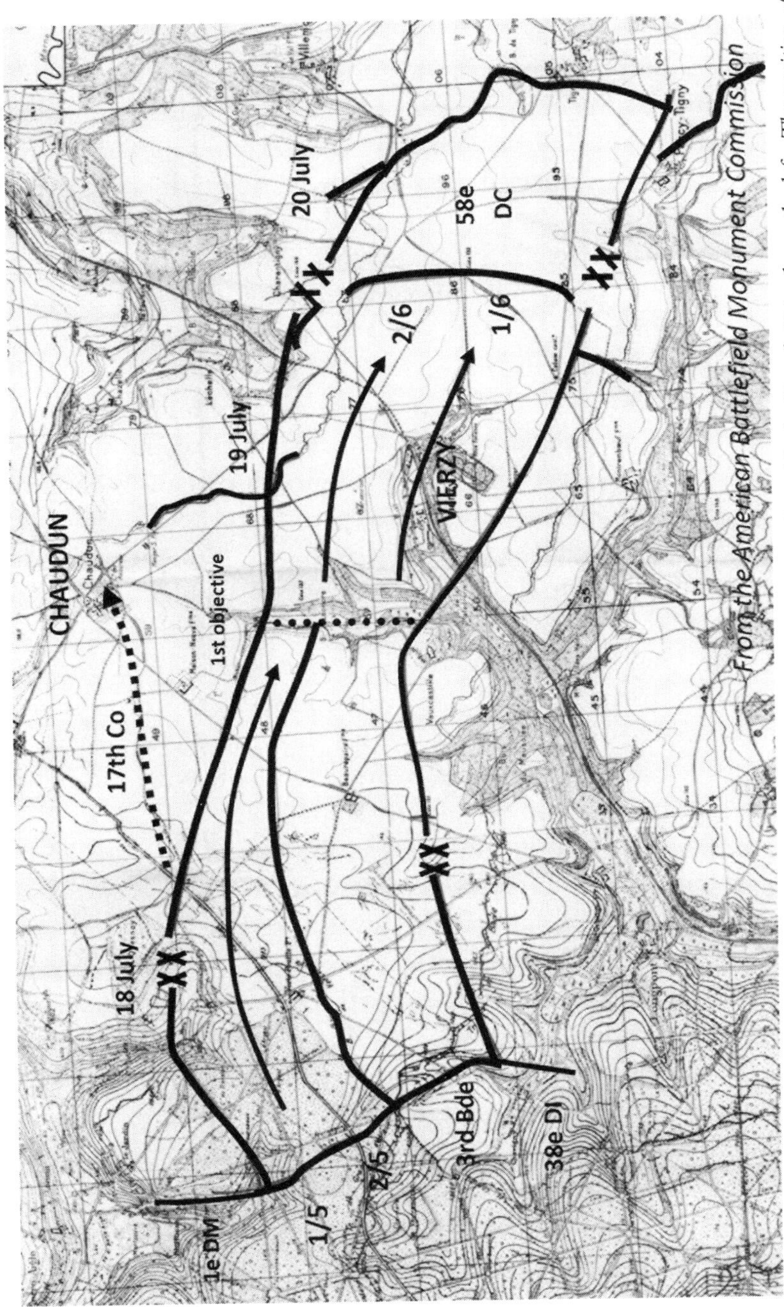

SOISSONS, JULY 1918. *The Second Division advanced rapidly across open terrain, with the Fourth Brigade on the left. The position of Vierzy in a deep ravine made the church steeple landmark invisible, so the 17th Company, 1/5 maintained its initial compass bearing and moved far into the zone of the 1ère Division Marocaine. On the second day the reserve Sixth Marines took over the entire division front until the division was relieved late on the third day by the 58ème Division Coloniale.*

Karl McCune (55th Company, 2/5) arrived at about 0330 h, passing a retiring French machine gun company, "bearded men, muddy from the trenches .... They appeared tired and glad to see the Marines."

At Soissons the Germans were not advancing so rapidly that their artillery trains could not keep up, as had happened at Belleau Wood. The German salient was well established, and the defenders liberally supplied with artillery and heavy machines guns. Even in reserve positions units were not safe from the powerful German artillery. Upon the commencement of the American preparatory barrage, the enemy artillery fired back in earnest even as the Marines were still moving up to their jump-off point. "As we were late, we began to double-time into position, panting, stumbling, well-nigh exhausted; the men ran quickly through the counter-barrage thrown over by the Germans. Men fell now and then, hit by shrapnel. A French infantry unit passed; newly made trenches with machine gun emplacements. Equipment lay everywhere, discarded by troops because it was too heavy and in the way. The second line position was passed. A French sentinel posted at the wire strung across the road, opened it to let the Marines through; shells dropped closer; several men were hit. Big trees cut by the artillery fire lay everywhere about the woods. Exhausted, the men dropped into holes constituting the line, and paused for breath. Exhausted as they were, the men arose and went over the top to meet the enemy."[14]

To add to the German advantages, the Americans had to advance across ground cut by ravines at right angles to the attack; each of these formed a natural trench line, spaced so that each supported the line in front.[15]

Almost immediately the massed enemy machine guns began to rake the attack waves. Again the Marines fell back on small-unit infiltration tactics. Sergeant Louis Cukela was born in Croatia, immigrated to America, and served two years in the US Army. He enlisted in the Marines in 1917, in the 66th Company, 1/5.

Cukela worked his way to the flank of one machine-gun position, killed part of one gun crew with his bayonet; the others fled. He took the enemy's grenades, and heaved them into another position nearby, capturing another machine gun and taking four prisoners. (Cukela received a field commission in September, and went on to become a major. Famous for his rages, and his fractured and creative English, he reportedly once told a runner who garbled his oral message "If I want to send a goddamned fool, I'd go myself.")

Another immigrant, Matek Kocak from Hungary, enlisted in 1907 and served at sea, in Santo Domingo, and at Veracruz. Like Cukela, he worked his way to the flank of a machine-gun position, and rushed it with his bayonet. Outnumbered, Kocak killed three, but as six other Germans closed in, the members of his squad—no longer pinned down—came to his aid and captured the remaining enemy. Later in the day Kocak took command of a group of leaderless Senegalese French colonials. Despite the language barrier, his little command captured two more machine-gun positions.[16]

The delay in the attack gave the opportunity to bring forward 15 tanks to support the Marines in the attack at Vierzy. By 1915 h the town was in American hands, and two Army battalions moved through to continue the advance. Unfortunately the units on either side of Vierzy were held up by heavy fire, and German artillery targeted French tanks as they withdrew, further punishing the American infantry. The artillery fire drove the Moroccans on the left flank back as the attacks stumbled to a stop.

For the Sixth Marines in reserve, the first part of the day was something of a lark, marred only by the fact that "We were horribly short of water. The horses and men had drunk up all the wells for miles around, and there was no water. We sent off details with canteens, and they were gone eight and ten hours before they could come back with their canteens full. That day lancers and Cuirassiers and the beautiful French Cavalry would go loping by. The artillery was displacing forward, at the gallop. On the side of the road the walking wounded were coming back."[17]

For all of Foch's planning, the actual distribution of the mass of supplies broke down. John Hughes was an old campaigner accustomed to operating with extemporized logistics, and knew the importance of food whenever or however he could get it. Gerald Thomas: "The next morning, old 'Johnny the Hard' sent for me at daybreak. He said, 'There's a ration dump up back down the road about half a mile or a mile.' He described where it was. 'You take a detail, and get all the chow you can carry.' I called for half a dozen men from each company, and we went back down. All the dump had was corned willy, which was very bad because there was no water; but we picked up what we could. Going back and forth, by that time, the artillery was firing in support of the attack that was going on. The Fifth Marines had jumped off and the Ninth Infantry. We got back though, and we had our chow. Along about eight o'clock in the morning we were in pretty good shape. I mean the troops were all in, so Hughes moved out. We followed him right up the road."

With the Fifth Marines advancing quickly, the Sixth were rushed forward. "Soon we crossed the old front line. Actually, our attack in that area had been a complete surprise. It had just gone through like cutting through a horn."[18]

Even so, given the powerful German artillery, some of the men in the division reserve did not make it very far. Lieutenant Graves Erskine, now company commander of the 79th Company, 2/6, was concussed during enemy shelling of the American reserve positions, and evacuated within the first hour.[19]

The ravines that had so concerned the planners proved to be no obstacles at all, though one history referred to the wooded areas as "diabolically fortified." By 0930 h the most formidable of the ravines, a Y-shaped feature about 5 km from the start line, had fallen to the Americans. In the plan the Third Brigade on the right was to halt there. The Sixth Marines would move through and assume responsibility for the entire division front. The division turned from a northeasterly to a southeasterly path when the division resumed the attack toward their objectives. The Americans were already racing toward Vierzy.

By mid-afternoon intermingled groups from the Twenty-third Infantry and the Fifth Marines were in position overlooking Vierzy, which was located in a deep ravine, but they were held up by heavy artillery fire and gas. The rapid advance exacerbated the usual confusion caused by poor communications, and General Harbord, went forward on a personal reconnaissance. After encountering the Third Brigade commander he returned to his P.C. and ordered a resumption of the attack, but the regimental commanders said 90 minutes was too short a notice. The slow tanks, still struggling to keep up, had been assigned to the attack, but the unit commander needed an additional hour past that. The attack was ordered for 1800 h, tanks or no tanks.

A hasty attack was planned with 2/5, 1/9, and 2/9 attacking to the north of Vierzy, and 1/23 and 2/23, supported by 1/5 were to attack Vierzy itself. Fifteen tanks and a regiment of artillery would support each attack. The slow-moving machine-gun battalions had finally begun to catch up with the infantry, but the movement of 1/5 across the division rear and the usual breakdown of communications slowed deployment. Worse, all the artillery had been usurped by I Corps for counter-battery fire.

The tanks were Schneider CA 1 heavy tanks of Groupement I. The Schneiders were one of the original heavy tank designs. Armed with a 75 mm *blockhaus* Schneider low-velocity gun and two heavy machine guns, it was slow (8 kph, about 5 mph), clumsy, and had difficulty negotiating obstacles like trenches, ditches, and streambeds. And worse for the crew, it had a nasty tendency to catch fire when hit. It was not a true tank in the usual sense, but had found its niche as an assault gun, an armored artillery piece providing close support for infantry to break through enemy lines. Unfortunately for the attackers, the Germans had grown accustomed to countering armored-vehicle attacks, and were issued armor-piercing ammunition for artillery and machine guns, and man-portable anti-tank rifles.

The movement on Vierzy was the cause of considerable confusion. The outdated maps did not correctly depict Vierzy's position in a deep valley, and the church steeple that would serve as a landmark was invisible to the Marines on the higher terrain.

Problems inherent in the complex division plan of maneuver, a sweeping right-angle turn, aggravated poorly understood orders, resulted in yet more confusion. Units became intermingled with others on their flanks as well as those overtaking them from behind. The leftmost company—the 17th Company, 1/5—unable to recognize landmarks without a map, continued straight along the original compass bearing, taking it toward the village of Chaudun and across the path of the 1ère Division Marocaine.[20]

Thomas: "About three o'clock in the afternoon, our regiment moved forward and deployed on the side of a hill. Down in front of us and off to the left was a line of artillery pieces as far as you could see standing hub to hub. I never saw anything like it before or since. The word was, 'We're going to attack.' We deployed. I'll never forget because as I sat with my platoon there, here came Burr, whom I hadn't seen for six weeks. He had come back from the hospital. He had been wounded and had come back so he came to see me. He wanted to know why I hadn't gotten my commission." Unknown to Thomas, "I had been slated to get one when he left." He quickly filled in Burr on all the scuttlebutt, and the word came to maintain position.[21]

While the Sixth Marines waited, "I saw the greatest spectacle of the War. The French formed for a mass cavalry attack … there were lancers and Cuirassiers and dragoons and everything. There were about 6,000 of them, and they formed them up on a plateau above us. I could see the most spectacular sight. For some reason they didn't get the word to move forward. Finally the Germans threw some shells in among them, and they began to mill around. They all just drifted away."[22]

Carl Brannen noticed not only the anachronistic French lancers with their "long spears", but that "Much airplane fighting was going on, and several planes got shot down. A battle in the air is interesting, and we always watched them if we were not too closely occupied."[23]

Under heavy artillery fire the Marines crossed the Vierzy valley, supported by tanks. For MCune the highlight was that in a bunker "We found hot coffee and the German war bread [*Kommißbrot*][24] and butter which the men devoured, after making the prisoners first sample it."[25]

By nightfall the Americans had driven a deep wedge into the German lines, but both flanks were exposed and there were no communications with the French units on either side. The infantry units were badly depleted by casualties, and reserves could not be moved forward until well into the next day.

As always, patrols continually probed the German positions, seeking intelligence for the continued attack. William Nice, 49th, Company 1/5: "While there I was sent out on patrol one night to locate the enemy. We found them all right and they found us. We had 56 men.

The Germans cut us off from our battalion and there was a lively scrap in which we sustained 37 casualties. The rest of us managed to fight our way back .... I was hit in the right forearm, but it was only a flesh wound and I stayed with the company. We had advanced over six miles, captured over 3,000 prisoners, 11 batteries of artillery, over 100 machine guns and the like. Some of those guns were turned on the retreating enemy."[26]

Catching the Germans by surprise—a rare thing—the brigade had gained six to seven kilometers on the first day.[27]

July 19

The Marines "lay on their arms" all night, and McCune said that "The night was cool and clear, the stars shining. Wounded Marines lay groaning in the fields because there were not enough stretchers to care for all." Corps headquarters was apparently unaware of the division's exposed position, and ordered an attack at 0400 h, but it was delayed until 0700 h.[28]

Louis Jones's company was sent from a reserve position into the line. Despite the massive stockpiles of supplies and munitions, they were so short of ammunition that each man carried only 48 rounds and orders were that additional ammunition was to be issued only in case of a German counterattack.[29]

Support units were still caught up in the traffic jams. McCune wrote that the company field kitchens came up with hot food, and prisoners carried the bulky aluminum food cans up to the front lines. In contrast, Carl Brannen noted that it was now 3 days since his men had last eaten.[30]

In the final phase the Sixth Marines, 3/5, and the late-arriving Sixth Machine Gun Battalion passed through the Fifth to press the attack. The ground over which the Marines advanced was subject to German observation, and the units were heavily shelled as they tried to organize for the attack. The passage of lines was again delayed, until about 0900 h.[31]

Gerald Thomas said that "Again there was no move toward chow, but we had gotten some water during the night. We moved down in the Vierzy Ravine, and then we went on forward, past Vierzy. My battalion came up out of the Vierzy Ravine and deployed on the edge of a wheat field. The Germans, who were over on the right on a hill, spotted us. They were about 1,800 yards away, but they started throwing machine gun bullets at us. We had a few casualties. It didn't worry anybody much.

"I could see Holcomb's battalion come out of the orchard way off to our left and deploy and move out. Then I would see another outfit on their left, that was Sibley. We lay there, and after awhile we heard rumbling. It was the tanks. We were waiting for the tanks to come. When the tanks passed through, the command came, 'Forward.' We got up and started going with them."[32]

Clifton Cates, 96th Company, 2/6: "The morning of the 19th we attacked from a position just east of Vierzy. Major Holcomb's battalion had the left flank and the First Moroccans [Division] were on our left .... So we formed for this attack and we were supposed to have had, I think it was, eight little old French tanks. So there we stayed for an hour or an hour and a half waiting for these French tanks to arrive. By that time, we were getting not only artillery fire but indirect machine gun fire. They were shooting indirect coming over the hill. In fact, one hit the back of my shoulder. I thought somebody had hit me with a rock. I finally pulled it out and it was a red hot bullet. I went right over to Major Holcomb and yelled to him, 'well, I got the first *blessé*. Here's the first wound' and I handed him this bullet and he dropped it, it was still hot."

When the attack finally commenced, "It was the most beautiful attack that I have ever seen. As far as you could see, up to the right, there were just waves and waves of men extending up to two miles I guess." These were the division's Third Brigade and another division. "The Moroccans that were supposed to have attacked on our left didn't appear at all. We broke the first German lines without too much trouble. By this time though we were catching billy-hell and I don't mean maybe—artillery fire and machine guns—and about that time I had just remarked to this Sergeant of mine close to me, I said, 'Look at Captains Woodward and Robertson getting right together there. That's bad business.' And I hadn't any more said it when a shell hit close to them and they both went down. By that time, the other Lieutenants had all been wounded and I was the only one left out of the company. I tried to take charge, but just about that time a whole bunch of Germans jumped up out of the trench and started running and our men went after them like a bunch of coyotes. With that, it was bedlam. I was never able to organize them again. I kept the attack going for about a kilometer, I guess. By that time, though, we were getting terrific fire from our left flank."[33]

Brannen: "we formed our lines and came out for a charge across a sugar beet field. The tanks were leading, with our lines right behind them. In trying to stop the charge, the Germans turned loose everything they had. It seemed to rain shells. One hit between me and the man on my left, Red Williams. It knocked a hole in the ground, half covered me with dirt, and left my hands and face powder-burned, but the shrapnel missed. Red was not quite so lucky and received his death wound. I left him writhing and groaning on the ground, and continued the attack." Lieutenant John W. Overton, a Yale track star from Tennessee, was walking backward, encouraging his men. "He was soon down, killed. The gunnery sergeant was killed." (There is a discrepancy in memories here, since Gerald Thomas described Overton as being alive later in the fighting).[34]

Almost every Marine vividly recalled that the tanks, "attracted considerable artillery fire" until about a third were disabled. Gaspar saw "tremendous" columns of prisoners marching four abreast. He spoke German, and "They answered my questions. The officers were more arrogant than the men. You take the old dedicated officer: he was inclined to be arrogant."[35]

Thomas: "The Germans had massed their artillery on a hill about three or four miles off in front of us. It was all direct fire. And, boy, they let us have it. Everybody, I don't think that anyone of those tanks went more than 1,500 yards. We just caught hell from the machine guns on the left, the artillery."

Although much of the fire was directed at the tanks, there was plenty to go around. Gerald Thomas: "Our attack collapsed. We just simply collapsed. A little fellow near me, J. P. White, who had been one of my original platoon boys with me .... I was [inaudible]. I was platoon sergeant. At that time I was still a sergeant. I couldn't see anybody. I saw people lying down. The attack was over. We saw a twelve-inch iron field roller that some Frenchman had left in the wheat field. J.P. and I got down behind that roller, and the goddamn machine gun bullets are clicking off of that roller. We started to dig, and we dug ourselves a little hole. It took a good time because the ground was like rock. We had to work on our bellies with a shovel. He had a pick and I had a shovel. We got ourselves a little hole so we could get a little depression behind the roller.

"About an hour and a half later, I looked up and there was still a lot going on. They were dropping hand grenades out of airplanes on us. We couldn't tell what was happening because some of them would explode in the air. The German planes were cruising around overhead and they were dropping grenades on us."[36]

The German air superiority was recalled by many veterans of the fighting, and Clifton Cates described being strafed as Marines fired back with all weapons. "So this one came right down our lines and I could see that gunner's eyes as clear as I see yours. And he couldn't get his gun depressed enough to get where we were .... I fired three shots with my pistol while that bird was going by and I know I saw the fabric fly from his plane."[37]

There is a tendency for men to pull together in groups for psychological reassurance, but Carl Brannen remembered his training and made an effort to avoid bunching up with other men. Then a shell hit a group near him, killing or wounding most. There was no shelter to be found for the units being shot to pieces in the open fields. "By this time, all the tanks had been crippled or stopped and all the men around me shot down. I was now nearing the woods across the field in front of our attack zone. Realizing this, I began to look for a stopping place and found it in an old sunken road less than a foot deep. A volley from a machine gun missed me by inches, and, falling where I stood in the road, I drew fire which barely cleared my body for the rest of the day.

"In thirty of forty minutes, our regiment had been almost annihilated. The field which had been recently crossed was strewn with dead and dying. Their cries for water and help got weaker as the hot July day wore on." German planes flew low overhead and as one plane flew past, "the pilot leaned his head over the side looking through his glasses, I lay feigning death. The hot sun made my thirst almost unbearable."[38]

Gerald Thomas: "What had caused us to be slaughtered was the fact that the Moroccan division which was supposed to have come up on our right, was delayed. The machine guns that were giving us hell were the one that the Moroccans should have taken .... There was nobody on our right except German machine guns.

"The Moroccans made an attack when they came up. Then they sent through an outfit trying to pass through their left and go down and take a little village in front of us. They lost all of their men. They lost the whole outfit. There must have been seventy-five of them. It wounded or killed every one of them.

"Maybe at noon or a little after, I was able to get up and peek around [the abandoned roller]. That's after the Moroccans came forward." Thomas spotted Overton. "He was sitting in a ditch, alongside of a sunken road. He was commander of the Seventy-sixth Company. He said, 'Come on over here.' I went over him. He said, 'I've got to go back and see Major Hughes. I'd like to take him the best information that I have of the line. I know that the situation is here directly in front of me, where what's left of my company is, but I don't know what's over in that other area so I want you to go and find out.'

"I moved up through the wheat and went along from one foxhole to another. There I found about one hundred men. I got to what I thought was the left of my battalion. I went back and told Overton that I had found about one hundred men, and that my company had about thirty-three men left in it as far as I could determine.

"There were perhaps 200 of them who started this attack."

"Overton went back during the afternoon to see Hughes. Hughes had had a tragic day too because the company commanders who had survived the attack went back to report to him. They were sitting with two members of his staff—Burr and Turner, the adjutant—in a sunken road when a German shell dropped right in the midst of them and killed or wounded every damn one of them and had killed Burr. It had blown off his head. My platoon commander, who by then was my company commander, Dave Redford, was wounded.

"Overton came back and told me all this; and then he said, 'We're going to be relieved at midnight by the French. When you are relieved, get your men together and go directly with them to Major Hughes because there are many wounded that have not been evacuated. We want to try to get them out.' At midnight the French came in. I got my thirty-three men; I went back to battalion headquarters. We made stretchers out of blankets wrapped around the rifles, and we carried the wounded out.

"Later we may have found another thirty-five or forty men at different places, but my company lost over fifty percent. There were a lot of them killed. Our battalion suffered very heavily because we were on the right flank where those Germans were before the Moroccans came. We really took a shellacking."[39]

In Walter Gaspar's newly minted company: "We were pretty well depleted in manpower and we only had about 170 enlisted. We had a full complement of officers. But we went over the top at nine o'clock in the morning, and by two o'clock the next morning we had two officers and 15 men in the 76th Company .... So Hughes—Johnny the Hard—raised Cain. I can hear him yet, walking up and down, cursing and what not, trying to get something done; not blaming us but blaming the rear." A unit of *tirailleurs* eventually relieved Gaspar's company. The senior officer was shell-shocked, "we kept him there on his feet but he didn't do anything."[40] Gaspar assumed temporary command of the company.

The German artillery fire reached a crescendo, most falling on supporting units along the roads, as did nocturnal air attacks. Some units, like the dressing stations and regimental headquarters, were able to shelter in a huge underground quarry in the ravine.[41]

Cates: "So we finally—the attack just petered out. We were up near an old sugar mill. And that's where I wrote that message, that you all have on file, to major Holcomb. I think it said 'I have twenty men out of my company or out of my battalion and a few stragglers', and I wound up by saying, 'I will hold.'" The full text of Cates's message was "I have only two men out of my company and 20 out of some other company. We need support, but it is almost suicide to try to get it here as we are swept by machine gun fire and a constant barrage is on us. I have no one on my left and only a few on my right. I will hold." This quote is often misattributed to the fighting at Belleau Wood.[42]

One of the stragglers was Carl Brannen. He had spotted a man crawling along the sunken road, and "Laboriously crawling to where he disappeared, I found my old friend Lieutenant Cates* of the 96th Company holding a trench with about twelve or fifteen men. He asked me where the where the rest of the 80th Company was, and I told

*Brannen only later became an "old friend" of Cates.

him that I didn't know, but thought most of them were hit." One of famished men crawled out between the lines and scavenged some black bread from the body of a German soldier. "I had a spoonful or two of sugar in my condiment can and with the sugar to sprinkle on the bread we got a bite around."[43]

Cates: "By that time though, I had had a pretty bad wound across my knee. A shell had broken off to my right and cut my knee. In fact, it tore my trousers out. That's when, after that, they started calling me 'Kiltie'. But anyway, we tried—I tried to form a line and as it turned out, I was one of about two officers left out of the battalion on the front lines. One of them, Captain Lloyd, was way off to the left front. He had gotten off out of position .... Anyway I was obsessed with the idea that I wanted to know where all our men were so I could establish a barrage line. A straggler told me, 'I think Captain Lloyd with eight or ten men is out to our left front some place.'

"So I sent a couple of runners out to try and see if they could locate him and they never came back—evidently casualties. So I decided, well, I was going to find out. So I took off my equipment, and I might say I had plenty of it on because I looked like a harness shop. I had two Sam Browne belts and all kind of leather. But I took off my equipment and took my pistol in my pocket and I worked down the trench to this road to the left and then I got to the road. I walked straight into the German lines, walking along-side the road. And when I got down fairly close to this sugar mill, I could see a couple of Dutchmen [Germans]—I caught three kneeling down—and I knew they had me covered. I was about 150 yards away. So I eased over the side of the road and I saw a little ditch and I made a dive for it just as they cut loose at me. So I lay there and I didn't know what to do with [inaudible] bullets clipping over me. There was a mound of earth over to the right and I got all set and made a dive up and over that and jumped on the other side of it. As I did, I went right square on some men. My first thought was that they were Germans. It turned out to be Captain Lloyd with the eight men that were in this fox hole. So I said, 'Well, I've been trying to find you so I could establish a barrage line so our artillery won't hit you.'

"So then I had to get back to my hole which was about two hundred yards away and, I might say, I had a tough time getting there, too." Later that night a detachment of Moroccan infantry relieved the handful of Marines.[44]

The Germans' lavish use of artillery ammunition had taken a heavy toll, sometimes indirectly. William Rogers, 84th Company 3/6: "We were pretty well shot up. We were pulled out of there [Tigny]." In a wooded area "We were not so much afraid of the shells as we were of the limbs falling off the trees, because the wind was blowing and there were high trees. Oh, it was a terrible time. We'd get up close to the trunk of the trees so we wouldn't get killed by a branch falling. We stayed there for a day or so."[45]

The falling trees actually could be quite deadly. Gunner William Nice: "And remember, we hadn't had food for two days and had gone three nights without sleep. That's where I lost my orderly, little Tritt. We found him dead under the branches of a fallen tree."[46]

The division had outrun its artillery, and it was thought to be dangerous to continue an advance without support. In addition, the division had long since outrun its telephone communications, and coordination was increasingly difficult. The Second Division was too badly battered to be effective. In the night hours of July 19/20, the division was relieved by the French 58e Division Coloniale.

July 20

Brannen: "The marines who left the battle line were a terrible looking bunch of people. They looked more like animals. They had almost a week's growth of beard and were dirty and ragged. Their eyes were sunk back in their heads. There had been very little sleep or rest for four days."

McCune said that when the Marines halted for a short interval, "the Marines 'bummed' coffee, wine, etc. from the Frenchmen. We passed a big pile of salvage which the men ransacked for needed articles. Exhausted soldiers were sleeping everywhere. Then the battalion halted; ate supper—cornbill [canned corned beef], French bread and coffee. The next morning breakfast was served—the same old stuff—slum!"

Brannen said that the survivors of the 2/5 were merged into a single understrength company, and sent into a temporary rest area. There the firing of a nearby artillery battery drove one man mad with shell shock.

Despite his violent ravings, "I dropped back down to sleep while he was being carried away."[47]

According to official sources the Marines suffered 189 dead and 1,153 wounded, with the most severe losses in the Sixth Marines. Cates later estimated his battalion had suffered around two-thirds of its strength in casualties.

When the Sixth Marines finally left the line, Jones said, "I went in as a senior lieutenant of this company and carried out the battalion, which was reduced to about 104 men, in one day … So we went in with 1,200 men and came out with about 104."[48]

After Soissons the Sixth Marines were sent to the relatively quiet Pont-à-Mousson sector near the Moselle River to recuperate and absorb replacements. Quiet was a relative term, as Walter Gaspar found out, when near dawn one day when he and his gunnery sergeant, Edward E. Steele were occupying a fighting hole "the Germans decide to send four shells over [Austrian 88s] … and the third hit our hole in the ground and we were buried, just covered. Fortunately neither one of us was hit. It just piled all the dirt in in top of us, but we got out of that. The doctor came along and he wanted to evacuate us. I said, 'What for? I'm not hurt.'"[49]

Lieutenant Erskine was temporarily absent with a mild case of influenza, and when he returned "went right back to my platoon." First Sergeant Barber was dead, Captain Zane wounded in Belleau Wood and evacuated (to die in hospital of influenza), and a new lieutenant had taken over Second Platoon. "I told him to get out, 'This is my platoon, I organized it, and goddamn it, that's that.'"

The sector abutted that of the American 1st Division, and the men had heard stories of German infiltrators disguised as Americans. Erskine was looking around, armed only with a pistol stuck in his trouser belt when he "heard somebody say, 'Halt.' I got up and looked around … and here was this great big husky fellow, with slightly reddish hair, and he wore an Army enlisted man's uniform with a major's leaves on, and he was giving this Marine hell there, 'I am your battalion commander.' So I stepped up and said, 'You are not my battalion commander, I know who my battalion commander is, and this is a Marine sector, and you get back up in the Army [sector], and stay up there.'"

The man was disposed to argue. "He got a little bit rough and I yanked out my pistol and made him stick his hands up. He said, 'I am Maj. E. C. Williams, commander of the 2nd Battalion of the Sixth Marines.' I said, 'Well, you don't look like my battalion commander'" and marched him to the rear.

"Capt. Van Dorn was the adjutant at that time and when I marched him in I could see Van Dorn's face just change, and I realized that something was wrong. And he [the prisoner], said, 'Tell this goddamn fool who I am.' And he [Van Dorn] said. 'This is the new battalion commander, Maj. Williams.'" Erskine tried to explain away his error, but "Bull" Williams "said 'About face … Now double time all the way back to your CP.' And I did."[50]

CHAPTER 9

The Women Marines

All women are created equal. Then some become Marines.

ANONYMOUS

The horrific casualty toll of the summer, 1918 fighting precipitated a manpower crisis for the Marine Corps. Even with the training cycle shortened to a ridiculous degree, and combing out every man from existing posts, the Corps could still not replace its losses. When an assessment revealed that about 40% of the clerical work could be performed by women, Commandant Barnett explored the idea of tapping a hitherto untapped resource—female clerical workers from the business world. On August 2 Barnett penned a request to the Secretary of the Navy Josephus Daniels requesting authorization to enroll women for clerical duties. (A sign of the women's ambiguous status was that they were "enrolled" rather than enlisted.) Six days later Daniels signed the authorization.[1]

The Navy Appropriations Act of 1916 had already created a Reserve category that opened a legalistic door for the enlistment of female Marines. Four months earlier the Navy had enlisted women as clerical workers (yeomen in naval terminology). But the law that authorized Army enlistment specifically specified "male persons", so the Army would lag behind in enlisting women. By the end of the war some 350 female Marines were employed in clerical duties.[2]

The trigger date for enlistment was set for August 13, and that morning thousands of women flooded recruiting offices. Motivations were mixed: Private Theresa Lake's husband had been killed in France, and others had husbands or male relatives in the service.[3]

Exactly how seniority was determined is unavoidably murky, but the first female Marine of record was Mrs. Opha May Johnson, a Civil Service clerical worker for the Interstate Commerce Commission.* On August 13 Johnson by happenstance was first in line at the Washington DC recruiting station. [4] Thirty-nine years old at the time of her enlistment, Johnson was immediately put to work in the Quartermaster General's office processing the paperwork of her fellow recruits.

Recruiting criteria specified women of excellent character (three letters of recommendation were required), neat appearance, with business or office experience, preferably as stenographers, bookkeepers, accountants, and typists, although general office workers might be considered. Applicants were to be between 18 and 40 years of age, though (like men) those under 18 might enlist with the consent of their parents.[5]

Like their male counterparts, most enlistment rejections were for physical reasons, and as of September 1, "So stringent are the physical requirements, though, that as of yet comparatively few have been accepted." The conduct of physicals, designed for men and conducted by Navy doctors, presented immediate problems. Detailed instructions on the conduct of examinations were promulgated, including the specification that "Corsets should invariably be removed." Only about one in 400 applicants were accepted.[6]

Many recruiting offices were overwhelmed by sheer numbers, and in New York Florence Gertler recalled that "Male noncommissioned officers went up and down the line asking questions about experience, family responsibilities, etc., and by the process of elimination got the line down to a few hundred." Applicants were interviewed and given a stenographic dictation test, required to read back their notes, and type them up. This process reduced the number of applicants to five.[7]

As with male recruits, sometimes sheer persistence paid off. Seventeen-year-old Elizabeth Shoemaker failed the typing test. Attempting to disguise herself, Shoemaker returned the next day but was recognized by a colonel (probably Albert McLemore), and she was asked if she had been

*Johnson's middle name is often cited as Mae, but she spelled it May on documents.

there the day before. When she admitted to the ruse "he got up and leaned over the desk and shook my hand and said, 'That's the spirit that will lick the German, I will allow you to take the test again.'" She passed.[8]

Martha L. Wilchinski, a straightforward young woman, unusually well-educated with a degree in journalism from New York University, enlisted in New York City. She quickly wrote to her fiancé in France: "Dear Bill: I've got the greatest news! No, have n't thrown you over; I'm still strong for you, Bill. No, it's no use; don't try to guess. You're not used to that much mental effort, and you might get brain-fag [mental fatigue]. Besides, you'd never guess anyway. Now, listen, and try to get this. I know it'll be hard at first, but it'll grow on you after a while. Are you ready? Well, then,—I'm a lady leatherneck; I'm the last word in Hun-hunters; I'm a real, live, honest-to-goodness Marine! The process was painful, I admit, and lasted for thirty-six hours, but I survived it all right. Our future together doesn't look so black to me now.... I'm not looking for sympathy or anything, but honest, I've been through an awful lot. They've done everything except punch my name out on my chest. That's coming soon, I guess."

She continued that a willingness to go anywhere duty required, and the requirement to be a skilled stenographer, thinned the group considerably. "And from what was left the lieutenant picked out twelve to go over to the colonel and have him give us the double O. I was one of them, of course. I'm not looking for applause, but you know I always said you could not keep a good man down. You're only a corporal, Bill, so you may not know what a colonel is. A colonel is a man who talks to you over the top of his glasses and looks through you as if you were a piece of smoked glass. You know me, I'm not afraid of anything this side of sudden death, but during the three seconds he looked at me I had everything from nervous prostration to paralysis agitans [an antiquated term for Parkinson's disease]. That's called psychological effect. I wouldn't admit it to a soul but you because it's scientific and will probably go over your head, anyway. The colonel gave us a pretty stiff examination, and out of the fifteen, five lived to break the news to mother." The colonel was Albert McLemore, the Officer In Charge of Marine Corps Recruiting.[9]

The next morning a physical examination winnowed the group down and "Well, only three of us came out alive." The group was sworn in by the colonel, and "Something kept sticking in my throat all the time. I don't know whether it was heart or my liver. I had to swallow it several times before I could say 'I do.'"

Wilchinski soon got a taste of military life, particularly what Marines call "police duty". She wrote Bill that "I've been so busy sweeping floors and picking up cigarette butts and washing windows and everything, I have n't had a chance [to write] …. What'll I say to my grandchildren, Bill? When they ask me: 'What did you do in the Great War, Grandma?' I'll have to say: 'Washing windows on the second floor'. That's a fine thing to have written on your tombstone, is n't it?"

She went on to express the complaints of any enlisted Marine of any era. An announced visit by a general led to a flurry of activity, with everyone "scrubbing and bumping into each other and stepping on each other's feet and everything. And just because I'm low in rank I have to do most of the work. The captain comes in and says: 'Here's where you ought to shine!' 'I am shining, Captain,' I says; 'I'm shining everything in sight.'" As is usually the case, the general never showed up.

Bill was wounded and sent to recuperate in a Paris hospital. "'You want to be careful about those French girls, Bill. They're terribly rough. I hear you can't take a peaceful walk by yourself without having one of them drape herself around your oesophagous and getting closer to you than your landlady on payday. I'm sending you a book on biology. It's called 'How to Tell the Wild Women.' You ought never to go to Paris without it."

Martha closed one letter with yet another complaint. "Well, I've got to stop now and start in picking up cigarette butts again. They're smoking them pretty short this year. I tell you, Bill, if I ever have a home of my own, there'll be no cigarettes in my house."[10]

An issue that quickly arose was what to call these unprecedented military personnel in an age of male domination. The Corps made it clear that "Marine Reserve (F)" was the official title, but the public and press was enamored of other names. Marinesse was one early term that appeared in the press, quickly superseded by Marinette. In any case,

Above: DeHavilland DH-4 bombers being made ready for a mission. Marine Corps aircraft operated in conjunction with the British from airfields near Calais. *(USMC HD)*

Right: In the final months of the war the Corps created a Women's Reserve to serve in various non-combat capacities, freeing men to fight in France. *(USMC HD)*

In the Allied Army of Occupation, the Marines were assigned to the Rhine River Patrol. These civilian excursion boats have been fitted with captured German heavy machine guns. *(USMC HD)*

as Corporal Avadney Hea noted, "they posted notices every once in a while on the bulletin board, that we were not to be referred to as 'Marinettes.' We were United States Marine Corps Reserves with 'F' in parenthesis after indicating female. And we were not to be called 'Marinettes.' The Marine Corps didn't like it."[11]

The hasty incorporation of women into the Corps resulted in confusion about clothing, and many served their first weeks or even months in civilian clothing. Eventually a uniform patterned after that of male Marines was adopted, and the wide-rimmed campaign hat was particularly popular. There was no formal dress blue uniform for women, only the winter "greens". Unlike men, the women mailed measurements to secure uniforms, and "they were horrible. We had to have a little tailoring done on them."

The summer uniform was not at all popular: "then in the summertime they sent us some of the most horrible khaki-colored things you ever saw in your life," and many of the women chose to wear the woolen winter greens year round. At least in some duty stations women also received dispensation to wear shoes rather than the prescribed high-top dress boots. Considerable uproar was created by women Marines wearing the Sam Browne belts (the mark of an officer; all female Marines were enlisted) and the authorized carrying of swagger sticks, another mark of an officer. The attractive uniform was widely emulated by civilian clothing designers.[12]

The Marine Reserves (F) went on to serve in a wide variety of roles other than office staff. These included recruiting, writing for Marine Corps publications, filmmaking (Sergeant Lela "Mackey" Leibrand[13] made the first military training film, *All In A Day's Work*), and messengers.[14]

Drill seems to have been a particularly difficult skill for the women recruits, and many other aspects of military life escaped the women. Two sisters from a socially prominent family bypassed the chain of command to complain directly to Colonel McLemore about being ordered to sweep and wash windows. The results were predictable. On another occasion Private Shoemaker overstayed her leave to attend a party, only to quickly find herself the guest of honor at a summary court martial. By the time proceedings ended "Through the grapevine word had gotten around and there was crowd of enlisted men waiting to congratulate me; the Marine Corps newspaper published the shameful story and I got letters from all over the world, including China, telling me not to worry, and saying 'Now you are a real Marine.'"[15]

CHAPTER 10

St. Mihiel

> An American Army was an accomplished fact, and the enemy had felt its power.
>
> GENERAL JOHN J. PERSHING

With no Marine Corps command billets open commensurate with his rank, John Lejeune had been posted to the Army's 64th Brigade, of the Thirty-fifth Division. Pershing was gravely concerned about the crucial but struggling Service of Supply, and decided to transfer James Harbord (an able administrator) from his Second Division command. This produced a ripple effect that led to Lejeune's July 25 transfer to the Second Division after only three weeks in command of the 64th Brigade.

Lejeune was by now a brigadier general, and there is speculation that perhaps Pershing thought that a Marine in a division command might at last put a stop to Barnett's and Daniels' meddling in AEF affairs. On July 28 Harbord sent for Lejeune, and told him he would command the Second Division.

Lejeune was "stunned", and his assignment created quite a kerfuffle. The new command called for a major general. Until the war the Corps rated only one major general, the Commandant, and his was a temporary rank: he reverted to the permanent rank of brigadier at the end of his term. The expansion of the Corps had required the creation of a second temporary billet. Lejeune's necessary promotion threw sand into the gears, and required the intervention of two admirals, and eventually an order from President Wilson. Lejeune would be the third major general in the Corps' history, and the first Marine to command a full division.[1]

Lejeune would prove to be an inspired choice, and Assistant Division Surgeon Richard Derby wrote that Lejeune "maintained among officers and men the same high standard of morale and cemented the ties of comradeship and respect between the two infantry brigades."[2]

Pershing was growing increasingly irritated by the patronizing attitude of the British and French commanders. The Allies thought the Americans inexperienced with poor staff work, and in turn the Americans thought their Allies tired, timid, and with such an ingrained trench mentality that they were psychologically unprepared for the mobile warfare required to exploit any breakthrough in the coming great offensives.

This next Allied offensive was intended to pinch off the St. Mihiel salient that threatened railway lines essential to any future Allied offensives in eastern France. The salient was asymmetric, with a deep western penetration that ran south from Fresnes to St. Mihiel, then narrowed with the front line trending easterly to the vicinity of Pont-à-Mousson. An important strategic feature of the salient was its mountainous spine. Mont Sec, a 760-m (2,500-ft) flat-topped peak near the nose of the salient dominated the local terrain and allowed unobstructed observation over a huge swath of Allied territory.[3]

Reduction of the salient would also bring about a major reversal of the strategic situation along this sector of the front. German possession of the salient allowed their artillery to interdict the Paris–Nancy rail line. Reduction of the salient would eliminate the threat and instead place the Allies in position to sever the Metz–Sedan rail line that allowed the Germans to shuffle reinforcements along the front, and would threaten German iron ore production in the Briey Basin.[4]

The offensive would be the first in which the new American Army would operate three multi-division corps, and under full American command. In the larger scheme of things the American effort was seen by the Allied commanders as a preliminary to a much greater offensive that would engulf the entire Western Front within a month.

Time was of the essence, particularly around the St. Mihiel salient. "On account of the swampy nature of the country it was especially important that the movement be undertaken and finished before the fall rains should begin, which was usually about the middle of September." In anticipation of the difficulties in moving through a ravaged no man's land with few usable roads, engineer supplies were stockpiled and support units reorganized. As an example, Derby said that "In order to have plenty of animal transportation on hand, in case the roads were impassable to motors, we ordered the medical cart which accompanied each battalion on the march, to report to the Director of Ambulance Companies at Noviant. These twelve carts, together with the animal drawn ambulance company, insured the medical department's being able to traverse No Man's Land as soon as the infantry and artillery had crossed."[5]

Fortunately for Lejeune, in his days at the Army War College he had studied another campaign fought over the same terrain in the Franco-Prussian War (1870–1871). Although he had no personal knowledge of the region, he still had a leg-up on most officers.[6]

Pershing and his staff labored tirelessly to formulate plans for an offensive by 13 American divisions and French forces to pinch off the salient, only to have Marshal Ferdinand Foch throw a monkey wrench into the plan at the last moment. Foch was looking ahead to the great Fall Offensive, and proposed a far more limited offensive to attack the tip of the salient head on. More significantly, Foch's plans were, once again, to break up Pershing's carefully crafted American Army. Eventually a compromise was reached. The American offensive would continue, but be limited in scope, restricted to pinching off the salient and not advancing upon the Metz–Verdun railway system. In return the French would withdraw their objections to the Americans fighting as an integrated whole in the great offensive planned for late September through November.

The Germans had held the salient for much of the war, with ample time to develop strong defenses. However German shortages of manpower were now limiting their capabilities. Armeeabteilung (Army Detachment) C, of some ten divisions, already planned to abandon the salient, and had formulated Plan Loki for a staged withdrawal. The goal was to anticipate the Allied attack, and withdraw over a period of days to leave the Allies punching an empty bag. As it turned out, the Germans commenced their withdrawal on September 11.

The overall Allied plan was for the French Colonial Corps to attack the southern nose of the salient, pinning German forces in place. The American V Corps would attack the western shoulder of the salient, while the American IV Corps and I Corps attacked the eastern shoulder.

The overly optimistic American expectation was that the Allies could recapture the strategic city of Metz and its transportation hub—definitely not part of Foch's plan.

The Second Division would be part of the American I Corps (Major General Hunter S. Liggett) of five divisions, part of the French Huitième Armée. The American I Corps and IV Corps would advance north, and then pivot west to cut off the nose of the salient. The Second Division, reinforced by an observation balloon company and the First Aero Squadron, would have to penetrate only as far as the transportation center at Thiacourt on the shallow east end of the salient. The observation aircraft of the Aero Squadron were tasked with observing colored cloth panels laid out by infantry to mark forward positions, allowing better tactical control of artillery.

The division would have abundant armored support: three light tank companies (45 Renault FTs from the 13e Bataillon de Chars Légers, 505e Régiment d'Artillerie Spéciale) and 18 Schneider medium tanks (from the Groupement XI). The medium tanks were tasked to help the division breach the enemy wire and first-line defenses, while the faster and far more agile FTs would assist in eliminating any centers of enemy resistance during the general advance.[7]

Overall the offensive would also see the first combat by American tanks, two battalions of Renault FTs operated by Colonel George Patton, as well as the 420 French light and medium tanks.

In the Second Division zone the Third Brigade would lead the assault in the usual two columns of battalions, with the Fourth Brigade in train.

Casualties in the Soissons battle had as usual been appalling, and hordes of partially trained replacements had to be quickly integrated. One such green man, Private Wilbur Brown, arrived as a replacement in Merwin Silverthorn's 20th Company, 3/5, just before the battle.

At last Leo Hermle was able to leave the replacement battalion when a captain was assigned to the 74th Company, 1/6 and took him along as Second Platoon leader. Other officers were simply shuttled around to replace casualties, like Louis Jones who was made the CO of the 83rd Company, 3/6.[8]

Officer casualties in particular were massive, so William Rogers was promoted to second lieutenant despite his lack of formal education. He had not attended the hasty officer training program at Gondecourt, and in fact his only advanced military training was a two-week gas warfare course. Against precedent, he was transferred to lead his old platoon. Then unable to evade his past, he was made battalion billeting officer, and then was ordered to scout the positions for the upcoming offensive.[9]

Upon his return from the hospital Graves Erskine was reassigned as battalion scout officer for 2/6 in August 1918.

Although his division was not yet in its attack position, Lejeune and some staff officers went forward to survey the terrain held by the division they were to replace. "We drove by automobile up a steep ridge to a point some distance below the crest where all vehicles were required to stop. As we drove up the ridge, we watched the bursting of shell after shell in a ravine about a hundred feet to our left. The Germans were evidently feeling for the road, as the range was slightly shortened after each burst. Just as we reached the crest of the ridge on foot, a shell burst in a group of men who were having a kit inspection. Eight of them were either killed or wounded. It was heartbreaking to see the poor mangled and bleeding bodies being carried into a shack which was used as the messroom of the battalion headquarters …."

It was also here that Lejeune witnessed his only mentioned example of the blind panic to which many succumbed. Walking down a communications trench "we heard sounds of a man's rapid footsteps. He soon appeared and almost knocked us down as he went by at a great rate of speed, shouting 'Run! -- --- it! Run! The Germans are shooting at us.'" Then they came across a lone man with pick and shovel calmly building a ramp for tanks and artillery to cross a trench in the coming attack. The man explained that "He is my buddy and was working here with me, but he got the idea in his head that all the guns in Germany were shooting at him, so he beat it."[10]

A period of rain and low clouds prohibited German air operations, so that for once Allied movements were unmolested by observed artillery fire. It was fortunate since the September 11/12 night march was the usual terrible snarl, with divisions moving across each other's paths, and Army traffic-control MPs uncertain of where to send units.

Perhaps as a joke gone wrong, Major Williams told Erskine that as scout officer he would take the battalion scout platoon and advance 1,000 yards ahead of the battalion and keep him apprised of the evolving situation. "So when we got ready to pass through I got ready to move out, because an order is an order, and he laughed and said, 'No, we won't do that now.'"[11]

The Second Division units held at rearward positions to avoid German detection, and "Come nightfall we all moved out—artillery, infantry, and everybody heading for the front line.... And of all the pandemonium you ever saw, that was it."[12]

September 12

The preliminary bombardment for the Second Division was prolonged—four hours, beginning at 0100 h—followed by a 30-minute machine-gun barrage by over 2,200 guns. The Sixth Machine Gun Battalion reported firing directly over the heads of the advancing Third Brigade troops, ceasing fire at 0548 h as the soldiers moved into the danger zone. The report of Company C of the Sixth Machine Gun Battalion was typical. Beginning at 0500 h the guns commenced a 28-minute raking of specified enemy positions. Fire was shifted forward as the infantry advanced; the company expended 30,000 rounds.[13]

At 0500 h the infantry and tanks attacked behind a rolling barrage under rain and a dense ground fog. The machine guns then packed up and advanced with the passing Fifth Marines.

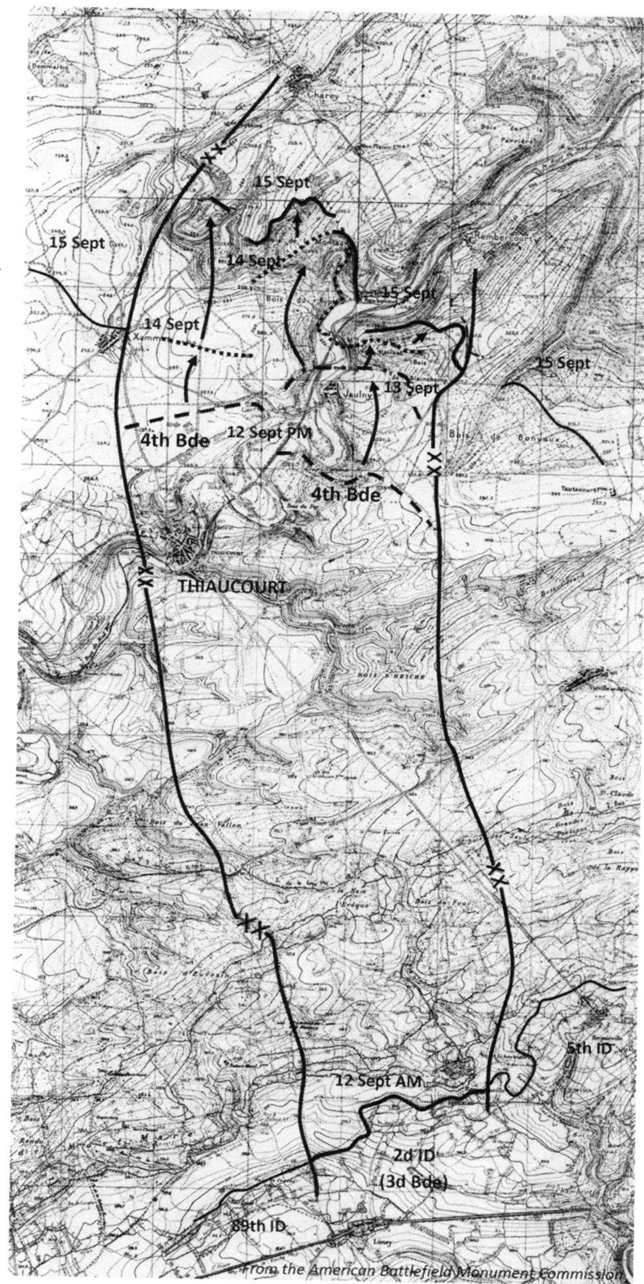

ST. MIHIEL, SEPTEMBER 1918. The Third Brigade led the division offensive, pursuing the rapidly retreating Germans to the transportation center of Thiacourt in a single day. In the more rugged terrain along the Rupt de Mad stream northeast of the town the offensive slowed as a result of stiffening German resistance and American logistical problems.

Hermle: "The Germans were on the run, planes were flying over us...." The entire operation was for most memorable for the miserable rain and chill.[14]

In his memoir, Lejeune described the attack plan or his division in detail, and it was typical of such an operation:

> The Division attacks in columns of Brigades, regiments side by side, each with one battalion in front line, one in support, and one in reserve.
> First line (attacking troops), Brigadier General Ely, commanding:
> 3rd Infantry Brigade
> 1st Battalion, 6th Marines, One Machine Gun Company 6th Marines
> 2nd Battalion, 12th Field Artillery
> Companies A and D, 2nd Engineers
> Two companies of light tanks
> One company medium tanks
> 6 x 4-in. Stokes Mortars
> Company E Gas and Flame Service
> A combat group of one battalion of infantry (6th Marines) and one machine gun company will maintain liaison with the 89th Division on the left.
> Second line (reserve), Brigadier-General Neville, commanding:
> 4th Marine Brigade (less 1 Bn. and 1 M.G. Co.)
> Companies B, C, E and F, 2nd Engineers
> 4th Machine Gun Battalion
> One company light tanks

In addition, the division was reinforced by three French artillery regiments, with pre-planned standing and rolling barrages. All these troops moved into position in "inky dark over unfamiliar ground, seamed with trenches and pockmarked with shellholes."[15]

Under unusually sporadic shelling the offensive was relatively rapid, and reached the first-phase objective by 0930 h. The attack was designed in such a way that the lead regiments had to extend their lines by shifting two battalions into the front line, but the Third Brigade quickly reached its objective. The Army units had taken heavy casualties, and Marine companies were used to reinforce the Army battalions. A problem that could not be remedied was that the German harassment shelling of American rear areas had caught the Second Ammunition Train, inflicting heavy losses of men and matériel.

From a sort of plateau Lejeune observed the division advance, and was pleased with the steady advance and the flood of prisoners moving to the rear. "They seemed more pleased than otherwise. They told us that for several days their artillery had been going to the rear, that many trainloads of supplies had left Thiacourt for the rear, and that they had expected the order of withdrawal from the salient within two or three days. When asked if they expected the attack on that morning, some of them replied that in the evening a few hours before the artillery bombardment begun, most of their officers had been ordered to the rear, and that they then guessed that the attack would soon take place. I had previously read in captured German documents that this precaution was sometimes taken owing to the serious shortage of company officers in the German armies. Its effect, however, was seriously detrimental to morale of the troops and was, therefore, unwise."[16]

The American onslaught simply crushed the German resistance. By 1300 h the Third Brigade had achieved he first day's final objective, a ridge overlooking Thiacourt. Measures of the rapid German disintegration were the Third Brigade's bag, including over 3,000 prisoners, and four railway trains loaded with artillery, ammunition, and a field hospital. The headlong rush to the rear prevented German sappers from detonating explosives set to destroy bridges over the Rupt de Mad brook. Surgeon Derby was surprised by the light casualties, and noted that "The wounded became fewer in numbers the further we advanced."[17]

The primary impediment to the Allied advance was the condition of the water-logged main road, now "swarming with men at work on the road. Material for the repairs was being taken from the heap of ruins which had been the village of Remenauville. Guns and caissons, ambulances, tanks and wagons were struggling to get forward through the maze." Ultimately Lejeune and a staff officer were forced to confiscate two horses to move forward through the mess.[18]

To secure the division's left flank, 2/6 was ordered up to the line. The 3/6 reached a hill overlooking Thiacourt, "and [battalion commander Berton] Sibley says 'You go out and reconnoiter the Army line.' The Army line was about a mile out ahead of where our companies were. We had the 82nd and 84th Companies on line on top of this ridge. I started out with about three men...." The 82nd Company commander could provide Rogers with no information. About halfway across no man's land Rogers spotted a file of men moving behind a ridge line, and decided to return to friendly lines. His path took him through the 83rd Company, 3/6, now commanded by Louis Jones. It turned out that in the confusion, Rogers had run afoul of another Marine patrol.

Rogers found that "For that, I got to take a patrol out the next morning."[19]

Rogers: "That night the battalion was ordered to take over the [inaudible] sector in the Army line.... I was sent out to see whether or not they did it. I had a couple of men with me. What happened was the 84th Company had all huddled up on the left, and the 97th Company had all huddled up on the right, and there was about a thousand yard gap in the middle." Sibley wanted a standard deployment with two companies up and two companies in reserve. Rogers tried to get the front line companies to thin out and close the gap. "There was a lot of flares going on and artillery and so forth, and they weren't very much inclined to move. So I finally got ahold of another company commander and got him to move into the interval between the two companies. I got back and told Sibley that was the best I could do."[20]

The 2/6 was in a reserve position near Thiacourt and sent to relieve another battalion. Erskine: "Maj. Williams was not the best map reader in the world, and he didn't listen to his junior officers very much." Erskine was familiar with the terrain from patrolling, and was dismayed to learn that the battalion column would cross a bridge over the small Rupt de Mad creek. "I asked the Major if he was going to cross the bridge and he said Yes. I said, 'By God, that's right in the middle of no man's land. I've been out there on patrol.' He said, 'You don't know what you are talking about.'" The battalion kept marching, led by guides from the battalion they were replacing. "Why the guides let these people go there, I don't know."

Insistently, "I kept pulling at the Major's leg while he was riding along and telling him, 'You are going right in the middle of no man's land.' Finally he stopped and halted the outfit down the road. He got off [his horse] and said, 'Come here and show me where you think we are. I know where I am.' I said, 'No, sir, the place is full of Germans right up there, I know. I am not coming near that flashlight.' He finally gave me a tongue lashing, got on his horse and started the march and we hadn't gone 50 yards before it seemed like every machine gun in the world opened up."

The battalion ambush drill was that the lead company would keep going out of the kill zone, the second would break to the right, third to the left, and the fourth would fall back as a reserve. The companies responded reflexively, "But fortunately his machine gun fire was too high and it missed."

The battalion kept moving, with Erskine, Sergeant Major Bill Ulrich, novice Lieutenant Tom Wirt, and a couple of scouts now in the lead. About dawn, the scouts spotted a large group of Germans falling back from a small wood. "So I went back and told the Major about this right away, and he said, 'Well, goddamn it, take a couple of people and go down there and capture them.'"

Erskine's small group of ten men went back, and Erskine told German-speaking Bill Ulrich to tell the enemy they were surrounded. "For a moment everything was sort of quiet, and some of them threw down their arms. There must have been 150 or 200 people in this woods."

The patrol started rounding up prisoners, but "Finally some wise German figured they were being fooled, and they started shooting, and we started firing back, and for some reason they started withdrawing and going up the hill. We started running after them, and taking the helmets off and banging them over the head with our pistols to disarm them, and thought we would see some more prisoners."

The Marines tossed grenades into a nearby house and about 20 more Germans came out. "I saw Tom Wirt, he got hit, I think in the hand. He had to go back. The first thing I know we are inside the German lines."

Farther up the hill "I had some people in front of me and I kept trying to stop them from chasing these Germans." Erskine finally reined in some of his men and redirected them.

Near a small patch of trees Erskine saw a column of Germans coming forward. "All I had was my pistol, and I got a few of them. The others sort of dispersed. I was hiding in these bushes, then I ran out into the open to try and get down under some cover." At the top of the hill was a German reserve machine-gun position, "but two machine guns opened on me and caught me in the leg and busted it up pretty badly...."

Erskine applied a tourniquet to his leg, but "In the meantime they'd take potshots at me, but I had just enough cover so that they couldn't get me. They hit my canteen. But I was so flattened out they couldn't really get me.

"Then about 10 o'clock I heard some voices coming and I pushed my helmet up with my hand and the Germans fired at it, and then pretty soon I heard a lot of firing all around me. These voices kept going right up the hill...." Eventually a Private Vale grabbed Erskine and started dragging him to the rear. "I said, 'I think you probably saved my life, and what in the world can I ever do for you?' He said, 'I've wanted a .45 caliber pistol ever since I've been in this outfit. You can give me that gun.' So I gave him my gun."

Erskine was carried back on an improvised stretcher by two prisoners. "I finally got back to the sick bay, and our regimental surgeon gave me first aid and fixed me up, and I really credit him now with having finally saved my leg, because both bones were broken right at the ankle, and the upper part was sticking out about six inches."[21]

Not all casualties were inflicted by the enemy. One of the men in Brannen's 80th Company, 2/6 "pulled a fork out of his coat pocket. One of the prongs caught in the pin of a hand grenade in the same pocket, setting of the detonator. After pulling the pin you have five or six seconds to throw it before the explosion, just as a firecracker after being lit. He was trying to get the grenade out of his pocket when the explosion occurred, killing him."[22]

Sensing the German collapse, General Pershing ordered an increase in the tempo of the offensive. The battle would now be a high-stakes race to the road junction at Jaulny.

September 13

In the shallow Second Division zone the Americans had already achieved the second day's operational objectives. They paused to consolidate positions and sent out patrols to probe German positions to their front. Lejeune rode to the Fourth Brigade headquarters in Thiacourt. While they conferred, General Neville hung his rain-soaked dress overcoat outside to dry, and it caught the eye of a passing Army teamster. "The overcoat being very different from the Army variety, the teamster assumed it had been left behind by an Austrian or German officer. So he cut off the sleeves at the elbows, proudly placed them on the ears of his mules, and went on his way rejoicing. Very soon Neville discovered the mutilated overcoat and learned the identity of the guilty party. He informed General Ely of the tragedy and the teamster was haled [sic] before the two irate Generals. Ely shouted at him, 'What did I tell all of you I would do to looters?' He replied in a weak voice, 'Shoot them, Sir.' The man was very penitent, and as Neville interceded in his behalf, no punishment of any kind was awarded."[23]

To the west, the Twenty-sixth Division was in a race to see who would be first to close the gap through which any remaining enemy might escape. The division was in a self-imposed competition with the First Division, known to be Pershing's favorite. The Twenty-sixth Division's 102nd Infantry, under the command of Marine Colonel "Hiking Hiram" Bearss, undertook an audacious night march through the heart of the remaining German resistance. The 0230-h arrival of the lead battalion of the 102nd was unexpected and threw the enemy formations retreating through the town into complete disarray. Most surrendered without a fight.[24]

When the First and Twenty-sixth divisions met at Vigneulles, it pinched off the bulk of the troops remaining in the salient.

In the east, the Fourth Brigade was ordered to resume the advance the next morning.

September 14

At 0400 h the Marine Brigade completed a passage of lines, replacing the Third Brigade along the division front. The Marines were instructed to consolidate the final objectives, push company-strength outposts forward, but not to make a general advance. Prisoner interrogations had suggested the possibility of a counterattack, so the brigade was instructed to take appropriate measures. On the division left the Sixth Marines were subjected to repeated German counterattacks, beginning a 2-day struggle for control of the Bois de la Montagne woodland.

The American plans were already a day ahead of schedule, but logistical issues, particularly food, seemed to bedevil the Marines at every turn. Captain Mathew Kingman, the CO of the15th Company, Sixth Machine Gun Battalion, received a message that "Your rations are at the ammunition dump. Kitchens have not yet arrived. Let me know what you want done with them. I have no idea where you are…."

In reply, Kingman promised to advise the logistics officer of their platoon positions—but they kept changing as the division tried to rectify its lines.[25]

Machine guns were instructed to fire at German aircraft, but in most cases the fire was ineffective even when the rounds were seen to penetrate the cloth and wood planes. An exception occurred when the 23rd Company of the Sixth Machine Gun Battalion reported that "At about 5:15 P.M. a German plane was brought down, presumably by machine gun fire from this Company, fell about 50 yards in rear of the 1st Platoon, the aviator was badly wounded and was taken prisoner by the infantry and evacuated."[26]

That night the staff of the 78th Division arrived at Lejeune's headquarters to arrange a relief in place. "They received an unpleasant welcome, as the Germans had gotten their second wind and had begun dropping gas shell on the woods. Soon the alarm was given and the smell of gas pervaded our dugouts. We had to put on masks, which with the dim candle light made seeing the maps and talking almost impossible. Finally however the odor of gas disappeared and, taking a chance, we removed the masks and were able to give an intelligible description of the situation."[27]

The unexpected successes of the American offensive had blown the enemy front wide open. Little remained to block their advance on Metz, but their orders were clear: no pursuit of the broken enemy. The bag included 16,000 prisoners, 443 artillery pieces (an important measure of success in this war), and masses of ammunition and other stores that the enemy had no time to remove.[28]

September 15

The supporting units were belatedly hitting their stride. Thanks to the efforts of the engineers on the roads, supplies were abundant and the medical services were positioned on the heels of the assault troops. Derby went forward and established a dressing station in a culvert north of Xammes. But "On the northern side of this culvert was an infantry ammunition dump discovered for us by a hostile plane, which flew low and played its machine gun upon it. As this made the culvert an undesirable refuge, we moved back to a dugout, but lately used by the enemy, in the side of an adjoining hill."[29]

As always, others were not so fortunate. Navy Hospital Apprentice First Class James E. Manning, attached to 1/5, "while attending to a wounded man in the dressing station was hit with a shell and the patient was wounded in two more places. Showing great devotion, dressed the new wounds and while doing so was knocked down by the explosion of another shell, striking the aid station. He refused to leave his post until he had finished dressing the wounded man and had removed him from the aid station, which was completely gutted a minute later by another shell. During the entire action Hospital Apprentice MANNING was conspicuous for his courage and promptness in the care of the wounded."[30]

In the Second Division zone the Marines were to keep pushing strong patrols out to screen the relief, with instructions from Lejeune to "go as far as they can go." In fact, though, the Marines continued to advance in order to adjust local lines, and the enemy launched local counterattacks. Carl Brannen's platoon was leading a 2/6 battalion advance guiding on a stream when they were ambushed by heavy machine guns in a large clearing west of the Bois de la Montagne. The survivors were able to withdraw to the battalion perimeter, but the entire battalion was surrounded and subjected to heavy shelling. When the shelling ceased and an enemy counterattack came on, the man next to Brannen was slow and unsteady as he rose. "I pulled down his shirt with one hand, handling my rifle with the other, and found a slug of shrapnel buried in his shoulder. He pulled himself together, however, and fought like an able-bodied man." Soon the battalions on either side fought their way through the forest, freeing the 2/6.[31]

Units were being relieved by the Seventy-sixth Division, so the Second could be thrown into yet another gruesome battle. By the early morning hours of 16 September the relief was completed, and the Second Division moved into reserve positions.

By Great War standards the Fourth Brigade losses had been miniscule: 76 killed, and 560 wounded.[32]

In the Forty-second Division zone a young Douglas MacArthur undertook a reconnaissance forward of the established lines, and could actually see Metz in the distance. Pleas to continue the advance toward that strategic city fell upon deaf ears: Marshal Ferdinand Foch had long ago decided how the remainder of the war would be prosecuted, and had no tolerance for proposed initiatives from junior staff officers.

With a large group of other Marines, Gerald Thomas was assigned to a school after the St. Mihiel battle. He had still not received his field commission. At the school the instructors assembled the Marines. "There were a lot of us—hundreds; and the school commander got up and said, 'Now I want to tell you fellows, this isn't the last battle of the War. They are in a battle, but they'll still be in it when you're through here. You only have to be here another four days so just go ahead with our course.' We all listened to him, went back and packed our gear, and just as soon as it was dark we shoved off.

"I was in a group of five Marines. We hadn't had any idea of what we were doing; but we knew where there was a railroad station. We went down and got a train to stop, and we got on. We found a railroad transport officer; and he told us how to get to Nancy, which was the last place that we knew of. We got to Nancy, and then we started talking to railway transport people. As a matter of fact, I saw a train of wounded with some boys from my company. We finally got back to the company as they were coming out of the lines. They were still shooting." Despite his unauthorized absence, Thomas finally received his commission.[33]

On September 18, the division moved back to its old familiar positions around Les Eparges to rest, refit, and absorb yet more replacements. Promotions were in order, including that of Richard Derby to Division Surgeon, replaced by Major Joel T. Boone. (Naval officers like Lieutenant Commander Boone typically adopted equivalent Army/Marine Corps rank designations for the sake of simplicity.)[34]

CHAPTER 11

Always on the Job: The Atlantic Fleet and Foreign Interventions

A ship without Marines is like a garment without buttons.

ADMIRAL DAVID DIXON PORTER

The land war had not relieved the Corps of its traditional duties of providing shipboard security on capital ships, guarding naval facilities, and acting as America's "colonial infantry".

The Mexico interventions had not resulted in permanent occupation, although the necessity of maintain a force for any future operation there tied down considerable manpower. In their latest Caribbean intervention in 1916, the Marines had occupied Santo Domingo (the modern Dominican Republic) with the 9th Company and a pair of 3-in. naval landing guns, with orders to support the established government. The operation turned out to be bloodless, as were most ensuing operations.[1] The occupation, and the long-established occupation of Haiti, continued to absorb badly needed manpower.

The war years saw significant increases in manpower in Cuba, Hawaii, the Philippines, Puerto Rico and the US Virgin Islands (the latter two for protection of the strategic Panama Canal). By far the greatest increase was in Stateside support and administrative services—566%. By late 1918 global commitments and administrative services absorbed 48,166 personnel, two-thirds of the Corps' total strength.[2]

After boot camp Albert Jensen was sent to Portsmouth, Virginia, for Sea School, the training for Marines of ship detachments. Jensen was supposed to be assigned to the 65-man detachment aboard the old battleship USS *Delaware*, but in fact his primary task was training 5-in. gun crews for transport vessels. The *Delaware* was sent to Boston to pick up a secret cargo, which the Marines had to guard in the Navy Yard until it was loaded aboard the ship as deck cargo. While slowly transporting the huge crates on trucks through the city, the Marines had to walk alongside the trucks to secure the cargo. A civilian climbed aboard one of the crates and despite a Marine private's warnings refused to get off. The guard went to the senior NCO, "a big Irishman named Gallagher." Gallagher climbed up and warned the man, who still refused to get off. Finally Gallagher just grabbed him by the seat of the pants, and "threw him out in the street. He lit out there on the cobblestones, and that guy finally got up and shook himself [inaudible]."

The trans-Atlantic voyage on the *Delaware* was rough, and most of the men had no actual seagoing experience. "My General Quarters station was on the three-inch anti-aircraft gun which sat on the top of a crane...." To access the position required climbing about 35 ft up the outside of the crane's support pedestal as the ship rolled, and "you might as well have been on a balloon up there." Worse, the Marines had been issued no winter or foul-weather gear.

Thanksgiving was celebrated in mid-Atlantic, but almost everyone was seasick. When it became Jensen's turn to eat, he had to negotiate an open deck with the ship taking waves over the deck, then a long passageway. The cooks were carrying Thanksgiving dinner down the passageway, with the ship rolling from side to side, and pitching as the bow and stern rose and fell.

"I fell down" as something hit him from behind and took his feet out from under him. "It was a turkey! A big roast turkey." With so many of the cooks sick, the mess attendants had been instructed to carry the bird to the Marine berthing space. When it arrived, "We just tore it apart with our knives and forks and ate it."[3]

On December 7, 1917 Division 9 of the US Atlantic Fleet (battleships *Delaware*,* *Florida*, flagship *New York*, and *Wyoming*) finally dropped anchor in the big British naval base of Scapa Flow in the Orkney Islands. The force was augmented by the USS *Texas* in February. Scapa Flow

* Replaced by *Arkansas* in July 1918.

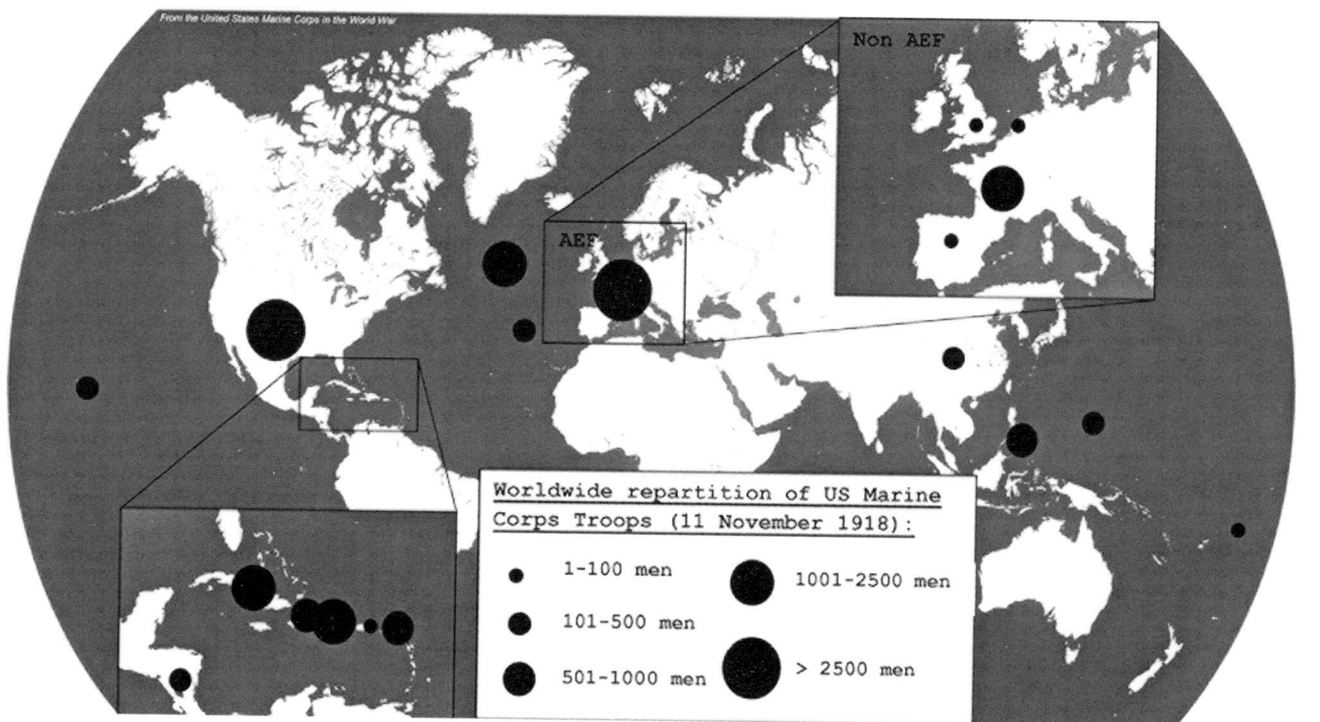

Despite the war the Marine Corps was burdened with global responsibilities. Forces in France constituted 34% of the Corps' total strength, with 51% in the continental US providing recruiting, training, administrative, security, and support functions. Some overseas detachments (Spain, American Samoa) consisted of a single Marine.

was to be the squadron's home base, with brief stays in the Firth of Forth, Scotland. Division 5 (battleships *Nevada*, *Oklahoma*, and flagship *Utah*) was based at Bantry Bay, Ireland to provide convoy security against German surface raiders.[4]

The ships also provided security for convoys carrying logs from Norway. "They had any old tub that could float. They'd get it up there and load it with logs and take it down the east coast of England. They'd maybe saw them up into timber; went to France for the trenches."

The only excitement came when the ship was issued an untested type of 5-in. ammunition, a blunt-nosed round to be fired at submarines; it contained a dye that would color the water and with any luck mark a position for a depth-charge attack. But the designers had failed to take into account the greater recoil. "We fired the first shot alright. The second shot the gun went back and the butt of the gun hit the deck and threw it way up." The gun hit the overhead and broke the sighting mechanism.

The Orkneys were (and are) a bleak place, so the most cherished liberties were in Edinburgh, where the troops could listen to concerts, and buy beer for two hours a day.

However Jensen's notable misadventure came in July 1915. He had just been promoted to sergeant, and was invited to "wet his chevrons" at the British sergeants' mess in a convalescent hospital at Scapa Flow. After several rounds of Scotch whisky, Jensen's host decided they should swap uniforms, and then venture to a photographer's shop to record the event.

Jensen got separated from his host, and quickly ran afoul of the Scots Military Police. He was stopped by an observant Jock MP with a rifle and bayonet. The Midwestern American and Scots dialects proved mutually incomprehensible. When the American finally made it clear his name was Jensen, it was too much. He was placed under arrest as a German spy. "'Take a look at yourself,' said the Jock MP scornfully. 'A kiltie named Jensen. A kiltie sergeant with his knees pink as a baby's neck.'"

The next morning Jensen was marched back to the *Delaware* under guard to make sure he ran afoul of no more patrols, and to make sure his commander understood why Jensen had not reported back aboard on time.[5]

By this time German ships seldom made forays into the North Sea, and their capital ships were nowhere to be seen as the result of the defeat at Jutland (May 31–June 1, 1916). Most activities were routine patrols, and occasional ceremonial duties, including the arrival of President Wilson aboard the Army transport USAT *George Washington* on December 13, 1918 for the Paris Peace Conference.

Marines aboard cruisers of the Asiatic Fleet intervened in the fighting in Vladivostok in June 1918. Czechoslovakian troops were fighting for control of the city against Bolsheviks reinforced by German and Austrian prisoners of war. On June 29 Marines from the cruiser *Brooklyn* were put ashore to provide for security of the US consulate and to act in conjunction with British, Japanese, Chinese, and Czechoslovakian troops to patrol the city. The *Brooklyn's* Marines would continue to be involved in the unrest through July, acting as guards over German and Austrian prisoners, and to keep order during unrest by workers at the Russian navy yard. The Marines of the Asiatic Fleet would remain involved for many months in providing local security as Bolshevik and White Russian forces vied for control of Siberia.[6]

CHAPTER 12

Blanc Mont Ridge[1]

> Why in the hell can't the Army do it if the Marines can? They are the same kind of men; why can't they be like Marines?
>
> GENERAL JOHN J. PERSHING

The long-awaited Hundred Days Offensive that stretched across the entire Western Front from the Swiss border to the North Sea was intended to overwhelm the German Army through sheer numbers. The American First and Second army zones stretched from the east bank of the Aisne River on the west, through the Argonne Forest, to Pont-à-Mousson on in the Alpine foothills on the east. The attack in the American sector commenced on September 26, but on the west bank of the Aisne the French faced a seemingly intractable problem.

In 1914 the Germans had easily captured a range of low hills called the Chemin des Dames for a royal carriage road that ran through parts of the hill complex. Though not particularly high, the hills dominated the lower terrain to the south. The German positions in the higher hills were one remnant of the old Hindenberg Line, with some of the most formidable defenses on the Western Front. The linchpin was the hill of Blanc Mont.

In a series of attacks in 1915 the French Army had bled itself to exhaustion in attempts to recapture the heights. Since then the front had been relatively inactive, and the ordinary French poilus regarded the Blanc Mont position as invincible. Senior French commanders largely shared the feeling.

German engineers had tunneled deep into the soft chalk bedrock to build deep trenches, and large galleries and bunkers in which troops could sit out any bombardment. The concrete-reinforced entrances were on the reverse (northern) slopes, immune to Allied artillery. Aerial observation was virtually impossible as the enemy maintained air superiority. Concrete pillboxes and bunkers dominated key points like road junctions and obvious approaches.

The depth of no-man's land here was not measured in yards or hundreds of meters, but in kilometers. Any attack would have to be mounted across a deep zone which, by a peculiarity of the geography, exposed both the northern and southern slopes to direct fire from the heights. The soil was seldom more than a few centimeters in thickness, with broad areas of bare rock: if an attack faltered, the attackers cold not even dig shallow scrapes for protection, much less trenches. Although virtually forgotten today, Blanc Mont Ridge saw some of the most intensive fighting of the war, with the usual brutal casualties. Walter Gaspar: "That was, I think, the nastiest from my point of view. We were right out in the open. We were the front; nothing ahead of us—nothing ahead of my platoon."[2]

By 1918 much of this fortification effort and tenacity was based upon the German Army's own strategic problem. The Blanc Mont line screened a major highway that led to a crucial railway junction at Charleville (and its twin city, Mézières, on the opposite bank of the Meuse). The railway network east of the Ardennes was far less dense than that to the west, and the city was the junction of the major east–west rail line east of the Ardennes, and a north–south line. In Allied hands the city would sever east–west German rail traffic, and worse, assure Allied rail transportation for an inconceivable invasion of Germany.

In the first stages of the huge German offensives of summer 1918 the French had stalled at Navarin Farm, south of Blanc Mont. The French had learned of the forthcoming attack, and withdrew out of the barrage zone, leaving only small sacrificial machine-gun units to slow the enemy. A French counter-barrage against German assembly areas commenced an hour before the German preparatory barrage. The enemy offensive failed miserably compared to those farther west, but had enabled the Germans to construct yet another strong series of defenses, their First Line of Resistance, a few kilometers south of the village of Somme-Py.

Even before the beginning of the offensive, the French had pressed Pershing for the use of American troops—still relatively fresh, full of fight, and presumably did not know of Blanc Mont's impregnability—to assault this key position. Pershing agreed, at first offering two inexperienced divisions but without their artillery. He later relented, and offered up the veteran Second Division, and the brand-new Thirty-sixth Division, composed largely of the Texas and Oklahoma National Guard.

When he reported to his new superior, the commander of the French Quatrième Armée, General Henri Gouraud, impressed Lejeune as "Tall, erect, with heavy dark brown beard and hair, and a complexion burnt dark by the blazing sun of Africa where he had seen so many years of army service, he would be a striking looking man in any company, especially as his distinguished appearance was enhanced by an empty sleeve and by a very prominent limp." (Growing up in Louisiana during the aftermath of the American Civil War, Lejeune would have been no stranger to amputees, and probably saw it as a sort of badge of honor.)[3]

Lejeune learned through the staff officer grapevine that the proposal had again been made to break up the Second Division (much larger than a French division) and employ it piecemeal. He promptly requested another audience with Gouraud.

Gouraud painstakingly laid out the plan for the greater scheme of the offensive. Laying his hand on the Blanc Mont sector of the map, he declared that "If I could take this position by assault, advance beyond it to the vicinity of St. Etienne-à-Arnes, and hold the ground gained against the counter-attacks which would be hurled against my troops, the enemy would be compelled to evacuate 'Notre Dame des Champs and Les Monts,' thereby freeing Rheims which he has been strangling for four years, and fall back to the line of the Aisne, a distance of nearly 30 km—as the terrain between the ridges and the Aisne does not lend itself well to defense.

"My divisions, however, are worn out from the long strain of continuous fighting and from the effects of the heavy casualties they have suffered, and it is doubtful if they are now equal to accomplishing this difficult task unless they be heavily re-enforced."

Inherent in Gouraud's speech was the suggestion that the Second Division might be used piecemeal under French command. But Pershing had on multiple occasions made it abundantly clear that he would never permit American forces to be broken up for replacements. Isolated and eager to prevent the breakup of his division Lejeune promised, "General, if you do not divide the Second Division, but put it in line as a unit on a narrow front, I am confident that it will be able to take Blanc Mont Ridge, advance beyond it, and hold its position there." (This exposition is longer and more detailed than that quoted by most historians, but they are Lejeune's own words.)[4]

Gouraud then added that he entertained no plans to break up the division, but would take the matter up with marshals Foch and Pétain. Lejeune had been subtly outmaneuvered, and made to promise the inconceivable.

By late 1918 the Corps was beginning to feel the pinch of heavy casualties and shrinking manpower. In a little known aspect of the war, men serving terms in naval prisons were given the opportunity to be released in return for serving as replacements in France. Gaspar: "But those kids did themselves well; a lot of them came over right out of Portsmouth Prison. They were given the opportunity to show themselves; and they did it."[5]

In this offensive new Lieutenant Gerald Thomas was chosen to be left in the rear. The Marines had learned from brutal experience that offensives commonly gutted their formations, and held back a cadre of men to serve as the nucleus of a reconstituted company. "So at Champagne I stayed behind in the ten percent, but was put in the M.P.s. We went back and forth to the front all of the time. We were in almost as much danger as though we had been with the front-line outfit. That's what I did for the Champagne fight."[6]

For the Blanc Mont operation the Marines were temporarily issued new weapons—BARs and M1917 Browning heavy machine guns—loaned from Army stocks.*

*Records are not entirely clear on this. There is no official record, only the memories of the participants.

Leo "Dutch" Hermle: "So everyone of our machine gunners had a machine gun out of the 6th Division or the 36th Division. Of course as soon as we got back in the rear areas, Col. Lee, the regimental commander, made us turn them all back."[7]

In late September Lejeune moved his forward division headquarters to a town just behind the French lines, and described the accommodations typical of such villages. "Suippes has been just inside the French lines ever since the first battle of the Marne, four years ago, and during all that time has been unoccupied except by troops, and it is certainly a dilapidated, desolated place. It has been shelled frequently and bombed often, and still some of the houses are in fairly good repair. The one we are in, except for the lack of window panes, is a pretty fair house. The old pictures are still hanging on the walls, and the religious images of the Holy Mother and Child, of Jesus on the Cross, and of the saints are still intact [Lejeune was Roman Catholic, and noticed such details], and there is a great deal of fine old furniture, more or less broken up. The filth of the house, however, and of the courtyard when we arrived was indescribable."

Being a general had its perquisites, of course, and when Lejeune returned a few hours later "The house had been swept, scrubbed and cleaned; furniture arranged, old beds and bedding put in the attic, electric lights and telephones installed; the courtyard was cleaned up, the kitchen scrubbed and polished, the table spread for lunch, and my room fixed comfortably."[8]

Just before moving forward, Wilburt Brown and others "made a raid on an estaminet [tavern] there one Saturday night and stole a couple of kegs of wine and hid them. We were told at breakfast the next day that we were moving up that night up on the lines again. We then found ourselves with a problem of what we were going to do with all that wine which we had stolen the night before. We took to drinking it all that day and, of course as you can guess by nightfall about half the platoon was as drunk as skunks. And of course, I guess I was the drunkest, it was my first experience with demon rum. When the company fell out that afternoon to move up, there were a number of people missing. Gilder Jackson [the company CO] said, 'Where are these people?' Someone said there were a lot of them still over in a certain red barn, so Gilder came over there. He came storming in and said, 'What the hell is going on here?' or something like that. My corporal who was a fellow named Henderson, killed a couple of days later, had come over after me and was trying to get me to come on and join the war. I said to him—or so I was later told—I said, something. I was still talking when the captain started to walk over toward me, and Henderson said, 'Shut up, Brown. Here comes the captain.' And I said, 'Just between you and me, to hell with that bastard.' And at that point, according to the story which I still can't testify to because I don't remember it, he, Gilder, spun me around with one hand and hit me on the chin with the other, and I went down like a poled ox. He said, 'Pick him up and throw him in the camion.' So I came to some time later in the bottom of a camion under the feet of a platoon of Marines and we were on our way to Blanc Mont. Somehow or other there was a blanket stuffed in my mouth though it turned out to be my tongue. I managed finally to stumble to me feet. My rifle and pack was in the camion somewhere, and we went riding and bouncing over these shell-pocked roads. I would have given a million dollars if I had it for a drink of water, but there was not a soul in the camion who would even let me have a sip of his canteen. If anybody was stupid enough to start to the front without water in that war, he died without it. As a matter of fact, I didn't get a drink of water until the middle of the night when I found a water cart.

"So I never will forget the horrors of the march into the battle of Blanc Mont. I, of course, swore off drinking forever. I wish I had kept it up."[9]

October 1

Despite the chaotic roads and problems caused by units becoming separated from their support trains of food, water, and ammunition, the Marine Brigade began to relieve French units defending Somme-Py at about 0200 h.

The Marine Brigade, the first to arrive, took over a long sector of the front from the French XIe Corps north of the Py Brook, from a strong ridge position the Americans called the Essen Hook, across in front of the Bois de la Vipère (Viper's wood). The Third Brigade moved into a reserve position a few kilometers to the south at Navarin Ferme. The Second Division was placed under the neighboring XXIe Corps' control.

Lejeune again shifted headquarters north to Souain, "completely destroyed, and the whole area north of it gave full evidence of the fact that it had been continually a battlefield for more than four years. It was the white chalk country, and not only was it a perfect maze of trenches and covered with a tangle of barbed wire, but the very soil was desiccated and pulverized. It had been shelled, and bombed and mined so frequently that it had lost all semblance of its former self. Not a tree was standing anywhere near Navarin Ferme, or elsewhere in its vicinity, nor was there even a brick on the site of the farm to show that buildings had once stood there. The debris of battle was still lying about—broken cannon and machine guns, rifles, bayonets, helmets, parts of uniforms, articles of military equipment, and partly buried horses; most grewsome of all, fragments of human bodies were often found. Arms and legs thrust out of the torn soil, and unrecognizable, long-buried human faces, thrown up to the surface of the ground by exploding shell, were frequently visible. The fearsome odors of the battlefield, too, were always present. P. C. [Command Post] Wagram was in the midst of the devastated area. It was not a home, but a horror."[10]

The original plan of attack was for October 2, but Lejeune was soon at loggerheads with his French superior. He successfully argued for a one-day delay. "The postponement was advised principally because the 2nd Field Artillery Brigade could not reach its position in time for the attack, also because I deemed it advisable for the 4th Brigade and the Artillery to have a look at the terrain during the daylight hours before making an attack, and for the additional reason that we believed it to be important that the portion of the trench which lay immediately in front of the Division, and which was then occupied by the enemy, should be mopped up, occupied and utilized as the 'jump off' line...." Leaving the Germans in possession of this lower trench complex would greatly slow and obstruct the American attack across the stony, barren terrain north of the trenches.[11]

Lejeune was summoned to XXI Corps headquarters, where Gouraud laid out General Naulin's new proposal for a very complex and risky attack. The French division on the American right had pushed well forward. Naulin's proposal was for the Third Brigade to use this salient as a start line, attacking in a westward direction and across the front of the Fourth Brigade attack. Lejeune liked this plan not at all. Quite aside from giving the laurels (dubious as they were) for a direct attack on the main position to the Army brigade, this plan posed the risk of artillery fired in support of the Marines striking the Third Brigade.

Lejeune instead made his own proposal that the Third Brigade leave the attack on the right to the French, and instead attack from the east of the potentially powerful Bois de la Vipère position, then swing to the right to avoid passing across the front of his Fourth Brigade. This simpler plan was relayed to Naulin, and approved.[12]

October 2

The Second Division shifted forward in the night, John Aasland's company moving into a position near a great old house. "Considerable shell fire all day—more holes in the wall and in the chateau. We shot at some airplanes now and then—that is the gang did; I haven't fired a shot yet and I'm not going to until I see something that I can hit. Our overcoats were brought in after dark and we worked around in the darkness getting as good a fit as possible."[13]

After midnight the Marine Brigade began to move into final defensive positions. The Germans had detailed knowledge of the terrain, and the advance went on under a rain of German heavy artillery fire directed at roads and known traffic chokepoints. Lejeune was advised by his staff to seek shelter in underground shelters but could not abide the stifling atmosphere. He watched from a doorway as the long columns of men and matériel flowed forward, and mused that "perhaps night battles will be just as essential and just as frequent during the next war. Attacks under cover of darkness may provide both the element of surprise and of reasonable security on the battlefield of the future."[14]

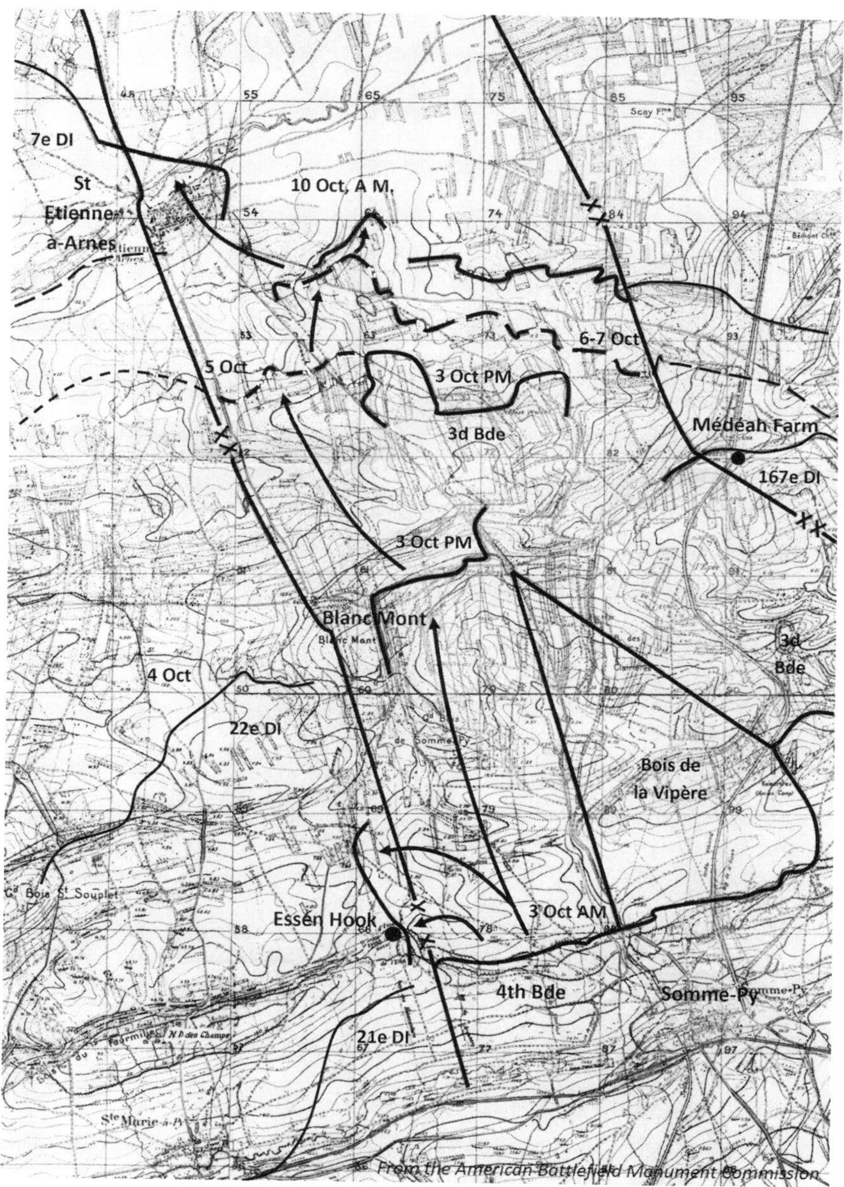

BLANC MONT RIDGE, OCTOBER 1918. Bypassing the Bois de la Vipère, the Second Division overwhelmed German resistance. The powerful Essen Hook position blocked the French 21e Division d'Infanterie, *dangerously exposing the Marines' left flank. At the end of the first day both brigades were like islands in a sea of German units. The Germans were finally able to organize a coherent defense along the Medeah Farm–St. Etienne-à-Arnes line, but the main German defense had been broken.*

As if Lejeune's problems were not complicated enough, a last-minute counterattack drove the French back about a kilometer.

A stroke of blind luck greatly aided the Americans. At about 2300 h First Lieutenant James M. Sellers of the 78th Company, 2/6 permitted Lieutenant Edward Fowler and Private John J. "Johnny" Kelly to reconnoiter the German forward trench line. They found the trench empty. "The Germans, as was often customary, had been in these trenches at night and then retreated to sleep in the rear during daylight." The entire battalion moved up to a more advantageous forward position in the Essen Trench, and captured the handful of German sentries. This trench had in part been taken on October 1 at 2100 h by the French 61e DI. There may have been communication issues due to the different languages when the Marines took over the 61e DI positions, and language problems remained an issue despite the presence of interpreters and bilingual liaison officers. Regardless, it placed the Marines in a far more advantageous position.

October 3

The end result of the last-minute wrangling over the plan of attack would cause considerable confusion. The Second Division's two brigades would attack around either flank of the Bois de la Vipère, leaving that potential hornet's nest to be mopped up later. Once past the northern margin of the wood the two brigades would converge, but on the right the Third Brigade would be required to execute a complex right-oblique change of direction. The Marine Brigade would attack with the two regiments in sequence, each in a typical column of battalions. The Sixth Marines' sequence would be 2nd, 1st, and 3rd battalions. As each battalion became depleted, the following battalion would pass through to maintain the momentum of the attack, and it was anticipated that the first passage of lines would come two or three hours into the attack.

The component companies of the Sixth Machine Gun Battalion were allocated to only four of the assault battalions: 2/5 (23rd Machine Gun Company), 3/5 (77th Machine Gun Company), 2/6 (81st Machine Gun Company) and 3/6 (15th Machine Gun Company). Platoons of machine guns would be spread across each battalion front.[15] Renault FT light tanks from the 2e BCL, 501RAS (2e Bataillon de Chars Légers, 501 Regiment Artillerie spéciale) would support the Second (10 tanks) and First battalions (20 tanks). The tanks assigned to the lead battalion, 2/6, would be spread across the battalion front. Tanks accompanying 1/6 would be positioned in the rear flanks of the battalion in case of German counterattack. The 5th Marines would follow in train, with its battalions in a 2nd, 3rd, 1st Battalion order.[16]

In the 80th Company of the 2/6, Carl Brannen was badly spooked, and not just by the sight of dead French soldiers draped over the dense wire entanglements near the base of the ridge. Twice his platoon had been wiped out, with him as the sole survivor. "Each man had two extra bandoliers of ammunition around his shoulders. I made sure the bandoliers of ammunition were in front of my chest. The issued razor was in the right-hand pocket of my blouse, and the YMCA-issued Bible was in the left-hand pocket. I was using all of the protection that I could think of."[17]

The Marines were already in the forward German trench, and the brief preliminary bombardment was to add an unusual element of surprise. John Aasland's 55th Company, Fifth Marines was in the support line, and saw that "by the time the Germans were half ready, the frontline was past the second and third lines and on their way to the Blanc Mont Ridge. We, in support, followed the 6th Marines by 600 yards; started from behind the railroad grade just before dawn and got into formation on the other side of the grade. We advanced in line of combat groups. Crossed a creek and waded in water a foot deep, just enough to get wet. Broad daylight arrived, the sun shining brightly, and we had no fog to screen us. The enemy balloons behind the lines were giving instructions to the artillery—which there was plenty of—so they started to shell us for fair. About a hundred yards from the German front line trench shell fire was so heavy that we made a run for the trench and had to stay there for about ten minutes waiting for it to ease up a little. When the fire became not so heavy we reached a narrow gauge railroad where we stopped again. On the barbed wire hung limbs of men who had been blown up before, around which lay blue cloth, the remains of the unsuccessful attacks of the French on this place."[18]

The Sixth Marines led the advance in the usual combat formation. Brannen: "The rows of men moved forward unhesitatingly but fell like tenpins before the deadly machine gun fire. I was a runner to carry messages from flank to flank of my company and the adjoining, trying to keep the units in contact with each other as the now thin lines swept over the crest."[19]

Captain Westover's company of the divisional machine-gun battalion was placed in support of the Marine Brigade. He watched the attack from an artillery observation post south of Somme-Py. "Ahead, the ridge, thinly wooded with pines, stretched across our front. Troops were crossing the valley in front, working their way up the slopes. Shells were throwing smoke and earth skyward in the valley and a low cloud hung over the ridge where our own artillery was concentrating its fire."

Westover was able to catch glimpses through the artillery's high-powered telescope when it was not in use. The impression was like being directly behind an infantry platoon. "The section was attacking a Boche machine gun, deployed in a long thin line; first a few men on one flank would rush forward a short distance, then, as the fire was directed at their attack, those on the other end would make a quick advance. The flanks were creeping outward and the line developing into an arc that would eventually envelop the gun position—that is if a sufficient number of survivors was left to reach it. This was no parade ground demonstration, even though nicely executed. Already five men lay still on the ground over which they had come. The right squad sprang up and forward. One, two, four men dropped; staggering, slumping forward to the ground. The rest threw themselves into shell holes and paused.

"They were close now, but where there had been thirty men a few moments before, only nine were still able to move. Of these, two more fell in the final assault. There was a pause at the gun, and they spread out and continued to advance—carrying on the attack under a new leader."

Westover must have seen the common fate of machine gunners. "Who shall plead that the machine gunners should have been taken prisoners? They that fed and fired the gun which took such toll, mowing down to the last moment, and only when bayonets in the hands of sweating, panting madmen threatened them in the final plunge, raised their hands and shouted, 'Kamerad.'"[20]

Almost immediately word came in Hermle's company that the CO, Captain Shields, and the XO, Lieutenant Shannon, had been wounded and evacuated. "Well, I had to get myself together and I sent for Mosher who was the senior lieutenant after me and had the 4th platoon. I told him he was the executive officer, and away we went." Apparently Shields was wounded but not evacuated, but the confusion persisted.[21]

Despite a protective smoke screen, from his vantage point near the wrecked Navarin Farm, Division Surgeon Derby and his assistant, Boone, observed the attack. "As the first gray of dawn appeared, I could make out some of the medium-sized French tanks climbing the steep slopes of Blanc Mont Ridge and spitting fire as they went. The small tanks, as usual, got no distance, and because of their drawing fire, were in many instances a menace rather than a help to the infantry."[22]

The Fourth Brigade swept the German 2. Bataillon, 235. Reserve Infanterieregiment back into the Bois de la Vipère. To the left the French 21e Division d'Infanterie was keeping the German 200. Infanteriedivision occupied, but they could not push the 2. Cologne Landsturm Bataillon (composed of expendable older reserves) off the eastern end of the Essen Hook.

The Marines had orders to press the attack up the ridge, but with the French held up on the left, intense machine-gun fire into the Marines' left flank and rear forced them to ground. Aasland: "Up again, and here comes machine gun fire from the left. We drop and lay perfectly still in the grass and weeds; someone from the extreme left will be sent after the machine guns. The firing stops. The whistle blows and we are up and start again. Sometimes when the whistle blew I got up real quick and looked around. Outside of the men right next to me, I could see no one. Six inches of grass and the color of the army uniform made us invisible. If we could lay still all the time it would be soft. Looks funny when the whole line stands up and starts to move again; just like they came from nowhere. Now and then a man was killed and a wounded man called 'First Aid'—then the call for the 55th Company stretcher bearers; but this isn't bad yet."[23]

By 0830 h the Marines had overrun the headquarters of the 2 Jager Brigade, though most of the staff escaped to the Sattelberg (French Grand Bois de Sommepy) and Petersburg positions, small hills to the east. Orders were issued to pull the 1. Bataillon, 368. IR (Group Langer) out of its positions to help defend Blanc Mont. It was the beginning of a mad scramble to assemble forces to resist the unexpectedly rapid American onslaught.

Sergeant Cecil B. Avery recalled Blanc Mont as the bloodiest day of the war. By about 0900 h the 96th Company, 2/6 had reached its first objective and taken numerous prisoners. Avery questioned one of the German lieutenants, "Asked him if he had any schnapps. He called to the rear of the ranks, and there was an old fellow there that came up forward, evidently his orderly…." The orderly led Avery into a dugout, "and under the bunk was a full bottle of schnapps, black bread, some cigars. I took the works."

Avery returned to his fighting hole on the extreme left of the line, and the Germans appeared to be counterattacking. "Then out of the woods, oh, maybe a hundred-fifty, two hundred yards away there seemed to be a group coming out with the intent to surrender." Avery stood up and began to wave them over. "And suddenly, wham! I got hit in the belly …. I knew I was hit. I didn't want the Heinies to see me fall, so I leaned on my rifle and let myself down. Got myself doubled up in the hole, and unbuckled my gear, and took stock of myself.

"I had a hole in my belly, and a hole in my back. I opened my first aid kit and of course it [the bandage] wouldn't go round my body so I had to use the two pads, stuck one on the back and one on the front. Held them there with my hands for a few minutes until they kinda stuck. Pulled my trousers round them. Laid there for some time.

"Every time it felt like I was gonna faint, I took a little schnapps, because they had these little French Whippet tanks* operating in the area. These things worked in units of five, and they scooted around and I was afraid one of them might run over me. I wanted to be able to wave my arms. So I stayed conscious. Finally a couple of hours later I was picked

*Avery is in error here: the Whippet was a British light tank, and totally unlike the Renault FT.

up, carried over to a first-aid station. On the way over the kid on the front of my litter was hit by a bullet in the head, and dropped dead over my feet. Dumped me out in the road. Little tarmac road we were crossing.

"I laid there a little while and yelled over the stone wall where I knew the dressing station was supposed to be. A couple of other guys came out and picked me up, pushed me back in the litter, and run me across. I got in there and Sandy, Sandy Sanderson, our first aid man, our medic, dressed my wound again, and stuck a red tag up in my blouse, up near my collar, near my neck. I looked at the tag and it said, 'Serious.' That made me feel good, so I took another snort.

"Then a French priest came along. Knelt down by the side of me, and heard my confession. I had no thought of dying. I knew I'd been hit, and hit bad, but I was just a casualty. I was going back, and I says, 'Great'. So they carried me down to a Ford ambulance." From that point on, Avery belonged to the division Sanitary and Medical Trains.[24]

The Sanitary Train had established its forward evacuation station just south of Somme-Py. At Somme-Py two main roads diverged to the north; these would serve as main arteries for bringing wounded to the evacuation point. As Derby moved forward he encountered the first wave of wounded south of Somme-Py, some walking, others carried by prisoners. Lavishly supplied with ammunition, the enemy was heavily shelling Somme-Py and the various road intersections. The road south out of the town to the Navarin Farm ran up a ridge, open ground clearly visible to observers atop the ridge. "During the first hours of the attack this exposed stretch of road was so heavily shelled that ambulances could not cross it, and it was necessary to interpose here a stretcher-bearer relay. They carried the wounded up over the hill to a point on its southern slope, to which the ambulances could safely be brought. From there it took the Fords only twenty minutes to get back to the main dressing station at Souain."

The field hospital at Souain shared a subterranean complex, constructed during the protracted fighting of 1915–1918, with a French hospital unit. There Derby was pleased to see that he had more ambulance capacity than needed, and the bigger G. M. C. ambulances were waiting for loads of wounded.[25]

Lejeune and one of his senior staff officers tried to observe the progress of the attack from a vantage point near Navarin Farm, but the haze, smoke, and chalk dust made that impossible. Then "Suddenly, both of us gave shouts of joy. We saw the signal lights being fired on the top of the ridge. They began on the right of the objective, and one by one we saw them until finally those on the extreme left became visible. The objective had been taken between 8 and 9 A.M." (On this point Lejeune's memory does not match the timing given in both official records and the memoirs of other participants.)[26]

Under the smoke and dust there was still considerable confusion. Hermle recalled that when the 1st Battalion executed its passage of lines, "He [Cates] tried to get me to go too far over on the left, and his commanding officer, Maj. Williams, also tried to give me orders, but I knew I was not to take orders from anybody but Maj. Barker, and I did as I wanted to."[27]

As the Marines pushed up the ridge, the galling fire from the left grew increasingly destructive. Aasland: "At noon we swung to the left, stopping our forward advance and jumped into a trench running the way we were going [a communication trench linking the fighting trenches]. Our battalion joined the 6th Marines in front, and the 10th Battalion of French Chasseurs [10e Bataillon de Chasseurs à Pied] in rear. We are strung out in a trench with the Germans in the woods ahead of us. Every now and then machine gun fire comes our way. About five o'clock we moved back in the trench to our original position. The French are coming up the communication trench and filing in with us. Then a heavy barrage began which plastered around us."[28]

By mid-afternoon the Marines were atop Blanc Mont, but not in strength. Carl Brannen: "I was with a lieutenant of the 78th Company [2/6] when we entered the forest of small pines which were along the crest and down its slopes on the other side. We were firing on the retreating enemy as we advanced, sometimes dropping to a knee for better aim. A bullet hit my bayonet about an inch from the muzzle of the rifle while I was carrying it at port arms, shattering the bayonet and leaving only a stub."

A man nearby flushed three Germans, and Brannen joined the rush. "They surrendered and then I noticed them looking at my bayonet. I tried to read their minds. They must have thought that I had broken off my bayonet in a man. Later a man in my company saw me with my stub of a bayonet and said, 'Old Brannen stuck his bayonet in one and broke it off.'"

Brannen had grabbed a fine set of binoculars off a dead German officer, and slung them around his neck. The Marines swept up onto the slopes across from Blanc Mont, and one of the enemy machine gunners there opened fire on Brannen. He jumped toward a nearby ditch but "a fusillade of bullets caught me below the heart on the left side, through one lens of the field glasses, and against my bandolier of ammunition. The best I can remember, ten bullets in my own belt exploded, but they had deflected the enemy bullets, saving my life. My own bullets ripped my coat to shreds as they exploded and went out over my left shoulder by the side of my face. My cloth bandolier and the field glasses caught on fire. I got them off of me and then replaced the field glasses around my neck again as they quit burning."

The Marines were forming a defensive line along a road when three enemy soldiers showed themselves, shouting "*Telephonique!*" They did not want to be misidentified as machine gunners, since in Brannen's words "Machine gunners were seldom taken prisoner by either side." [29]

The division's success began to work against them. Naulin misinterpreted the result as a complete German débâcle, and ordered a pursuit as far as Machault, 10 km to the north. Lejeune quickly disabused him of that notion. Blanc Mont was precariously held, and the Ninth Infantry was stalled. The Twenty-ninth Infantry had encountered less opposition, and shying away from the fire coming from in front of the Ninth had veered left and slightly across the front of the Fourth Brigade. Lejeune did not even know where his units and his front were, and would have to order up aerial reconnaissance to find his own division. He ordered a cancellation of the ill-advised afternoon attack and set out to reorganize his division.

The worst of the situation was that on the Marines' left the French had failed to make headway, and the brigade flank was completely exposed.

Hermle: "So Major Barker ordered me to take the 74th Company over there and close the flank. There I first met Maj. Henry Larsen who was in command of the 3rd battalion of the 5th. He was very glad to see me and told me what to do with my company."[30]

Though only slightly injured—a cut lip and minor burns—Brannen had an excuse to go to the rear, escorting a band of prisoners. Along the way he came upon a French artillery battery that had been hard hit, with many dead and wounded. His prisoners were pressed into service as litter bearers until he could turn them over to the division Military Police. At the dressing station Brannen was tagged for evacuation, much to his surprise.[31]

From his vantage point Westover could only watch as "Wounded were coming back along the road, dropping to the ground at frequent intervals as the Boche machine gun nests from Blanc Mont raked the highway. Even stretcher bearers were subjected to the fire—the Boche instilled the desire to kill by showing no mercy, even to those who hovered between life and death from wounds."[32]

The situation was sufficiently grave that the French 170e DI was transferred to the rear left of the XXI Corps, and ordered out of its second-line position to move to the Second Division's left to keep pressure on the enemy.

The Marines who survived were nearing total exhaustion. Gunner William Nice found Captain George Hamilton of the 49th Company and stumbled into his P.C. in a crater: "I've organized the company sector with 20 men, captain. They're all we got left—you and I make 22. Lord I'm tired, but what I can't see is why we didn't get ours too."[33]

The Second Division had punched a deep wedge into the German defense. On the left the Marines were still held up by the Blanc Mont heights, but the French on the left had failed to make any headway against the stubborn 2. "Cologne" Landsturm Bataillon defending the Essen Hook.

The French were debilitated by 4 years of unceasingly brutal casualties, and French doctrine was now to relieve their shrunken divisions for rest after 1–4 days in battle. Since mid-September the French had been fighting their way through the stubborn enemy defenses around Somme-Py;

they were simply exhausted. Westover complained but did not fault the French. "They were old men, thirty-five to forty-five years of age. All had families. All had been under fire for years; nerves subjected to the never-ceasing strain of high-explosive. They were mentally lacking that last ounce of devil-may-care spirit that takes men forward because they have no thought of death, nor will to live; and they were nearing that point of physical exhaustion which allows the body to move but refuses the power to push on against a hail of fire."[34]

In the center the 23rd Infantry had driven more deeply against lighter opposition, and in part veered across the front into the Fourth Brigade zone north on Blanc Mont. But a 1½-km gap exposed their left flank where the line stepped back to the Marine positions. On the right the Ninth Infantry was also partially stalled, exposing the Twenty-third's right flank. Captain John Thomason aptly described the Fourth Brigade situation as "Four little islands in a turbulent Boche sea, and the old Boche doing his damnedest." The description applied equally to all four of the division's infantry regiments.[35]

All night the Marines were wary of a counterattack into the thinly held left flank, but none ever came. The French 22e DI was ordered to relieve the 21e DI to renew the attack on the left flank.

October 4

In the pre-dawn hours the Army's 4th Machine Gun Battalion was ordered forward to defend against a possible German counterattack into the open west flank, and Westover could see the prices the French and Germans, and then the Americans, had paid for the possession of the first trench lines north of Somme-Py. "Losses had been severe. Every effort had been directed towards defense; there had been no time for taking care of the dead.

"In consequence the trenches were choked with days-old bodies, often dismembered, which were turning green under the sun during the day and molding at night. They lay ghastly under the night light. Those which fire had permitted to be thrown from the trenches were only in a better position to feed the soft breeze. The whole place stank to such a degree that only the critical nature of the situation prevented prompt change of location. Gas masks were called into use, and the horrors for the guard and inspecting officers during their long vigil formed unfortunate memories…."[36]

Positions of various units remain uncertain. Official accounts indicate that during the night the Sixth Marines had misinterpreted a division order and partially drawn back from the crest of Blanc Mont proper. John Aasland of the Fifth Marines wrote in his diary that "As the sun went down we started to make ourselves comfortable. At 1.00 A.M. word was passed: '55th Company chow one kilometer back.' I was detailed with five men to go after it." On the return trip, "On our way up the trench it was evident that other points in the woods had caught it also. Here and there were dead men lying in the trench. Soon we reached the top of Blanc Mont Ridge, where the 6th Marines and 9th Infantry had been since yesterday at noon. They were dug in in a shallow trench right on top of the hill, but with trees to screen them from the air."[37]

The enemy used the respite offered by the darkness to concentrate forces atop the ridge. Their problem was that most of the formation that faced the American onslaught had simply ceased to exist. By this stage of the war the German Army had come to regard staff work as a partial solution to their manpower woes. Small units from various divisions would be thrown together to form a *kampgruppe*, or battlegroup. The German command responsible for Blanc Mont assembled any available units they could find, but the hastily assembled force was not a coherent fighting unit. German communications had completely broken down, with no real chain of command.

Hermle: "As daylight appeared you could see little blue [French] uniforms going through the woods, and we heaved a sigh of relief."[38]

At 0600 h the Fifth Marines, supported by elements of the Army's 4th Machine Gun Battalion, executed a passage of lines and continued the northward attack. C Company advanced with the 3/5 attack waves, with—from left to right—20th Company with 1st Platoon machine guns as security for the open left flank; 16th Company with 2nd Platoon machine guns on the left of the main wave; and the 45th Company reinforced by 3rd Platoon machine guns on the right.

Merwin Silverthorn, Gilder Jackson, and Wilburt Brown were all wounded on the same day. Sergeant Matek Kocak who had won the Medal of Honor at Soissons attempted to repeat his feat of outflanking a German machine-gun position. He was spotted and riddled with bullets.[39]

The enemy's artillery control was now suppressed enough that Field Hospital One was shifted north into Somme-Py. Derby: "The stretch of road between Somme-Py and Souain, in spite of the hard work done upon it by our engineers during the last four days, was still very rough. This section of road represented No Man's Land of the past four years. The enemy, in withdrawing, had mined it in several places on the crest of the ridge which separated the two villages, and extensive detours had to be made around the resulting craters. The practically new road which had to be constructed was necessarily narrow and correspondingly congested."

The new location of the hospital was near the shelter of the railroad embankment, and handy to the new road. But the enemy had registered every terrain feature for artillery fire. "About a hundred yards to the south of this site was a road intersection, which later turned out to be much too popular for the enemy's artillery." Unfortunately the hospital was forced to remain in the town, near the only reliable clean water supply, from the communal well.[40]

From the beginning there was heavy resistance. The worst carnage was on the left, where German machine guns and light infantry guns fired into the left flank, inflicting heavy casualties. About a kilometer southeast of the village fortress of St.-Etienne-à-Arnes, Major George W. Hamilton spotted a German counterattack forming on the far left, and a prolonged and bloody fight held off the German threat. The German counterattack nearly overwhelmed the 16th Company and accompanying machine guns, and the machine gunners had to fight off the attackers with grenades and pistols until the guns could be set up. Held up on the left, the regiment wheeled and pushed ahead on the right.

At 1700 h the Fifth Marines, with A Company machine guns in support, advanced against machine-gun positions on Blanc Mont, but were again forced back by intense fire from their front, left, and even the rear.[41]

Wilburt Brown said that Gilder Jackson had "always bragged that he had a terrific company, that 20th Company [3/5]. There weren't so many of them left the night of the 4th of October, though. I think the company came off the front when that battle of Blanc Mont was over with slightly less than half the strength it had at the beginning of the fight."[42]

Lejeune was still fending off Naulin's unrealistic demands for a more vigorous attack. By afternoon the French had broken through the powerful enemy positions on the lower ridge and made headway on the left, achieving a lodgment on the western slopes of Blanc Mont. But the tactical problem remained the machine-gun positions atop Blanc Mont. On the right the XXI Corps was still foundering on the positions north of Médéah Farm.

In a hasty conference Naulin and Gouraud were finally convinced that the division was not on the verge of a breakthrough. But to the west the enemy was in full retreat from the Suippe River to Reims; now their desperate defense at Blanc Mont was to cover a retreat.

October 5

German resistance was rapidly evaporating, and at 0600 h a battalion of the Sixth Marines and French troops closed in on the last enemy positions on the Blanc Mont crest, following so closely on the heels of a terrific barrage that neither suffered any casualties. This relieved the threat to the left flank, and deprived the enemy of direct artillery observation not only of the fighting forces, but also of the mass of support units flowing to and fro along the roads.[43]

William Rogers, 3/6, was to act as liaison officer with the French on the left. "We finally got upon top of the hill overlooking St. Etienne. Along the axis of our advance there was an underground telephone line, and every hundred yards or so there would be a ladder and a space to get down in there, a space underneath, where they could work to fix the lines and so forth. We had a battalion headquarters in one, and

Marshall and I appropriated the one forward of that, about a hundred yards forward of that. So one day Marshall said, 'Let's go out and look over our front lines.'"

The two went several hundred yards when "All of a sudden a shell hit right amongst us. I dropped. I had learned to duck long before that. He didn't duck at all. He said 'You'll duck into one of those one of these days.' He was the bravest man I ever saw in my life. I said, 'I haven't got any business I know of up in that part [unintelligible], I'll go back and look after my own.'"[44]

The Second Division continued to be bombarded with unrealistic instructions to exploit their stunning success. Lejeune: "no sooner was the successful operation against the stronghold on Blanc Mont completed, than we were required to give our attention to the preparation of the order directing an attack in the direction of Machault."

Machault was the next significant village and road junction to the north. It was also a major depot for the defenders, with a network of narrow-gauge rail lines connecting it to the defensive positions. It also held huge stockpiles of ammunition and matériel that were impossible to remove. Enemy resistance in the XXI Corps zone was rapidly crumbling as the Germans retreated, but to the east the French were still blocked by stubborn resistance north of Médéah Farm. The main axis for the preplanned German retreat, the Gudrun Operation, was along the major north–south road through Machault. The town played no planned role in the withdrawal, but now the enemy elected to make a stand there.

October 6

The Germans might be withdrawing, but their rearguards were stubborn and the spent Second Division was in no condition to exploit success. Both sides licked their wounds. For the Americans significant operations were limited to an attack on a trench system in front of the juncture of the two brigades that required two hours to clear. On the bigger scale the situation was slowly being resolved, and to the east troops from the 21e Division d'Infanterie pushed the enemy back, and now covered the Third Brigade's right flank.

Rogers: "That next day I was ordered to go down in St. Etienne and get in touch with our troops down there...." The town itself was still disputed, with both Germans and Marines in the streets and houses, with the French supposedly on the left (west) of the town. "So I got down there and about that time shells started falling around, and they dusted me off all the way back. I'd run up that line to one of these telephone holes, and get down in that thing and stay there for a few minutes 'til I thought they'd get out of synchronizing. I'd get up and run to the next one."[45]

Like the enemy, the Second Division was at the end of its rope: heavy casualties, limited food and water, and no sleep had taken their toll. Lejeune reluctantly requested that the division be relieved. He assumed that the typical practice would be followed, that the inexperienced Seventy-first Brigade of the Thirty-sixth "Arrowhead" Division (Texas and Oklahoma National Guard) would conduct a relief in place. The new men would move in and the old remain for a day to familiarize the new formation with the situation.

Instead, he was advised that the untested National Guardsmen, under his command, would launch an attack as part of a more general offensive the next morning. When Lejeune argued back (he seems to have made a general practice of it), he was told that "Tomorrow will be another great day for the 21st Corps." The best Lejeune could do was to call his brigade commanders together and explain the situation, with clear verbal instructions that the attack orders be promulgated downward to battalion level. [46]

October 8

The plan called for the two fresh National Guard regiments, with two of the less battered Second Division battalions to maintain liaison with French divisions of either flank. The Marines' 1/6 would fulfill this function on the left, where the 7e Division d'Infanterie had just replaced the 22e DI, but still no one knew where the front line actually lay.

Rogers: "I was told to go get in touch with the French down in St. Etienne. I didn't like the idea of that telephone line much, so I went over to the left ... and I saw the French line there. It never occurred to me to ask them. I just assumed they told me the French were down in the outskirts of St. Etienne. I just assumed this was a support line someplace." Rogers crawled and ran forward, following an embankment that provided cover and concealment until he was about 300 yards from the town. He crossed a dirt road, "played possum" for a while, and then started forward again. "Just about that time I got hit. I thought I'd been shot in the back. I looked around and couldn't find anybody, and I laid there and played possum for a minute or two. I finally got up enough strength to run back across the road to the others side. So I finally worked my way back up on hands and knees up to where this French line was....

"So they got a stretcher and carried me back over to the headquarters." Rogers had been shot through the chest, the round exiting his back but missing his lungs. "They carried me back by stretcher for maybe four or five miles back to the field hospital, and [from] there I was sent on back to an evacuation hospital."[47]

When the novice regiments attacked, the One-Forty-second Regiment was able to make good headway, pushing units in to relieve the beleaguered Second Engineers—fighting as infantry—in the St. Etienne cemetery. On its right the One-Forty First Regiment was in a terrible snarl. With the 2/9 they finally cleared the stubborn enemy machine-gun positions north of the St. Etienne–Orfeuil Road. In the slow process they fell behind the rolling barrage, and worse, the reserve battalions kept moving forward according to plan and became intermingled with the assault battalions. With no artillery support and disorganized units, a further advance would have been suicidal. Their limited gains—500 m.—left the right flank of the One-Forty Second exposed. Although things started well, reports from the National Guard brigade grew increasingly pessimistic as the day wore on. After a trip to the brigade headquarters, Lejeune felt he had no choice but to order the Second Division back into the lines.

That night the enemy launched a series of frenetic counterattacks, with mixed success. The One-Forty second Regiment was pushed back onto reserve lines held by the 3/6, where Major George Shuler reported that "We shot the tar out of the Boche."[48]

The 76th Company, 1/6, moved into St. Etienne and found that the Germans had evacuated the town. The Marines moved past it onto the northern slope. The Germans decided to counterattack, and Walter Gaspar sent up a flare to call for artillery support, but the shells began to strike the Marines. Gaspar sent up the appropriate colored flare to lift the fire, "And I'll be doggoned if the artillery didn't answer that one and hit the Germans broadside...."[49]

October 9

Despite the need to press the retreating enemy, the day was devoted to reorganization and rationalizing positions, and establishing solid liaison with the adjacent French units. The only real advance came when the 76th Company of 2/6 and E Company of the Second Engineers pushed into a complex of old German practice trenches on the slopes of the next ridge north of St. Etienne, The other units of the Second Division were relieved piecemeal that night, leaving only the artillery and engineers at the disposal of the new division.

October 10

Units began to move out of the line again, recovering their marching packs that had been piled in rearward positions during the approach march.

A handful of officers was left behind to familiarize the National Guardsmen with the situation. Like other units, the War Diary of the Marines' 6th Machine Gun Battalion noted that "This relief was badly bungled, the relieving division having no orders, instructions or idea of what they were to do.... The Battalion Commander of the machine gun battalion relieving this battalion was never seen, nor could he be located."[50]

October 11–12

In the wee hours of morning Karl McCune thought that "It was a good night for hiking and the men covered the ground rapidly. A brigade of the 36th [Division] was lined up along the roadside in Somme-Py waiting the order to go forward. Outside the towns were long lines of escort wagons, field kitchens, and auto trucks of the 2d Div." The Thirty-Sixth Division was short of transport, so most of the Second Division trucks had been allocated to that division. "The battalion proceeded in single file winding in and out between mules and wagons. Having passed the traffic the battalion reformed."

At the end of their role in the offensive the Second Division marched to the rear. It was axiomatic that going into battle you rode, coming out—battered and exhausted—you walked. After several long marches, "On Oct. 12th we marched to Suippes where every man ran his clothes through the cootie machine, took a bath, and received new underwear. The next day the company prepared to march to a new area."

Total Brigade casualties for the operation had been 292 killed and 2,016 wounded. Lejeune noted that while it might be easy to form a negative opinion of both the French divisions and the American National Guardsmen, he did not share that opinion. Touring the Essen Hook position, he remarked on the sheer density of French bodies still lying on the contested hill, and counted over a hundred French dead in a two-acre area (about 8,000 m^2). The number did not include those dead in the trenches themselves or entombed in bunkers. As for the Guardsmen, he thought they lacked only experience.[51]

The hard-fighting Second Division had now been designated by the French commander in chief as his "special reserve". This carried with it a risk, since, quoting Surgeon Derby, "The French were very likely to attach their tentacles firmly to an American unit when it had once entered their sphere of influence. And what was even more trying, they had a way of splitting up a division and using the two brigades at different points on the line."

Karl McCune was a bit more vivid. "On Oct. 20th the battalion packed up to move and at 1.30 [p.m.] shoved off for the front lines.... Splashing through the mud and rain for three hours the column reached the highway which it followed for three kilometers. Here billeting sergeants met their companies and guided them to their barracks—old dugouts abounding in rats and vermin. It was now nine o'clock and everybody turned in regardless of the fact that they had had nothing to eat. Eating wasn't essential then; what they wanted was sleep."[52]

CHAPTER 13

Marine Aviation

> The British did not care whether you called an aviator a Marine, or a Siamese piccolo player, so long as he could fly. They were "jolly" glad to have us.
>
> KENNETH COLLINGS, *JUST FOR THE HELL OF IT*

The Marine Corps was not immune to the aviation craze sweeping the nation and world in the first decades of the new century. On November 14, 1910 Eugene Ely, a test pilot for Glenn Curtis's fledgling aircraft company, made the world's first takeoff from a naval vessel. The primitive aircraft, taking off from a platform on a gun turret of the cruiser USS *Birmingham*, could not land back on the ship, but it foretold a revolution in naval scouting and gunfire observation.[1]

Curtis trained the first two naval aviators at his own expense, and in 1911 the Navy purchased three aircraft (two from Curtis, one from the Wright brothers), with a Navy mechanic and pilot for each aircraft trained by the manufacturers. By autumn of that year these first three aviators had established their own primitive flight school alongside the Navy's Engineering Experiment Station near Annapolis, Maryland. Unfortunately the site chosen was behind the targets of the Naval Academy's rifle range, and the occasional errant bullet from inept midshipmen added to the already considerable hazards of aviation.

In December training was temporarily relocated to the Curtis test field near San Diego, California to avoid Maryland's winter weather. Over the winter months the new pilots wrecked all three of the primitive aircraft.

In the spring of 1912 training was moved back to a more permanent (and safer) site near Annapolis. While the wrecked aircraft were being rebuilt, a new crop of potential aviators reported for duty.

There was at that time no official Marine Corps interest in aviation, so Lieutenant Alfred A. Cunningham joined the civilian Aero Club of Philadelphia. He launched a campaign to interest the Marine Corps in aviation, and through the Aero Club enlisted prominent members of Philadelphia society in his efforts to convince the Corps that it should have a Marine Corps aviation facility. He also rented a home-made aircraft, which he afterward referred to as "Noisy Nan", and persuaded the Navy Yard commander to let him use an open space for his dangerous personal experiments. Cunningham's experiences with the primitive aircraft did nothing to build actual flying skills. "I called her everything in God's name to go up. I pleaded with her. I caressed her, I prayed to her, and I cursed that flighty old maid to lift up her skirts and hike, but she never would."

Marine Corps Commandant William P. Biddle (February 3, 1911 through February 24, 1914) was himself a native of Philadelphia, and socially connected to those whom Cunningham was lobbying. It is impossible to determine whether the activities of a lowly lieutenant had any effect on official policy, but Biddle eventually concluded that "great benefit to an advanced base force … might result from trained aviators" who could serve in reconnaissance and naval gunfire control. Accordingly, two Marine Corps officers, lieutenants Cunningham and Bernard L. "Banney" Smith, were assigned from the newly formed Advanced Base School at the Philadelphia Naval Yard.

Considered by most as the "father" of Marine Corps aviation, Cunningham had an unusual career. After enlisting in the Army infantry in the Spanish-American War, he served primarily on occupation duty in newly conquered Cuba. After leaving the Army in 1901, Cunningham spent ten years selling real estate in his birthplace of Atlanta, Georgia, where in 1903 he made his first flight, in a balloon. In 1911 he enlisted in the Marine Corps, and served ashore and aboard battleships until promoted to first lieutenant and assigned to the new Advanced Base School in late 1911.

The first Marine to report for flight training, Cunningham arrived at Annapolis on May 22, 1912, but there were no aircraft available for training. When he returned from a temporary assignment to expeditionary duty, there were still no aircraft, so Cunningham finagled an assignment to the Curtis manufacturing plant in Marblehead, Massachusetts, where there were aircraft and a few highly qualified (and extravagantly paid) civilian instructors/test pilots. Under these cost constraints, Cunningham received two hours and forty minutes of supervised flight training, mostly under adverse, windy conditions.

Cunningham later wrote that "one calm day they decided to risk the plane rather than continue to pay any instructors large salaries. I was asked if I was willing to try it alone, and said I was." Cunningham's first solo flight was one familiar to every novice pilot. "I took off safely and felt confident in the air until I thought of landing and wondered what would happen when I tried to do it alone. Every time I decided to land I would think of some good excuse to make another circle of the bay. The gas tank was mounted between the wings in plain view, and a small stick attached to a float protruded from the top of it for a gasoline gage. As the gas was used, this stick gradually disappeared within the tank...."

As his fuel was slowly consumed, Cunningham was forced to steel himself to approach the ground, no doubt bearing in mind the old adage that all crashes occur at ground level. "I became more and more perturbed at having to land with little idea of how to do it. Just as the end of the little gasoline gage stick was disappearing, I got up my nerve and made a good landing, how I don't know."

Cunningham was officially designated "Naval Aviator No. 5", and the first Marine Corps aviator.

Banney Smith did not arrive at Annapolis until September, but proved to be an adept student. He quickly learned to fly in one of the now-repaired Curtis aircraft, and became Naval Aviator No. 6. With four aircraft now available, the first enlisted Marine aviator, Sergeant James Maguire, underwent training.

By 1913 Cunningham's assigned aircraft, the original Wright machine with a single engine driving two propellers through a complex chain drive, had been wrecked and repaired several times, and was beginning to show its age. On numerous occasions the old engine simply quit in mid-flight. In an official letter he described in detail how the plane was now a Frankenstein's monster of mismatched parts, and listed a string of complaints: "in spite of unusual care of myself and men, something seems to vibrate loose or off a majority of flights made," and "It is impossible to climb over a hundred feet with a passenger." He concluded by noting that "Lt. Arnold [future General Henry H. "Hap" Arnold, commander of the Army Air Forces in World War II] of the Army, after seeing the machine run and examining it, said that none of the Army fliers would go up in it."

Despite these handicaps, Cunningham and Smith participated in the January 1913 fleet exercises at Guantanamo Bay, demonstrating that aviators could spot submerged submarines in the clear waters. Aerial observers could also fulfill scouting duties better than the traditional cruisers, since the small aircraft were themselves difficult to spot, and were not betrayed by the coal smoke generated by ships. Here and at Annapolis they carried over 150 Navy and Marine Corps officers on familiarization flights, including Lieutenant Colonel John A. Lejeune.

In August Cunningham requested reassignment (his fiancé would not marry him unless he gave up flying), leaving two aviators and seven enlisted men undergoing training as mechanics. In October Commandant Biddle recommended that aviation functions be relocated to Philadelphia to operate with the new Advanced Base Force.

In August a Navy guidance board recommended the establishment of a formal naval aviation branch. In October Secretary of the Navy Josephus Daniels established a board of officers to create a naval air service: lowly but outspoken Lieutenant Cunningham represented the Marines. The recommendations included a Marine force of six aircraft to serve with the Advanced Base Force. In January 1914 the still-small Marine aviation arm (pilots Banney Smith and Second Lieutenant William H. McIlvain, ten mechanics, a Curtiss "F" seaplane and an OWL—Over Water or Land—amphibian aircraft) joined the fleet for the annual maneuvers at Culebra, a small island off eastern Puerto Rico. The OWL proved underpowered, incapable of carrying an observer.

The exercise simulated seizure and defense of an advanced base, so the aviation group had to clear a mangrove thicket to serve as a base. The two fliers took ground officers on demonstration flights to demonstrate aerial observation. Most telling, during bombardment by an "enemy" naval counterattack, the Curtiss flying boat circled over the battleships (which lacked high-angle guns) at 5,000 ft with total impunity, out of defensive range of small-arms fire. In a portent of things to come, Banney Smith observed that this demonstrated "the possibility of aeroplanes for defense using bombs of high explosive." It was an idea that predated Army Brigadier General William L. "Billy" Mitchell's still-disputed July 1921 demonstration of the vulnerability of battleships to air attack. The end of the Culebra exercise marked the end of the brief existence of an independent Marine air group, and the small squadron was merged back into the Navy arm at the new base of Pensacola, Florida.

The Marines, including Smith, deployed in support of the 1914 Mexican expedition. Based at Tampico, they played no significant role.

With the outbreak of war in Europe, Smith was dispatched to France to report on the French development of military aviation and garner intelligence about German capabilities. In this role he occasionally flew combat missions with French squadrons, but to what extent is unclear.

Development of Navy—and Marine Corps—aviation faltered as allocated funds went unspent by senior officers of a "battleship Navy", and the Marine air arm (consisting now of only McIlvain and few enlisted men) and an antiquated aircraft. Eventually an agreement between the Secretary of the Navy and the Army Signal Corps (in charge of Army aviation) resulted in additional pilots being trained at the Army's flying school at San Diego; among them were McIlvain and Cunningham, who had returned to flight duty.

As the nation began to belatedly prepare for war, naval and Marine aviation underwent a major expansion. August 1916 legislation created a Naval Reserve program. Senior naval officers still resisted creation of a separate naval aviation branch, and most of the aviation expansion would be in the Reserve, outside the usual Navy structure. By the end of 1916 the Navy had received 25 modern aircraft, Curtiss N-9s, a floatplane version of the famed JN "Jenny". By late 1916 the Commandant had determined that the time had arrived for development of an aviation company to support the Advanced Base Force. In late February 1917 Cunningham received orders to stand up the new unit at Philadelphia.

In early 1917 First Lieutenant Francis T. ("Cocky") Evans inadvertently made aviation history. Evans was trying to resolve an argument about whether the awkward N-9, with its huge pontoons, could loop. Evans attempted a loop; the plane stalled, and went into a flat spin. No pilot had ever recovered from such a spin, and it was an all too common cause of crashes. As the plane spun out of control, Evans instinctively pushed the nose down to regain airspeed and regained control with the rudder. Finally achieving a loop, he repeated the series of maneuvers over the Pensacola base (so as to have witnesses). It was not until he landed that he found that his spin recovery technique was of vastly more interest than looping an N-9. Evans was sent on a tour of military bases to teach his revolutionary technique, and in 1936 was eventually awarded the Distinguished Flying Cross for his discovery that saved the lives of thousands of pilots.

Men like Karl Schmolsmire ("it's spelled 40 different ways") Day, born in southeastern Indiana, was a graduate of Ohio State University and its obligatory officer training program. He was not interested in an Army officer's commission. Then the company he was working for sent him to New York, where an officer of the company advised him to join the Marine Corps: "It's the finest military organization, bar none."

Day took the train to Washington to see his friend (and later Commandant) Major Thomas Holcomb, who "was in a hell of a dither because Secretary [of the Navy, Josephus] Daniels had ordered them all back in uniform, and Holcomb said, 'Gosh, I haven't had a uniform on in four years, I haven't got any that fit me!'" Holcomb advised him to take the competitive examination for a regular commission, and Day was in the top four of 75 candidates. Day was quickly sworn in and told to report to Winthrop, Maryland until the new base at Quantico was ready.[2]

Francis P. Mulcahy was the son of Irish immigrants, a 1914 graduate of Notre Dame, and an Army National Guard enlisted man when he requested leave to apply for an officer's commission in the Marines. The base adjutant refused, so Mulcahy went to the base commander's home. The colonel replied "Oh, you want to go into the Marine Corps? Go ahead. Why sure, [if] that's what you want to do. Go right ahead."

Mulcahy did not consider aviation, as he was not a "daredevil", but after a few sessions of bayonet training the 135-pound Mulcahy "went back to my tent and I got to thinking, 'What chance have I got if I run into some big heinie over there?' I sat down and wrote an application for aviation."[3]

At the outbreak of war the Marine aviation center was still at Pensacola, but over the next three months was transferred back to Philadelphia again, with greater emphasis on land aviation. Observation balloon training was added to the curriculum, conducted at Army bases in St. Louis, Missouri and Omaha, Nebraska. On October 12 the Marine Aeronautic Company was administratively divided into the First Aviation Squadron (land planes) with 24 officers and 237 enlisted men, and the First Marine Aeronautic Company (floatplanes) with 10 officers and 93 enlisted men.[4]

Kenneth Collings grew up as the son of a Republican Party appointee and a privileged member of Washington society, hobnobbing with the likes of President Teddy Roosevelt's son and the sons of senators and Supreme Court justices. Failing in his efforts to cadge a ride on an early Orville Wright demonstration flight for the Army at Fort Myer, he nonetheless caught the aviation bug early. His privileged life was soon interrupted by the loss of his father's patronage job and eventual disintegration of the family, so he left high school without graduating.[5]

After a brief period of life "on the road" including stints as a piano player in New Orleans and Honduras, Collings drifted back home and joined the District of Columbia National Guard, but he still had the flying bug. After a short deployment to Texas during the 1916/early 1917 confrontation with Pancho Villa, Collings experienced a brief failed marriage, completed high school, and worked as a railway surveyor. Called back for National Guard service once again, he asked for a leave of absence to be privately tutored for an examination that would give him the equivalent of the university degree required for officer candidate school. Collings requested the Marine Corps examination. "Why did I pick the Marines? I am not entirely sure. There was a possibility of getting into the flying branch of either service and the Marines were—well, they were the Marines."

Collings's aspirations appeared to be thwarted again—this time by his tonsils—but intervention by a friendly Lieutenant Colonel Charles Lyman skirted the rules and allowed Collings to be commissioned after a hasty tonsillectomy at Walter Reed Army Hospital.

Reporting to the new base at Quantico, Collings found "a quagmire studded with Dixie huts,* and seething with the activity of thousands of troops.

"The keynote was mud. Troops drilled in it; they executed open order and flopped on their faces in it. As the emphasis was on trench warfare, they dug trenches and waded in it. They slip-slopped through mud to the rifle range where the barking reports of the firing were indistinguishable from the backfires of the churning trucks mired to their axles in the mud. Three-fourths of the officers in the school had only one object in mind: to finish their training in the shortest possible time and get into the trenches in France—to stand in some more mud!" The vast majority of new officers were champing at the bit to get to France as quickly as possible.

"That attitude on their part suited me! Rumors were flying around to the effect that at the conclusion of our course Major Cunningham would come down from Washington and select a limited number of officers for the aviation section. The more who went to the trenches, the less competition for the flying jobs!"

At Quantico Alfred Cunningham recruited new officers for aviation. Day recalled that everybody was talking about "the Lafayette Escadrille, and the Richthofen Circus, and things like that. It was a daring thing to do. As I say, everybody put in for it, and we didn't hear any more until the end of school, when 18 of us were assigned to the First Aeronautic Company at the Navy Yard in Philadelphia." Six were assigned to the Azores seaplane group, the other 12 to learn to fly land-based planes.[6]

Collings thought Cunningham was "a fine-looking soldier, slightly gray at forty or so. The flash of gold wings on his left breast was enough to set him apart from the other senior officers I had encountered, but

*Crude, unpainted wood and tarpaper buildings.

there was more. He was actually laughing and I thought that was against the rules in this war. Evidently the major had not met our hard-boiled instructors who frowned on levity and imported grisly veterans of the front line trenches to pep up our hatred for the Huns by pounding fists into palms and thundering 'Remember, men, they crucified Belgians!'

"Oh well, maybe the major did not like Belgians."

As Collings watched rejected candidates emerge from the interview room, he desperately cast about for something to set him apart. "Fighting! That was the answer."

Rather than waxing enthusiastic upon the future of aviation, he "barged in the door.

"'Major,' I said, 'from what I've seen of trench warfare, it's about one percent fighting and ninety-nine percent standing around in water up to your ears. I figure that I will be killed in this war anyway, but if I get into aviation at least I won't have to live in an aquarium while I'm waiting to get it in the neck.'

"'Fine,' said the major. 'You are the first man who has told me the truth. You're picked.'"[7]

The flight training, often by civilian contractors, was inconsistent and Day recalled an instructor who was "scared to death. He wouldn't let anybody touch the controls.

"I had four or five rides with him, and he never once let me touch the throttle, the wheel, or touch the rudder."

The next instructor, "He just went to the other extreme. After one hour and 53 minutes of dual instruction one morning he staggered out of the airplane, he was drunk as hell. He nearly put his foot through the wing.

"He said, 'All right, you sons of bitches, go up and kill yourselves.' That was my first flight solo."[8]

In mid-1917 more capable planes and equipment like gun cameras to evaluate mock air-to-air combat began to appear.

Alfred Cunningham—now the de facto leader of Marine Corps aviation—was dispatched to France in November 1917. After seeing the wreckage of a torpedoed ship en route, he finally made his way from England to France on November 17. After a brief stay in Paris (which he hated), Cunningham noted that "Paris is simply filled with U. S. Army officers who have nothing to do. It is the biggest graft I ever saw. Why don't they send them to the front and make them work." He spent three weeks touring French aviation training bases and examining aircraft, and on December 12 arrived at the AEF Headquarters at Chaumont, observing that "the closer we got to the front the fewer people you see and there are none of the usual loafers at the [train] stations." After much jousting with military bureaucracy, he was finally able to get permission to arrive at the French Quatrième Armée front on December 17.[9]

On December 18 Cunningham got his first taste of aerial combat when he persuaded a French pilot to take him along as an observer in a Spad two-seater. "The archies [anti-aircraft shells] bursting near us worried me some and made it hard to look all the time for boches." Sighting a German two-seater "We made for him. It was the finest excitement I ever had. I got my machine gun ready. Before we got to him he dived and headed for home. On 1 of our rolls I let loose a couple of strings of 6 at him but it was too far for good shooting."[10]

On Wednesday, December 19 Cunningham joined French front-line troops near Suippes. "Walked six miles before daylight and went in the trenches. They are filthy and horrible. Don't see how the men stand it. The stink of dead Huns in front is awful even in this cold weather. Soon after daylight I followed a party cleaning out an old communicating trench with hand grenades. I went until I saw 4 dead boches killed by grenades and 2 bayoneted and 1 poilu shot through the head. It was sickening but I suppose I would get used to it. Everyone does."[11]

A major obstacle to Cunningham's mission was the attitude among AEF leadership. Despite a desperate shortage of aircrews, the Army wanted no more of what they perceived as glory-seeking Marines in France. Of course Cunningham was not about to take this lying down. He offered the services of Marine aviators to the British, who had a surfeit of aircraft but had suffered heavy losses among aircrews. The US Navy could transport personnel and crated aircraft to Europe, independently of the resentful AEF.

Back in the US the land aviation component was leading a peripatetic existence, transferred from one Marine Corps or Army base to another:

Philadelphia, Long Island, New York and Lake Charles, Louisiana. Then in March 1918 the Marines' own facility was finally established near Miami, Florida.[12]

When Collings and the other would-be aviators reported at Miami, Major Roy S. Geiger greeted them in his typical staccato fashion: "How d'you do gentlemen; this is war; no time to waste; meet Lieutenants Burlingame and Davy who'll be your instructors when you start flying land planes this afternoon out in the Everglades; orderly, tell the officers' mess caterer to fix six extra places for early lunch; good day, gentlemen; stop by the supply office and draw helmets and goggles; the car leaves for field at eleven-thirty; don't miss it!" With that Geiger strode away.[13]

The Marine Corps air base was a flat stretch of drained swampland, blinding-white coral sand and dust covered with a few bits of sparse grass, and bounded by drainage ditches. The aircraft consisted of a pair of badly worn Curtis JN-4 "Jennys" powered by the already obsolete OX-5 90-horsepower V-8 engine.

The student aviators had been discouraged by the prospect of 6 months of ground school. Burlingame went through a very brief spiel on the stick and rudder, and Collings made the mistake of asking about ground school. "Davy flicked his cigarette butt away and froze me with a glance. 'Ground school? Ground school? Weren't you listening to Lieutenant Burlingame, man? You just finished ground school. What do you want? Raised letters, a diagram, and a club to beat it into your brains—if any?'" And away the first candidates flew.[14]

Training was hampered by the lack of any means of communication between instructors and students except shouting over the deafening engine noise. This resulted in considerable raging and shouting on the part of the instructors.

More student aviators flooded in, and the Marine contingent moved from distant barracks near Biscayne Bay into tents on the dusty airfield. As more new men flooded in, pressure increased to accelerate training. After a few more flights Burlingame asked Collings if he was ready to solo, then instructed him to take off, fly a figure eight over the field, and land. In his elation, Collings took off, flew a circle over the field, and made a near perfect landing. Burlingame came storming across the sand to puncture Collings's pride in his achievement. "Get-out-of-that-airplane-before-I-brain-you!" he snarled. "When I say a figure eight, I mean a figure eight—not a circle. You're grounded for five days."[15]

Washington bureaucracy also hampered training in its own strange ways. It had already been decided that the Marines would fly land-based planes in France, but now the Treasury Department decided to have a say in the matter. Since the Marines were technically *naval* aviators, all must qualify to fly floatplanes! One hundred and twenty aviation candidates moved back to the Biscayne Bay base for floatplane qualification.[16]

After struggling with inter-service rivalries, bureaucratic travails, and illnesses, Cunningham returned from France with the news that the Army aviation branch did not want them, and that the Marines would be operating under British command. The exact role of the Marines was still undetermined, but they began training to fly scout planes as escorts for day bombers.

A notable aircraft used for training in this role was the British-designed Thomas-Morse S-4 Scout, a single-seat advanced trainer used by both the Army and Navy/Marine Corps to train pursuit pilots. Although it was their most successful advanced combat trainer, the 75 hp Gnome rotary engine lubricated by castor oil (a laxative if inhaled or swallowed) made the "Tommy" unpopular.

The Tommy was exceedingly difficult to fly, and the rotary engines hard to maintain. Collings recalled his first flight after waiting in line for his turn in one of the few Scouts. "I took off—only to have my camera-gun jam before I had been up five minutes. Before I could orient myself and head for the field, the motor choked up and deluged me with castor oil. It coated my goggles with a thick, gummy film. I tried to wipe it off but only smeared the oil and made my visibility worse.

"I stripped off my goggles. Half-blinded I groped my way to the ground, my head and shoulders veneered with castor oil. The oil was in my eyes and my ears, had seeped under my helmet and saturated my hair; it was oozing down my neck and spreading over my shoulders. The smell of it was atrocious, nauseating. Then—

"'Jump, Lieutenant,' yelled a mechanic. 'She's on fire!'

"'That's the best news I've heard today,' I growled, scrambling to safety. 'Let the bastard burn.'"[17]

After incomplete training with the Morse Scouts, the squadron was suddenly reassigned as heavy fighters to escort Navy day bombers. Day: "Anyway, we were to furnish the escort for them, and for that purpose we had been ordered Bristol fighters."*

The American Liberty engine proved inadequate in the Bristol airframe, "So they canceled that and ordered DH-4s for us with Liberty engines" but as yet none had arrived.[18]

Given the mission of escorting bombers with heavy fighters, the necessity was to train the rear-seat gunners, but a shortage of aircraft forced risky measures. The Marines cobbled together some gunnery training ships out of wrecked aircraft. Day decided to take one up. "We had the gunners always crouch down in landings and takeoffs because otherwise they would deflect the airflow from our tail surfaces, particularly the rudder." On landing, "I saw I was going to overshoot, I began sideslipping to kill it [momentum], I looked back and here was my gunner, 6 ft 2, standing as big as life looking over the side. There went my control, and we slipped into a spin at about 50 ft.

"Then we cracked up. The plane broke in two between me and the engine and between me and the gunner. As a matter of fact the [machine gun] scarf ring went through the two rear cylinders of the engine, which was about the height of my neck. The only thing that saved my life was that I hadn't had time to buckle my seat belt.

"So I am a little allergic to seat belts today...."[19]

With overseas deployment looming, the mission changed again. The Marines were to be bombing squadrons, and were re-equipped with 72 brand-new Army DH-4 bombers.

Geoffrey de Havilland designed the DH-4 for the British firm Airco as the first two-seat daylight bombing aircraft with an effective defensive armament against German scout (fighter) aircraft. A 375 hp Rolls-Royce Eagle engine allowed a top speed of 143 mph (230 kph) and a typical payload of two 130 lb (100 kg) or four 112 lb (51 kg) bombs. Highly

* The F.2 "Brisfit" was an agile two-seat fighter/reconnaissance plane that could hold its own against contemporary single-seat fighters.

maneuverable with a forward-firing .303-caliber (7.7 mm) Vickers gun and a ring-mounted .303 Lewis gun for the observer, it was capable of holding its own in a dogfight and very popular with its crews. The DH-4 was being built in large numbers in the United States for use of American forces.

The primary drawback of the DH-4 was the pressurized fuel system with the tank located between the pilot and observer, which led to the nickname Flaming Coffin when it was penetrated by enemy fire or a fuel line broke. The long speaking tube required by the large fuel tank also limited communication between pilot and observer.

The first crop of Marine aviators was at last ready for graduation, and the night before set out to party in Miami. At the base gate Roy Geiger stopped them to offer some hard-won advice: "Gentlemen, you are now Naval aviators—live ones—so far. But you would be surprised how easy it is to become dead ones. The best formula I know about is overconfidence. My advice to you is that you never try to be the best aviator in the world—leave that to the other fellow. Just try to be the oldest. That's all; have a good time."[20]

Marine aviation in France

At long last the aviators departed for France, destined for Brest.[21] The only excitement came when the escorts opened fire on what turned out to be a floating crate. In the confusion *DeKalb's* steering engine broke, and the rudder jammed hard to starboard. The big troopship careened through the convoy at right angles, narrowly avoiding two collisions. It took a half-day to repair the engine and reassemble the scattered convoy.[22]

A, B, and C squadrons, and Headquarters Company of the First Aviation Force, arrived aboard the *DeKalb* on July 18, 1918. When D Squadron joined them in October the Force reached its full strength of 107 officers and 842 men.[23]

Collings was assigned to Geiger's squadron, based in an abandoned beet field: the giant beets were like stones protruding from the ground. On the first night the Marines learned what it was like to be on the receiving end when German Gotha night bombers struck the area. The men could hear the approaching line of bombs, but were spared only by the interval between bombs. A bomb struck a nearby munitions dump. "The place blew up with an earth-filling roar!.... Glowing balls of fire arched sizzling through the heavens; the sky was alight, now bloody-red, now multi-colored, now shot through with flashes of supernatural lightning.... The Gothas bombed our field every clear night until the end of the war."[24]

The real problem was planes. It was discovered that their planes were structurally unsound (Collings attributed it to sabotage) and had to be shipped to England for extensive repairs. The flyers sat in muddy fields, worrying about German raids and whether they would receive flight pay since they could not fly. Meanwhile the British aircrews at nearby bases were "walking shadows, gaunt and haggard, mere bundles of nerves existing on whiskey and sheer will power." Meanwhile the idle Marines cadged flights from British and French squadrons as best they could.[25]

The confusion and bureaucratic absence of coordination continued in France, and Cunningham continued to operate outside channels to get his force into combat. When the first contingent landed at Brest, no arrangements had been made to move the unit and its gear from the port to operational bases in the vicinity of Calais, 400 miles to the north. He found that the unit's trucks "had gotten mixed up and gotten into the Army pool, and I had to go down there, drag 'em out of the pool, and find drivers, and send those things North."[26]

Karl Day was assigned to locate the wayward trucks. "So we got there, and our motor transport had gotten to Paulliac, which was of course a big naval base in southern France, near Bordeaux. Roben [the squadron commander] sent me and some people to get the motor transport out. Then we had to find it, buried in Army pools, they had to steal a lot of it too, they stole six Cadillacs, right smack under the Army's eyes." The raid also netted a dozen Dodge sedans.[27]

The Marines were eventually scattered among three bases: squadrons A and B at Oye (now Oye-Plage) between Calais and Dunkirk, Squadron C at Le Fresne, 12 km southwest of Calais, and Headquarters at Bois-en-Ardres, about 12 km southeast of Calais (only a ten-minute drive today, in 1918 this was a much longer trip). The Marine aviators were to be the daylight bombing force, the Navy night bombing.

A few aircraft were assembled, and the indefatigable Cunningham went to work striking more deals. Airco had designed the DH-9 derivative of the DH-4, with the fuel tank in a position between the cockpits, and improved defensive guns. But suitable Rolls-Royce engines were not available and the performance was poor. US aircraft manufacturers were already producing the DH-9B, a redesign that used an American 400 hp V-12 Liberty engine. It had a longer wingspan and greater fuselage rigidity, with a top speed of 125 mph (200 kph) and a bomb load of 460 lb (210 kg). With four machine guns, its defensive armament was formidable. In yet more confusion, the British had a surplus of redesigned DH-9A airframes, but no engines while the US was shipping extra Liberty engines to England. Another deal was struck, under which for every four Liberty engines supplied, the British would turn over one completely equipped DH-9B to the Marines. But no matter what his machinations, Cunningham's air group never reached full strength of 72 aircraft: the maximum strength was 20 DH9s and 16 DH-4s.

Unable to equip his unit, Cunningham approached the British who by 1918 had more aircraft than trained pilots. Marine aviators would receive combat training with the RAF 217 and 218 squadrons. Day was assigned to 218 Squadron, and along the way checked out in Sopwith Camels, "That was an airplane I would have loved to have flown."

Canadian Major Bert Wemp's 218 Squadron was "this collection of misfits, and about the only thing they had in common was that they could speak English.... They could have given Hell's Angels many tips on how to raise hell, and Wemp handled them beautifully. He taught me what it means to be an officer and a gentleman."[28]

The RAF flyers had a reputation for hard partying, but Francis Mulcahy did not recall much alcohol abuse. "If a person was off and had nothing to do and got into town. I wouldn't say that everybody was loaded up, but once in a while you'd find somebody who'd had a little too much to drink."[29]

On one of Day's more memorable raids with the RAF 218 Squadron, "Instead of the usual bomb load of four 50s, they gave me a 230 pound bomb and hung it under the fuselage." The big bomb completely blocked the primitive bombsight mounted in the floor "So I told Frank [Corporal Frank Smith], 'When you see the other guys drop their eggs, I'll drop mine.'"

"So we came to our objective which was a railway junction in Belgium. I think the place was Deynze. And so Frank tapped me on the shoulder, and I could see the guys ahead dropping their eggs, so I reached over and dropped mine, and the next day we had a report from British intelligence ... one large bomb had scored a direct hit on a German troop train."[30]

The Marines quickly settled into a dangerous routine that would last the remainder of the war: "bombing enemy bases, aerodromes, submarine bases, ammunition dumps, railroad junctions, etc."[31]

Veteran pilots, the British commanders usually assigned the Marines to the "tail end Charlie" positions. "They put us—always the newcomers were the last on the right—in the 'V', because if you got shot you hadn't lost anything."[32]

The peril of this position in the formation is attested to by the disproportionate number of awards for heroism in this period. The first Marine aviator to be so decorated was Sergeant Thomas L. McCullough. On September 9 "while flying over Cortemarck, Belgium, was attacked by eight enemy scouts. Sergeant McCullough shot down one of the enemy planes and fought off the others until his gun jammed and he was forced out of action."[33]

Pilot Francis Mulcahy described the incident more vividly, and remembered that McCullough shot down two enemy fighters. "McCullough my gunner in the rear cockpit shot them down. I was just riding—I was all alone—and maneuvering as best I could, but they filled the damn thing full of bullets. They must have been very much surprised that we did not go down.... The only thing I could compare the sound to ... was it sounded like lightning looks. It was the nastiest kind of crackling sound."

One went through his [McCullough's] flying suit. "This old plane had a wind-driven propeller, two of them, because they had two main tanks to suck the gas from the tank to the carburetor. It was sitting up ahead there, and one bullet must have just barely missed my head, because it hit one of those things and put it out of commission. The engine stopped. And I thought, 'Oh, oh, here I go in Germany, Holland, or some place with no engine.' And then I thought, 'Well, I'll try the other tank.' And—whoop!—she jumped. I was glad to hear that sound."[34]

On September 26 Second Lieutenant Chapin C. Barr "was attacked by a superior number of enemy scouts. In the fight which ensued he behaved with conspicuous gallantry and intrepidity, and despite having been mortally wounded, he drove off the enemy and brought his plane safely back to the aerodrome."[35]

On September 28 First Lieutenant Everett R. Brewer "in company with Squadron 218, Royal Air Force. Lieutenant Brewer was attacked over Cortemarck, Belgium by fifteen enemy scout planes. During the severe fight which followed, his plane was shot down and although both himself and his observer were very seriously wounded, he brought the plane safely back to the aerodrome.... Considering the distance from Cortemarck to his aerodrome this is a remarkable instance." His observer, Gunnery Sergeant Harry B. Wershiner, "shot down two enemy scouts (one officially allowed) and although he was himself shot through the lungs and his pilot shot through the hips, he continued to fight until he was able to shake the enemy."[36] Wershiner's experience was particularly hair-raising. As Brewer desperately maneuvered their aircraft in the dog-fight with the 15 enemy planes, Wershiner's leather restraining harness snapped, and he was thrown from the aircraft. He somehow landed on the tail assembly. As Brewer tried to evade the enemy, Wershiner pulled himself slowly forward until he could tumble into the rear cockpit. Somehow in the fracas the two enemy planes were shot down.[37]

The plane(s) downed by Wershiner were the first credited to Marine aviators. On the same day four others (pilots Captain Francis P. Mulcahy and Captain Robert S. Lytle, and observers Gunnery Sergeant Thomas L. McCullough and Gunnery Sergeant Amil Wiman) were the first to accomplish what was to become a sort of Marine aviation specialty, when they helped drop 2,600 pounds (1,182 kg) of supplies to a surrounded French infantry unit.

In all the Marines flew 43 raids with the RAF.

In early October Squadron Leader Major Roy Geiger managed to acquire one of the new DH-9As just arrived from England; with Navy Lieutenant Commander Harold Grow as an observer, the two decided to try the new plane on an impromptu solo raid. At a British ordnance dump the plane was fitted with Lewis guns and four 100-lb bombs.

In a bit of showboating, Geiger decided to climb steeply away from the British field. Too steeply. At less than 400 ft the overtaxed aircraft side-slipped and went into a steep dive, with Geiger fighting to level the aircraft. It smacked into the grass at high speed, tearing away the landing gear, propeller, and lower wing with its load of bombs. The aircraft bounced up, engine racing, and flew another hundred yards before skidding to a stop on the grass. Both men scrambled out seconds before the aircraft burst into flames. It was not an auspicious beginning for Geiger's career.[38]

Not until October 8 were the Marines able to mount an air operation of their own. Captain Robert S. Lytle led five DH-4s and three DH-9As from C Squadron, dropping over a ton of bombs on the railway yards at Thielt, Belgium. The formation was jumped by nine enemy fighters who concentrated on the tail-end Charlie, a DH-4 flown by Second Lieutenant Ralph Talbot with observer Gunnery Sergeant Robert G. Robinson. Despite the odds, Talbot downed one of the attackers.

The two aviators' luck could not last forever. On October 14 the squadron attacked the town of Pittham, Belgium. "Second Lieutenant Talbot and another plane became detached from the formation on account engine trouble and were attacked by 12 enemy scouts." Robinson quickly downed one of the fighters, but two others closed in from behind and below. "Gunnery Sergeant Robinson, after shooting down one of the enemy planes, was struck by a bullet that carried away most of his elbow. At the same time his gun jammed." Despite excruciating pain, "While his pilot maneuvered for position, he cleared the jam with one hand and returned to the fight. Although his left arm was useless, he fought off the enemy scouts until he collapsed after receiving two more bullet wounds, one in the stomach and one in the thigh." In the mêlée Talbot "attacked the nearest enemy scout with his front guns and shot him down." With his plane now relatively helpless against the nimble

German fighters, Talbot took advantage of the remaining weight of his powerful engine. "With his observer unconscious and his motor failing, he dived to escape the balance of the enemy and crossed the German trenches at an altitude of 50 ft, landing at the nearest hospital to leave his observer, and then returning to his aerodrome." Both were awarded the Medal of Honor.[39]

As Captain Lytle tried to come to Talbot's rescue, his engine failed. Gliding to a crash landing in front of Belgian lines, Lytle and his observer scrambled to the dubious safety of a trench. That night Marine ground crewmen crept into no-man's land to disassemble and salvage the aircraft, a harrowing undertaking more dangerous than aerial combat.

On October 22 the Marines lost their first aircraft to enemy action. An aircraft piloted by Second Lieutenant Harvey C. Norman with observer Second Lieutenant Caleb W. Taylor "became separated from the other planes of his formation, owing to heavy fog and while so cut off was attacked by seven enemy scout planes. In the engagement which ensued he behaved with conspicuous gallantry and intrepidity, continuing the fight against overwhelming odds until he himself was killed and his plane shot down."[40]

The bland official document omitted what angered the Marines most. "The Germans had their victory, and should have been satisfied. They were not. Circling the wreckage at tree-top altitude, they riddled it with machine-gun fire, ground it to mince-meat, just to make sure that no one escaped. Why they did it I do not know, because they were usually not like that."[41]

Not all bravery was in the air. On October 28 C Squadron had received a huge consignment of crated bombs. "An aeroplane piloted by Lieutenant Ralph Talbot crashed into this pile of live bombs, caught fire and was completely burned. The fire spread to the crates of bombs and an explosion was imminent. Sergeant McGraw impressed the nearest men into service and dragged the burning crates of bombs off the pile while other men rolled them in the mud until the fire was extinguished. Sergeant McGraw's presence of mind and courage undoubtedly prevented a serious explosion, which would unquestionably have resulted in the destruction of the entire aerodrome and probable loss of life as well...."[42]

Because of the 1918 influenza epidemic that disrupted operations, the First Aviation Force flew only 14 raids in its brief existence as an independent unit, dropping about nine tons (8,180 kg) of bombs in addition to seven and one-half tons (6,818 kg) while cooperating with the RAF.

Combat casualties were only four pilots killed and a pilot and two observers wounded; Lieutenant Lytle was killed on a test flight. Non-combat deaths were significantly greater, with four officers and 21 enlisted men dead of influenza. Day: "When the Spanish influenza epidemic struck, the D Squadron camp was in a low, damp area. [C Squadron commander] Roban had the flu but wouldn't admit it, and he got out to pull stakes and move canvas to get us out of there, and died that night. God, what a man he was!" With Roban dead, Day was ordered back to his squadron as Executive Officer, but came down with the flu and only made one raid with the squadron.[43]

Like all too many, Collings was destined not to take an active part in combat. Spanish Influenza ravaged the camps. Cunningham arranged to loan aircrews to the hard-hit British, but Geiger refused to let his younger flyers participate. Finally struck down by the flu, Collings could only watch from his sickbed as planes came and went.

When the Armistice came "At Calais that night there was the most unrestrained exhibition I've ever seen. Many of these people had been subject to night bombing for four or five years. There hadn't been a light showing in Calais for four or five years. Most of them had spent their nights down in bomb shelters ... And Boy, the lid was off!!! We were surrounded by a whole gangs of pretty girls, and we'd kiss our way out of 'em, and so forth."

A few days later Day and another officer got an interpreter and slipped into German territory. In Bruges they looked forward to sleeping in a hotel's feather bed only to discover the mattress was straw: the retreating Germans had taken the mattresses. The two bluffed their way into Brussels, and "We spent the night in a hotel right across from the North Station, and the Germans completed their evacuation that night and as the last train pulled out they dynamited the station." Upon returning, the two were ordered to report to Major Cunningham, and placed on ten-day punishment for Unauthorized Absence.[44]

The Marines of the Aviation Force had their hopes of seeing Paris and Germany dashed. Cunningham expressed a desire to avoid the coming winter in their tent housing, but his eagerness was probably more driven by his ambitions for aviation. "I think we could accomplish much more at home, getting our Aviation service established...." In December 1918 the First Aviation force sailed for home.

The forgotten Azores

The strategic role of the Portuguese Azores in World War II remains largely unknown, and in World War I is even more obscure. The Azores archipelago dominates the most direct shipping lanes from Europe around Africa to India and the Orient, and its small islands provide the most strategic land base locations in the central Atlantic.

Before the war Britain and Germany had cynically engaged in secret communications over a possible dismemberment of Portugal's African empire. After the outbreak of war, Portuguese and German troops skirmished in an undeclared war along colonial boundaries, but Portugal remained a "belligerent neutral". On February 23, 1916 Portugal complied with a British request to seize German and Austro-Hungarian ships interned at Lisbon, and on March 9 Germany declared war on Portugal.

Portuguese participation on the Western Front remained largely symbolic and plagued by mismanagement, but on December 3 the German submarine *U-38* sank three ships in Funchal Harbor on the island of Madeira, including a French gunboat, and briefly bombarded the town. At 0300 h on July 4, 1917 the *U-155* shelled the port of Ponta Delgada on Sao Miguel, and the only effective resistance was offered by the collier USS *Orion*, undergoing repair in the harbor. *Orion* drove off the submarine with her 3-in. deck gum, and damage was insignificant (except to the four civilians killed). By December German U-boats were operating with near impunity, again shelling Funchal (December 12), and sinking Portuguese ships (December 17 and 26). By early 1918

U-boats were ranging far into the South Atlantic, and particularly in the small coves of the vulnerable northwestern Azores that provided shelter for U-boats making repairs, and secretive rendezvous points for blockade-running German supply ships.

All these actions alarmed Allied naval planners. It was decided that American forces would be responsible for defense of the Azores. Navy submarines and patrol craft, with a Marine aviation detachment would patrol out of Ponta Delgada. A contingent of 150 Marine infantry and two coastal guns would defend the base against further attacks.

Marine aviation in the Azores

The 1st Aeronautic Company under Captain "Cocky" Evans arrived on January 21, 1918, both the first Marine unit and the first American aviation unit to see actual overseas service. The company was designated for anti-submarine patrols, with ten Curtiss R-6 seaplanes and a pair of N-9 aircraft, the latter trainers hastily fitted with rear-cockpit machine guns. Personnel included 12 officers and 133 enlisted men. The unit later received six more capable Curtiss HS-2L flying boats, a single-engine pusher aircraft with a forward-mounted observer's cockpit that provided far better forward vision for patrol work. The cruising range of 400 miles at 90 mph also made the HS-2L far more suitable for long-range patrols.[45]

Duty at Punta Delgado was far cushier than in dangerous France. Christian Schilt had been interested in aviation before his enlistment. Probably because of his two years as an engineering student, he was trained "on the job" as a mechanic, and assigned as an aircraft crew chief and gunner. "Oh, it was a beautiful place. There was wonderful flying weather, [and] people were very friendly.... They took us right into their homes and did everything they could for us, so it was good to be there. Of course they had an ulterior motive because they were expecting submarines to come right out of the water all the time. They were really scared."

On February 23 the Marines began aerial patrols. Based at Naval Base Number 13 in Punta Delgada, the planes could effectively patrol only within a 70-mile radius of their base, but it was sufficient to disrupt German submarine operations and deny the U-boats temporary refuge in isolated bays and inlets. "We saw a few out there; in fact we dropped a few bombs, but as far as we know we didn't damage anything. We had 125 and 200 pound bombs, which wasn't very much. You'd have to get a direct hit, and then be lucky to sink one."

"But we kept them submerged, I think."[46]

A small Marine detachment was belatedly established at Naval Base Number 29 at Cardiff, Wales on September 30, 1918 for antisubmarine patrols. It saw no known action.

The near demise of aviation

The Marine aviation units were some of the first to face near extinction in the breakneck demobilization. In February 1919 the 1st Marine Aviation Force was disbanded, and the 1st Aeronautic Company followed in March. The Miami base was closed and personnel were transferred to Parris Island and Quantico. The number of Marine aviators was drastically cut.

Still, Marine aviators were the only American flyers to see combat between the major wars, in Santo Domingo (modern Dominican Republic, 1919–1924), Haiti (1919–1934), and Nicaragua (1927–1933). In these places the tiny Marine air arm pioneered close air support, aerial evacuation of wounded, dive bombing (a Navy innovation) in combat, air-to-ground communications, and aerial transport of combat personnel.[47]

CHAPTER 14

Meuse-Argonne

But God would never be cruel enough to create a cyclone as terrible as Argonne battle. Only man would ever think of doing an awful thing like that.[1]

SERGEANT ALVIN C. YORK

The Meuse-Argonne Offensive would be the first (and as it turned out, only) major, purely American offensive of the war. It was to be but part of the Allies' great Hundred Days Offensive, designed to overtax Germany's already reeling army by attacking along the entire Western Front from the Swiss border to the North Sea. Allied resources were enormous.

After the fall of the Blanc Mont position, the Allied threat to the Sedan–Mézières lateral railway line, and the great communications center at Sedan itself, loomed larger than ever in German planning. The American First Army would advance down the valley of the Meuse River as the French Quatrième Armée advanced toward Mézières. The two forces would converge to outflank and force the enemy to evacuate the Argonne, and to eventually outflank the final remnants of the old Hindenburg Line.

To counter this, the Germans began to strip reserves from fronts facing the British and French. The Hundred Days plan was working as desired.

In the Argonne the Americans would have a massive superiority in artillery, including more heavy howitzers and huge railway guns like those mounted on battleships.

The primary problem was that the local terrain favored the defenders. The enemy fought for the forested hills with the usual skill and tenacity, and Westover wrote that "Machine guns seemed to grow like bushes on the hillsides, in the woods, along the borders of fields; they covered the roads, they swept the contour of the ground; the Boche were using them to great effect, and with knowledge born of experience and study of defensive actions."[2]

By late October the American Army offensive was grinding to a stop. Casualties were heavy, and units needed rest and reorganization.

Logistics were also strangling the advance. The preparation for the offensive had been the biggest in American history: 600,000 men, 4,000 artillery pieces, 90,000 draft animals and a million tons of supplies—not to mention tanks and trucks—had been shifted eastward to a new front. At the same time 220,000 French troops, with all their heavy equipment, had passed back through the Americans.[3]

All the movement was done under cover of night, amid massive traffic jams. Now, as the attack advanced into contested terrain, the transportation infrastructure was collapsing under the weight. The rail lines were ancient and few, and the road net mainly a series of unconnected tracks. Even the construction of new roads was hampered by incessant rain and swampy ground in the valleys.

While the Second and Thirty-sixth divisions fought at Blanc Mont, the major American force battered itself almost to pieces on the Kriehilde Stellung defensive line in the Argonne. The heavy casualties resulted in far too many soldiers being sent into battle poorly trained, some unable to use their rifles or bayonets.

The Second Division was granted only a brief rest period. The Marine Corps seemed to have remedied its manpower problems with the administrative skills of Smedley Butler, who was at last in France. Lejeune complained that the Fourth Brigade was quickly brought up to strength, but it was difficult to obtain Army replacements, though in fairness the Army was straining to replace losses in several dozen divisions.[4]

When Lejeune reported to the American First Army, he found that his new corps commander, Major General Charles P. Summerall, was cut from the same cloth as Pershing. Summerall was confident—even arrogant—to the point that he would argue even with Pershing, but his superior abilities made him valuable. Like Pershing, he would immediately relieve officers who failed to meet any measure of his exacting standards, and never let them forget it.

Lejeune was told that not only were Army replacements hard to provide, but that while the supporting arms remained with the Thirty-sixth Division, his division would be supported by the artillery of the First Division and an unfamiliar regiment of engineers. It seemed that the Army was to some extent adopting the *kampfgruppe* concept that the German unit commanders found so counterproductive. "I insisted that the Second Division as a unit could accomplish far more than could a conglomeration of infantry, artillery and other units hastily thrown together on the battlefield, as it was the *esprit* of the Division which made it such a formidable antagonist. I explained too that our Artillery, for its part, would overcome insuperable obstacles in order to give effective support to the Infantry and Marine regiments." The argument was bumped all the way up to American I Corps commander General Hunter Liggett, who secured the return of Lejeune's support units from Gouraud's command.

Lejeune was knowledgeable enough to ruthlessly exploit his connections from among Army school contacts. With his Assistant Chief of Staff he called on Pershing's staff officer in charge of personnel, who explained the shortage of replacements and "mentioned in the most casual way that 2,500 replacements were then on their way by rail to join the Third Division. He gave us a significant look which we clearly understood, and without further delay we went back to the Chief of Staff's office intent on obtaining those replacements by any means in our power." The personnel were transferred to Lejeune's division.

Lejeune was pleased to have put one over on the Third Division's commander, but as he rode back his car passed the slow-moving *camions* carrying the Fourth Brigade. He slowed the car "so that I could see and be seen by each of the 8,000 men. The thought that in a few days the lives of these men and of many others would be dependent on my acts was enough to banish gaiety or mirth from my soul ... and to put in their places seriousness and earnestness of purpose and the determination to do all in my power to direct the operation of the Division [so] as to achieve victory with the minimum loss of life."

On October 26 the Second Division began moving into the lines, on foot.

After arrival at his new headquarters a member of Lejeune's staff ushered in a young private from the Fourth Brigade, wet, exhausted and suffering from a bad cough. The man explained that he brought letters from officers back home who explained that he was underage, and requested fellow officers to keep an eye on him. Lejeune quizzed him as to why he brought the letters just now, and the private explained that "All my buddies were killed at Blanc Mont and I am worn out from the forced marches. I saw you drive by us on the road today, so I got permission from our Captain to bring the letters to you."

Lejeune arranged to have him transferred to the regimental headquarter as physically unfit for field service, and he proved to be a capable clerical worker. The man later met with Lejeune after the war, when he was studying medicine.[5]

Despite all their travails, the Second was to be accorded the "post of honor" as spearhead of the renewed offensive in the Meuse-Argonne.

Security was tight and effective, but the enemy was still quite aware that something was going on. The reaction was the usual probing bombardments of potential assembly areas with gas and high-explosive artillery rounds.

Despite early Allied successes in September and early October, the Germans were able to withdraw from some key positions in good order, preserving forces that would later prove important. By early October advancing divisions were ensnared in massive traffic jams along the limited road network, inexperienced divisions suffered from poor organization and staff work, and the American tanks thought to be critical found the going too difficult.

Enemy counterattacks negated some gains, and led to local withdrawals. One such retreat left the Lost Battalion of the Seventy-seventh Division (actually seven companies from the Three-hundred-seventh and Three-hundred-eighth regiments, plus two companies from the 306th Machine Gun Battalion) isolated in enemy territory for a week.

The see-saw battles continued through October with heavy losses. In the closing days of the Blanc Mont Ridge battle, on October 27 the

French Quatrième Armée finally advanced west of the River Aisne to align with the Americans in the Argonne Forest east of the river.

The hastily reconstituted Second Division was not officially plugged into the V Corps until November 1.

By late October the American offensive had pushed the Germans nearly to the Meuse. It was common knowledge that the war was all but over, but the deadly Spanish influenza pandemic was beginning to ravage the front-line troops with more effect than the Germans. Clifton Cates: "By that time, our company in the Meuse-Argonne had only three men killed but for some reason we had a lot of wounded. We had, as I remember it, thirty-six wounded. But we were wet, cold and I don't think we had over thirty men in the company left at the Armistice. I mean cold, dysentery, and flu."[6]

The problems were poor (or no) food, and the fatigue and debilitation of prolonged combat and marching which weakened resistance to disease. Division Surgeon Derby recorded that "The men began to succumb to influenza and intestinal inflammation, and during the coming week sickness claimed many more victims than did the machine gun bullet. The evacuation mounted to four or five hundred a day, of which only a fifth were battle casualties."[7]

Late October found the Second Division scattered, with the Second Engineers and the Second Field Artillery Brigade still supporting the Thirty-sixth Division north of Blanc Mont. The infantry had begun its slow march to the Argonne on October, but the slower engineers and artillery were not reunited with the division until October 30.

The Second Division, in strict secrecy, moved into positions on the nights of October 25 and 26.

Orders were issued for a November 1 attack, with the Sixth Marines on the left, and the Fifth Marines in the center. Both were to attack in the usual column of battalions. On the right the Twenty-third Infantry would attack with the First and Third battalions in line, and the Second Battalion in support. The Ninth Infantry and the Fourth Machine Gun Battalion made up the division reserve.

The plan was another ambitious one, with the Second Division expected to advance 9 km in the first 48 hours, seizing five fortified towns as well as breaking through two major German defensive lines. The division artillery would be augmented by the artillery brigades of two other divisions, as well as French guns. This deep penetration was intended to bring Allied artillery within range of the Sedan–Metz rail line, and at last sever German lateral communications.

Resistance was expected to be heaviest on the right, facing three forested areas, and so after the Twenty-third Infantry cleared them the regiment would pass into division reserve. The Marine Brigade was to extend its line to form the full division front.

Fire support would be lavish, with the artillery brigades of the First and Forty-second Divisions, and the machine guns of the Forty-second Division added. A small contingent of FT light tanks would support the attack.[8]

For this last, great push the Second Division relieved the Forty-second Division on the night of October 30/31, with the Marine Brigade and the Twenty-third Infantry taking over the forward positions. The Forty-second Division occupants remained in place to provide security as the new division organized for its attack.

Repeated experience like that at Blanc Mont had taught the Americans about the German practice of sending sacrificial machine-gun detachments forward of their main line to inflict losses and hinder the momentum of an attack. This time the attackers would be held behind the jump-off line while a standing barrage smothered such potential positions before the attack. Since the heaviest resistance was to be expected at the enemy front line, the Marine Brigade would attack with the two regiments abreast, with the Twenty-third Infantry on their right. The Ninth Infantry would follow to eliminate remaining enemy resistance in the many wooded plots. After the first objective (a line 400 m from the start) the Marine Brigade would fall into a support line and the Marines would spread right to cover the entire division front. Once the final day's objective, near Barricourt, had been reached, the advance would halt while strong patrols probed toward the exploitation line.

Sleepless and worrying at 0200 h, Lejeune's spirits were buoyed by the knowledge that the Second Artillery Brigade—and its highly competent commander—were back.[9]

November 1

After a two-hour bombardment the attack commenced at 0530 h. The first phase of the battle was to be across relatively open country.

Leo Hermle was impressed by the sheer scale of the operation: "we had what was known as a million dollar barrage behind us that day: some 13 battalions. It was terrific. The rolling barrage was terrific."[10]

Machine gun barrages also beat the ground in front of the advance at ranges up to 2,000 yards, and as the attacking infantry moved through, the machine gunners joined the attack waves. The infantry battalions continually moved through each other to maintain momentum. Artillery support was detailed and effective, with rolling barrages to precede the infantry, and whenever the infantry paused, standing barrages to keep the enemy from organizing an effective defense.

Apparently the campaign was not one of the more memorable compared to Belleau Wood or Banc Mont, and does not figure greatly in period memoirs. McCune, 55th Company, 2/5: "At nine o'clock on the night of Oct. 3d [*sic* October 30/31] the battalion set out for the front line.... Then we came upon a ridge lined with artillery, and all along the road lay bodies of Germans and Americans who had made the complete sacrifice and were still unburied. About a half kilometer further the battalion reached the main road running parallel to the lines which it followed going to the left. The 1st Battalion was digging in on the right side. Then we turned off to the right into an open field, formed the two-wave of skirmish line about a hundred yards in advance of the '75s."

Under a thunderous Allied barrage and German counter-barrage, "the 1st Battalion of the 5th passed through the 2nd Battalion positions, advancing to the attack. At distance of between 600 to 800 yards the 2nd Battalion went over, the 55th Company in support."

McCune described in detail sweeping through the forest, crossing one ridge after another, and impeded by relatively weak resistance.[11]

The Marines again fell back on the harsh lessons of counterinsurgency warfare, as well as experience at Belleau Wood. Fritz Wise gave instructions to his battalion that every German body would be bayoneted to neutralize those feigning death. All machine guns would be disabled to

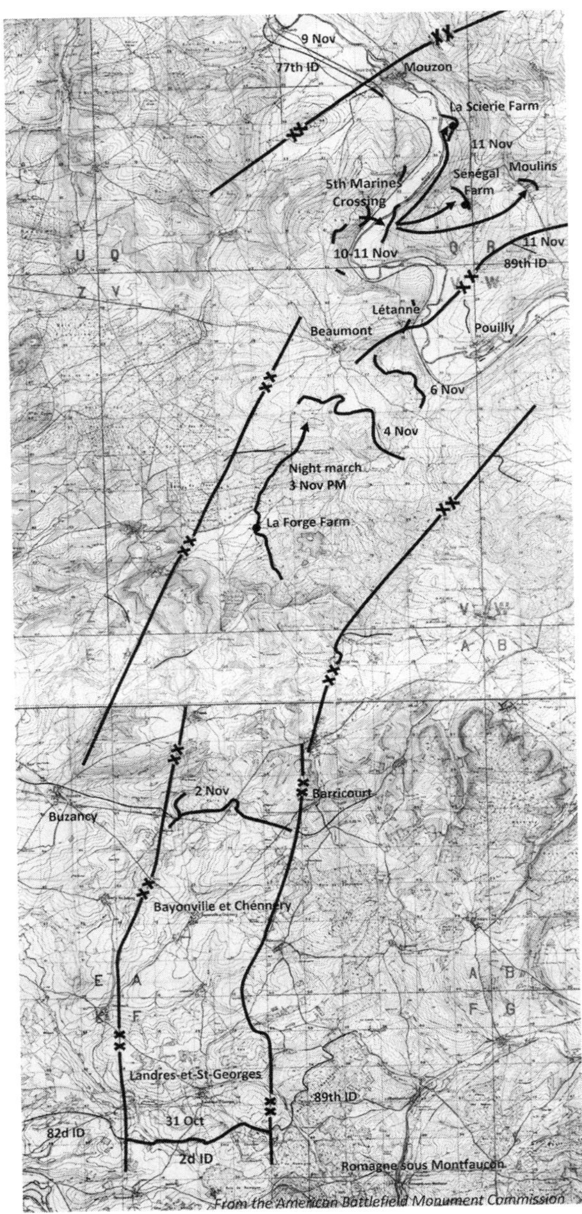

MEUSE-ARGONNE OFFENSIVE, NOVEMBER 1918. The rapid advance of the Second Division's Third Brigade was slowed more by weather conditions than by German resistance. After a brief rest while engineer equipment was brought forward, the Marine Brigade forced a crossing of the River Meuse on the night of 10–11 November.

prevent infiltrators from reusing them. Special "squirrel squads" would follow behind the advance, killing snipers that had waited to fire at the Marines from behind.[12]

By 1520 h the brigade had attained its first day's objective.[13]

Walter Noble was also impressed by the vast scale intended to overpower the enemy. "I remember getting up on a hill, and as far as I could see to the right and to the left was open country and as far to the rear as I could see there was nothing but men and equipment moving deployed across the country like a bunch of locusts.... I remember my first sergeant saying, Looks like nothing could stop that movement...."[14]

Hermle recalled the cold, and wading through the streams: "when you stepped in the water it was a little cool." Then, "We were held up on a ridge, and I went over and talked to Lieutenant Overton of the 76th Company [1/6] and just as I left a shell hit him and killed him. He was a very much loved man. His outfit about went crazy, I know mine did. On the ridge to our left were machine guns firing at us, and I walked over to Lt. Summerall* and I said, 'Happy, let's go get them.' Well, we did. We lost a few men, yes, but the record shows that we captured 155 prisoners and 17 machine guns. Summerall actually led the platoon. I am credited with leading it, but I didn't lead it. I was the company commander.

"In the meantime the 76th on our left had cleared out everything in front and away we went."[15]

That night Hermle "noticed that there was a lot of blood on my right leg, and I put my hand down there and a small shell splinter was in my leg. So I went over to the doctor, he said, 'You got to go for tetanus shots.' I said, 'I am all right, doctor.' And I walked away. He caught up with me and ordered me to go back and take a shot of tetanus."

In that era the men were not inoculated against tetanus, but if wounded were given a massive dose of tetanus antitoxin serum. "I remember going back on a machine gun truck with a lot of seriously wounded men and I felt like 30 cents going with them." He took the injection and went back to his company, "not because I was a great hero, but because the war was over and I wanted to be with my outfit."[16]

---

*Hermle may have his platoon leader confused with the corps commander, Charles P. Summerall.

As the division advanced rapidly, Lejeune shifted his headquarters forward several times. In the process he observed the constant flow of wounded to the rear, although casualties were unexpectedly light. "First there were the walking wounded, and then a considerable number being carried on stretchers by German prisoners." He was undoubtedly exaggerating when he added that "Each of these seemed greatly to enjoy the experience of being borne in state by four husky Germans, and took great delight in giving them orders."

Last came the ambulances with more serious cases, and Lejeune remarked that the Division Surgeon, Colonel Richard Derby, and his assistant seemed to be everywhere, coordinating the evacuation.[17]

On the division left the Eighty-ninth Division had not kept pace. The division artillery laid down heavy barrages in the unsecured zone. Parts of the Sixth Marines and Ninth Infantry moved into their zone to secure the open flank until that division advanced by fighting far into the night. Word came down for a renewed morning attack, then another order at 1900 h adding an attack westward into the Eightieth Division zone, directed at the town of Buzancy. Lejeune pointed out the risks of an attack across another division's front, and then it was discovered that the attack (across the boundary with I Corps) would run headlong into that corps' attack. The attack was not called off until 0400 h, after the staffs and troops had spent a sleepless night.

November 2

McCune recorded the morning was "foggy and drizzling and the battalion continued to hold the position. At noon a German plane swooped down through the clouds, flying low over the two battalions, and then returned to its lines. Hostile batteries were now firing upon us and it was pouring rain."[18]

In fact the confusion of the rapid advance had rendered it impossible to reorganize the Fourth Brigade for the planned attack, so instead it was revised so that the Third Brigade would carry the brunt. This attack would be different in that most began near dawn.

At about 1800 h the Third Brigade executed a passage of lines and lay silently in position, ready to resume the offensive, with the Marines in tow. The weather remained miserable, and Carl Brannen observed that "We were drenched to the skin, and it was freezing. At night we lay in the mud, tired and hungry and in the morning would take up the advance again."[19]

November 3

Commencing in the middle of the night, the offensive was more like an armored thrust or an infantry movement in jungle of a later era. The plan used surprise, and deep piercing attacks, to break the enemy's will, rather than just inflict casualties. Under a heavy rain and in darkness that helped conceal them, the American soldiers broke through the thin enemy defensive crust, right through the remnants of the Hindenburg Line and the Freya Stellung. The two Army regiments advanced in extended columns along major roads, with an advance guard and flankers to the sides. The rapid advance "moved through the enemy lines, capturing many prisoners, a number of whom they found asleep. Those more alert were surrounded."

The Army brigade commander told Lejeune that "perfect quiet reigned after the advance began, not a word above a whisper being spoken. Many German soldiers were made prisoner while lying asleep on the ground, and at La Forge Ferme the buildings were filled with sleeping men." The columns moved stealthily onward, past enemy artillery batteries firing at where the Americans were still believed to be. At one headquarters the American soldiers arrived only minutes after a German division commander and his staff had departed. Even among the reserve units morale was high as they marched through the rain and darkness, not having to fight for every inch of ground.[20]

The attack was one of the most notable of the campaign—8 km in a single day.

Many dangerous German positions had been bypassed. That afternoon, McCune recalls: "An '88 gun crew, missed by the 9th Infantry in its advance, planted shells on the line until a one pounder crew brought up and put it out of action. Rations arrived at nine, and it was still raining."[21]

November 4

The rain that had aided the original attack now worked against the Americans. The few roads through the forest quickly became bottomless pits of mud, and resupply ground to a nearly complete stop. "Animals died in their traces trying to pull loads through. Tractors were being used continuously to pull out stalled trucks. During the day casualties piled up in the advanced positions with no ambulances available for evacuation; they were not able to get forward. To add to the "horrors of war", men were becoming ravaged by dysentery. Slightly wounded men sent to the rear by walking, died on the way from the combination of wounds, exposure, and dysentery."[22]

Food ran short and forward units plundered gardens planted by the Germans, consuming raw cabbages.

The Marines were in supporting position, but were called forward to help protect the division's exposed flanks. But even in reserve units still suffered losses as the ever-alert German artillery sought out rest positions. B Company of the 6th Machine Gun Battalion suffered losses of 20% when caught by one such barrage.[23]

November 5

American units had reached positions overlooking Sedan. For reasons of prestige the French Quatrième Armée was to liberate the city. The American First Army veered eastward, aligning its advance perpendicular to the River Meuse. It was not a great issue: the enemy had destroyed all the bridges. The Marine Brigade was withdrawn from the line to rest and refit in preparation for the river crossing.

November 9

The rapid advance hindered the assembly of engineer logistics necessary to force a river crossing. Lejeune learned that all the pontoons were allocated to the Eighty-ninth Division; the long-suffering Second Engineers would have to bridge the river under hostile fire.

Summerall's callous bluntness enraged the officers. "Rumors of enemy capitulation come from our successes. Only by increasing pressure can we bring about his defeat. We will not pause.... I don't expect to see any of you again. But that doesn't matter. You have the honor of definite success [so] give yourselves to that. Report to your commands."[24]

November 10

Despite rumors of a pending armistice, offensive operations continued. The Americans stood poised to cross the Meuse. The Sixth Marines were to cross at Mouzon, the Fifth at Léthanne. As a preliminary, engineers constructed crude foot bridges, building sections of raft at a sheltered position. The rafts were carried to the river and lashed end to end on the near shore. When complete the undulating raft was swung across the stream and engineers secured the other end to the far shore. Bridge guards—usually an infantry platoon reinforced by a machine gun—were pushed across the frigid river to secure the far bank while the engineers completed the bridge. These undulating bridges often sank below the water line under the weight of men, so troops loosened all their pack and helmet straps, and carried things like ammunition and weapons in their hands, for fear of falling into the icy water heavily laden with gear.[25]

The enemy was completely aware of what was going on, but darkness and thick fog provided some protection. Periodic shelling delayed bridging and sometimes destroyed the bridges, leaving the bridge guards isolated on the enemy bank.

In the Fifth Marines' sector the Marines were able to push across the river. By day's end the sizeable main bridgehead included 1/2, 2/2, the 23rd Machine Gun Company, the 1/9 Infantry and a company of the 5th Machine Gun Battalion, and the 1/356 Infantry and Company C, 342nd Machine Gun Battalion (Eighty-ninth Division).[26]

The history of the 49th Company recorded that "Crossing under heavy fire of shore batteries on foot bridges, which sunk below the water line, with their live weight, the marines, by desperate fighting, reached the opposite shore by 10 P.M., aided by a heavy fog." [27]

As it turned out, only a few Sixth Marines units crossed the river. Clifton Cates: "I was very glad not to cross the river, I can tell you that.... We would have to cross on little foot bridges and the Germans were putting down heavy fire and no sooner than the engineers would get the bridges down than the Germans would blow them up. Then when the men got on the bridge, you can imagine, it sank down, and they would flounder off in the water. "In the bitter cold, and heavily burdened with weapons and equipment, survival was a matter of sheer luck.[28]

The southern bank offered little cover or concealment from enemy artillery observation. For the Sixth Marines "Every time we put a bridge across they'd shoot it down. At daylight the sixth was ordered back to the woods. This was the morning of the 11th." In many places this necessitated a withdrawal of up to 3 miles.[29]

November 11

On the morning of November 11 the anticipated news of the Armistice was promulgated. At 0605 h Lejeune received a radio message that hostilities would cease at 1100 h, but many were concerned that it was a German hoax.[30] After confirmation, the message was quickly sent down:

> November 11, 1918—9:10 A.M.
> To Major Hamilton:
> All firing will cease at 11 A.M. today. Hold every inch of ground that you have gained, including that gained by patrols. Send as soon as possible a sketch showing positions of all units at 11 A.M.
> (Signed) Feland[31]

Hermle was called to his battalion headquarters and instructed to make no noise or anything that might draw fire. "I remember I went back, and my first sergeant, Charles Connett ... said, 'Well, Captain, you can stop me from hollering but you can't stop me from standing on my head.' Which he did."[32]

But the casualties continued. Lejeune later encountered a man in a hospital who had been a telephonist in the division artillery: "the message came over the wire, 'It is 11 o'clock and the war is ----.' At this point, he said, a shell landed and burst in the room, killing his 'buddy' and wounding him. So far as I have been able to learn, these were the last casualties of the war. The shell was doubtless fired a second or so before 11 o'clock and reached its mark a few seconds after the clock had struck…."[33]

Carried by runner, the late-arriving order was slow to reach the men in the bridgeheads on the enemy side of the Meuse. There firing continued until 1130 h, but with no casualties on either side. "So it happened that although the Marines were not the first to fight in the World War, they were the last to stop."[34]

The brigade's cost in the Meuse-Argonne had been astonishingly light, with 185 killed and 1,033 wounded.[35]

CHAPTER 15

Victory and Occupation

> At eleven o'clock this morning came to an end the cruellest and most terrible War that has ever scourged mankind. I hope we may say that thus, this fateful morning, came to an end all wars.
>
> DAVID LLOYD GEORGE, NOVEMBER 11, 1918

The Fifth Marines reported suspending their advance and digging in at 1100 h, with the last units crossing the river at 1800 h on November 10. "In compliance with telephonic instructions from Headquarters, Fifth Army Corps, transmitted through Headquarters, 4th Brigade, hostilities ceased at 11 am. "The brigade was to remain in position until November 14, when they were relieved by the Army's 308th Infantry.[1]

The Allies elected to maintain a cautious attitude, and orders continued to be issued for organization of defensive positions.[2]

Decades later Alfred Noble was still bitter about the decision to push across the Meuse at the last moment. When the celebration ended, "Then we went down and looked at our casualties all over the place. And we called it an unnecessary slaughter. I talked to General Summerall [Charles P. Summerall, commander of the Second Field Artillery Brigade] later when he was the president of the Citadel. He was telling me the reasons which were logical to him, that although the Armistice was about to be signed he thought the pressure should be kept up until the thing was absolutely complete. I never saw it that way. The thing was going to happen anyway, and we were there to prevent the Germans coming across the river. I still think it was an unnecessary action."[3]

Hermle said that "about five minutes to 11 all hell broke loose on both sides. Both sides burned up everything they had." Inevitably, there were casualties, probably unintentional. "I saw a lieutenant killed on a horse out in front of the woods. Luckily we didn't suffer any casualties."[4]

The celebrations reached a crescendo that night. Cates: "on the night it came it was a beautiful sight, I can tell you that, because each side broke out and shot up a lot of their ammunition, shot off their flares, started bonfires as far as you could see in each direction. The Germans on the other side of the river and we were on the south side. The men, you might say, thawed out for the first time in weeks.

"We got clothing and got cleaned up a little bit and then started the hike into Germany."[5]

Oddly enough, in the rear many were not aware of the impending Armistice. DeWitt Peck had been wounded and gassed at Blanc Mont, and was on his way to rejoining his unit. With another officer he was waiting for a train "when everything broke loose in Paris. We found out we were in the middle of a celebration." Nevertheless, "I caught a train out that night and joined my unit in time for the march into Germany."[6]

For those still in hospitals, the scuttlebutt had gotten around about the impending Armistice. Cecil Avery was sitting on a terrace at the hospital. "Eleven o'clock in the morning the bells rang, and the guns went off, and people yelling, kissing, carrying on to beat the band. I wheeled back into the ward, and I said to the nurse, 'Can I get a uniform today?'" Eventually he was able to secure a badly used uniform, and "I looked like the very devil in it." There were no taxis and the streetcars were packed, so Avery set off on his crutches to see the sights.

He sat on a bench at the Place de la Concorde, and then decided to go into the famous bar Maxime's for a cocktail. "The place was mobbed. Generals, colonels, all brass, and they were four or five deep." After working his way up to the bar, he ordered a martini, "It was the first I ever drank." After dinner and the Folies Bergère, he worked his way back to the hospital.

In mid-December Avery was shipped to Brest aboard a modern American hospital train, a far cry from the forty-men-or-eight-horses boxcars. From there he was shipped home on a luxurious French liner, with "the lights blazing, and that was a grand and glorious feeling."[7]

William Rogers was discharged from hospital after being wounded at Blanc Mont and rejoined 3/6 on the thirteenth of November.[8]

The abrupt end of hostilities, welcome as it was to the troops in the field, caught the Allied leaders off guard. The immediate task of the combat troops would now be to shadow the German Army as it retreated back across its own borders. The terms of the Armistice decreed that German troops vacate occupied territories, but there was as yet no realization by the Germans that the terms would not be the relatively benevolent terms of President Wilson's Fourteen Points.

The terms stipulated that the Allies were to cross the German border no sooner than December 1, so several days were set aside for rest and recuperation. Roland Thomas had been assigned to deal with his battalion's errant baggage train. "When I got back from the baggage the word was out that we were going to be in the Army of Occupation. We did not move until the seventeenth of November. Our first day's march took us to a village in Belgium. Two days later we were in Luxembourg. We just cut through a corner of Belgium, and we were in at least two places (Arlons) where we stopped en route in Luxembourg.... There was an agreement between the German Army and the allies that we would allow them withdrawal time. We were not to cross this river into Germany until the first day of December. We stayed and were very nicely housed in this little place in Luxembourg on the Sauer until the morning of the first of December. Then we started off."[9]

A major problem was that the division was depleted, not only by the casualties from months of relentless fighting, but also the epidemic of Spanish Influenza then sweeping the globe. Everyone was painfully aware that a long march awaited. The condition of the men caused considerable concern, with about four or five hundred men evacuated each day from disease and exhaustion. Fortunately, "This high rate kept up for the day or two following [the Armistice], and then sharply dropped. It was surprising to see what a large part hot food and dry clothing, not to mention the cessation of hard, physical labor, played in the prevention of disease. The men's vitality was at once increased, and in a few days they were a different looking lot."[10]

There were acute shortages of horses. To make the situation even worse, an epidemic of mange—a skin parasite—was sweeping through the equine population. The French railway system was grinding to a stop under the burden of supplying the huge mass of troops, and it was difficult to supply even enough to maintain positions. The division had to be supplied over roads that Lejeune described as "villainous", by truck convoys from railheads far to the rear.

To flesh out the division for the march into Germany, the nearby Seventy-seventh and Eighty-ninth were cannibalized for draft animals and equipment. Derby wrote that "During these days I saw a great deal of Lieutenant Colonel Hugh Matthews, the G1 of our division, whose numerous duties included those of re-equipment. He was a marine officer who had been on the division staff since the beginning and had been G1 since the early summer fighting. To him more than to any one man was due the smooth running and reliable supply system of the Division. It is not an exaggeration to say that he was on his job for twenty-one out of the 24 h."[11]

Lejeune again found himself in conflict with higher headquarters and their unrealistic expectations. On November 13 he received instructions that the division was to march 40 km out of its way to reach specific bridges across the Meuse, and then backtrack 20 km on the far bank just to reach its planned starting point for the march into Germany. This was to avoid passing through German ceasefire positions. Lejeune offered to have his division engineers repair bridges that would cut some 40 km off the march distance. "I then told him that my persistence was due to the exhausted and weakened condition of the troops and to the necessity of reequipping and reclothing them, which could not be done while they were on the march. He answered that he was without authority to make any change in the orders, but was simply repeating them to me as they were given to him by higher authority." All the higher officers were asleep, and the staff officer did not want to awaken them. "I replied, 'It is better to wake up one General than to have twenty-five thousand sick and exhausted men march sixty kilometers, and I will do so myself.'"

The stubborn Lejeune had won another battle. The staff officer woke up a general, and the march was not only rerouted to cross the river at the closer crossings, but the start of the march was delayed by three days.[12]

On November 17 the Second Division finally commenced its march through Belgium and Luxembourg. Karl McCune: "Nov. 17th, at 5.00 A.M., reveille sounded. For a brief time the quiet of the sleeping village was broken by the preparations for departure. Packs were rolled up immediately and wagons loaded. Breakfast was served at 5.00 A.M. with night still over-shadowing. At 6.40 all companies formed for departure. Wagons and mules crowded the streets, making it almost impossible for movement of troops. Finally the battalion left town proceeding in a column of twos along the heights skirting the northern banks of the Meuse.... Malandry, the first village of the repatriated area, was reached about 10.30. A sign of 'Welcome' stretched over the road. Civilians rushed out to greet the Marines with cries of 'Vive les Américains' and 'Vive l'Amérique.'"[13]

The two brigades moved in separate columns. The march was to be conducted as if through hostile territory, and there was a strict schedule at which the division was to each certain points.

Each of the infantrymen, mostly exhausted and debilitated by extended combat, carried a load of some 80 pounds (36 kg). Draft animals had been requisitioned from other divisions, and they took the opportunity to dump all their sick and worn-out mules and horses on those divisions.

A major problem proved to be the new boots issued just before the march. The British footwear was poorly made and ill-fitting. The boots pinched and broke apart, and some men marched barefoot through light rain and snow, on roads that were mud in daytime and frozen at night. Supplies to maintain the march were difficult to move: new rail lines had to be laid through the old combat zone, and much of the traffic was directed by sometimes uncooperative German railway officials. Slowed by these conditions and the need to lag behind the retreating Germans, the average day's march was about 25 km.[14]

The long march was grueling. Lieutenant Clifton Cates had spent two days in the hospital with dysentery and a mild case of influenza, but the battalion Executive Officer, Major Clyde Metcalf, let him ride his horse—the only one in the battalion—for short periods. "I always appreciated a thing like that because I couldn't have made it otherwise."[15]

Walter Gaspar: "every day one officer and a detail of men (perhaps a dozen) had to follow the brigade. We had to pick up all stragglers; had an ambulance with us. Sometimes it took all night to do this. After a brigade had settled down for the night, we were still picking up stragglers."[16]

The German Army was still considered potentially hostile, so march security was emphasized. Gerald Thomas: "when that column halted every night, it had to be outposted in true rule-book fashion. If our regiment happened to be in advance guard that day, we would catch an outpost zone. After the column had marched for the day, we might go five or six miles way up in the woods and put out an outpost. The next morning we had to march back and join the column. On many nights, the rolling kitchens didn't get up. We really had a rough time. They didn't even make any pretense of feeding us a meal. Sometimes we would eat at night and in the morning, but sometimes we wouldn't. I remember that one night the kitchens didn't get up until the next day. When they didn't get up, we just didn't have anything to eat. However, we continued the march for about eleven days; and my company was on outpost the last night, which was probably the eighth or ninth of December."[17]

The worn appearance of the men and draft animals in Lejeune's division did not escape the ever-critical eye of Pershing, an old cavalryman, and his observers. One criticized the seeming lack of ambulances intermixed with the columns, but Derby had deliberately placed them at the rear "on the theory that an ambulance out of sight is out of mind" to reduce temptation to report sick for a ride.[18]

Pershing himself stormed into the III Corps offices and dictated a laundry list of complaints and shortcomings. He was particularly outraged at the appearance of the Third Brigade troops, probably recalling the earlier periods when the Marines always seemed more impressive. In his usual way Lejeune was not about to take the criticism without a fight. He fired back his own critique that if Pershing wanted a better appearance, perhaps a period of rest and refitting prior to the grueling march might have been in order.[19]

It is really difficult to grasp why Pershing never retaliated against Lejeune—he had relieved other officers for far lesser crimes. The answer probably lies in the fact that the Second Division was simply too effective, and that he admired men like Lejeune and Summerall who would not buckle in the face of his threats.

The liberated townspeople met the advancing Americans with arches of garlands over the entrances to villages, rather fanciful versions of American flags, and carefully hoarded wine and spirits. The welcomes accorded the advancing Americans, as earlier described by Karl McCune, were repeated many times. One notable event took place in Medernach. "Thanksgiving was spent here, the dinner consisting of bacon and mashed potatoes." [20]

From period accounts it is interesting how many locals the Marines encountered who had lived in America. Hermle: "One of my lieutenants met an American who had been in Chicago most of his life. I guess he was an Luxemburger who'd lived in America. He gave us a beautiful Thanksgiving dinner."[21]

In the small town of Ettlebruck, Luxembourg one of the battalion commanders proved to have no tolerance for alcohol. Cates: "We got into this town and all these people met us with high silk hats and one greeted me as I went in. A bartender opened the door and said, 'Where have you been? We've been waiting for you for the last five years.' I said, 'Where are you from? Chicago?' And he said, 'No, Newark.'"

After a tour of city hall Major Ernest Williams "must have snapped down two good bottles of champagne." After getting the troops billeted, Williams, Cates, an intelligence officer named Hawkins, and a Lieutenant van Dorn returned to a small café and ordered more drinks.

"But about this time a Major General walked in—an Army Major General. He said, 'Who's in charge here?' Williams looked up and said, 'I am,' and didn't get up. We sat there too. And the Major General said, 'Have you seen that all your men are billeted?' Williams said, 'Nope.' The General said, 'Why not?' 'Just got in' [Williams]. The General said,

'Did you start washing your rolling stock?' 'Nope.' 'Well, why haven't you?' Williams said 'Just got in.' About that time, Williams got up and pointed to his stars. He said, 'I can see that you're a Major General but who the hell are you anyway?' With that, the Major General says, 'Why, young man, I'm Major General [John L.] Hines, your [III] Corps Commander. You're under arrest, you're relieved.' We made a bee line out the door…."[22]

Harsh as the conditions were, there were lighter moments. On November 19 at Virton, Belgium, the mayor and the division's senior chaplain arranged a ceremony for the liberators. A large crowd assembled, bands played the national anthems, and speeches were made. At the conclusion the chaplain, Doctor Jason Pierce, announced that Mademoiselle Clementine, a famous French dancer travelling with Lejeune, would entertain the crowd.

"To my horror, the dancer appeared, arrayed in ballet costume, with cheeks well rouged and with head covered in long golden curls." The dancer went through the routine, while the crowd roared and demanded encores, "while I sat there horror-stricken, with cold perspiration running down my back and with thoughts running through my head that my reputation was in shreds, that the action of the Chaplain was unpardonable, and that he had certainly secured the services of a most skilled dancer. Finally, to my unspeakable relief, the dancer as a last encore bowed, took of the very pretentious wig, and I recognized the close-cropped black head and smiling countenance of my very masculine soldier cook, who excelled not only in the terpsichorean but the culinary art as well. It was an episode characteristic of our Chaplain…."[23]

Once in Germany, the civilians proved unexpectedly docile. One issue that likely facilitated cooperation was the extreme shortage of food in Germany. Louis Jones: "you could get almost anything for a bar of chocolate, and if you had an animal that was sick and was dying they would ask for it, and so forth. They had no fats, you see."[24]

Hermle said that when going through a town "They lined up." But unlike the civilians in occupied countries "They didn't cheer us. The Germans were retreating right in front of us. One day I had the advance guard, I could see the German rear guard. We were right behind them.... When we stopped at night in their town they were pretty nice to us."

The problem remained: how would the German Army react, once the true nature of the peace that Allies were determined to enforce upon Germany became known? Plans for counterattacks and a deeper advance into Germany were formulated. Detailed orders were issued for defensive positions after each day's march.

A rotating duty for officers, and one much disliked, was billeting officer, responsible for scouting ahead and arranging housing. William Rogers recalled that, with four or so enlisted men, "I was ordered out every day to go out ahead. Some days I'd have a motorcycle and sometimes I'd have a horse. There was a law against going ahead of the front lines, but we had to go anyway, because I had to get there anyway."[25]

At one point Lieutenant Walter Gaspar was the billeting officer for 1/6. The *burgermeisters* had orders to meet the billeting details and toured the town, marking buildings with chalk to indicate how many men or horses were to be billeted in each. The billeting officer provided a receipt for reimbursement by the German government.

The billeting parties were often far head of the advancing troops, actually mingling with the Germans. William Rogers' group crossed the Rhine in a rowboat, and then took local trains to search for their destination.[26]

Pushing on into Germany, the division arrived at its occupation zone along the Rhine between December 1 and 13. Gerald Thomas's 1/6 was at last lucky in that "We had a shortcut into the Rhine. Instead of going up and going down to Nauheim and then coming down, we shortcutted and got into Brohl ahead of the rest of the Army. It was the only day that we got a decent break. We stayed in this town just a few hours, and they then moved us down to a village on the Rhine River. This was about the ninth, and we were not to cross the river, according to agreement, until the thirteenth.

"On the thirteenth we moved to Andernach on the Rhine, the west left bank of the river. I was appointed by my regiment to be the embarkation officer. I saw the whole Army and the whole Sixth

Marines embark and go across the river on the ferry from Andernach to Leutesdorf [Leudesdorf]."[27]

Cates said that "So we had always said we were going to celebrate the day when we could urinate in the Rhine. And it was quite a cold day. All the officers went down to the Rhine and took a pee."[28]

Units were assigned specific occupation sectors. Cates's company billeting NCO had lost his way and it seemed that all the good billets were taken, but instead they found a pontoon factory in Rheinbrohl "that couldn't have been more ideal" with a workers' club with bowling, billiards, and a tennis court. "About half a dozen Generals tried to kick us out of that billet—I was a Captain by that time. But they never did. I had squatter's rights."[29]

Other officers had even better accommodations. Alfred Noble found his final billet at Leudesdorf just before Christmas. "I landed at my billet with an architect and his family who lived in a rather nice house with his wife and three daughters; he had a son in the German Army who came sneaking around about a week later—afraid I was going to capture him I suppose, and make him a prisoner of war."[30]

Detailed orders were issued for construction of defensive positions. The Americans were painfully aware that they were immersed in a sea of Germans, as reflected by ominous instructions that in the event of a surprise attack "Troops of the Outpost Line will fight in place to the end." Detailed plans were formulated for counterattacks on multiple objectives.[31]

As the occupation troops settled in, a problem was that all the hospitals were choked with German casualties, and the division had to continue the use of its field tentage. Worse, the big, slow moving steam disinfestor trucks had been left behind in France. "A medical officer attached to one of the marine regiments constructed a clever disinfestor out of a pontoon boat, into which he conducted live steam from a neighboring boiler. It was not perfect but it served its purpose in disinfesting the clothing of the men of his battalion. We obtained a number of shower baths and set them up where they would serve the greatest number of men."[32]

The Armistice was merely a cessation of active hostilities, not a peace, and the Allies had no clear idea how to occupy and administer Germany. The primary goal was to occupy the primary industrial area and the seat of its war-making capability, the Rhineland, while a final peace was negotiated. Presumably because of their maritime connection, a main responsibility of the Marine Brigade was the Rhine River patrol. This duty consisted of both land and boat patrols, and photographs depict the use of civilian craft like ferries and excursion boats, armed with captured German heavy machine guns.

The occupation zones were enclaves on the north bank of the Rhine, divided up among the Allies. These occupation zones were large semi-circular areas, 30 km in radius, along the river. In the American sector the Fourth Brigade's assigned area consisted of an outpost zone manned primarily by the Fifth Marines, with the Sixth responsible for the area along the Rhine bank.

Neutral zones separated the various Allies and German forces. The neutral zone separating the Americans and British was about 6 km wide. Hermle: "In the middle of that neutral zone down near the Rhine was a town called Linz. One of my company's jobs was to tour that town to see what the Germans were doing there."[33]

Quartered in towns and villages, the Americans fraternized fairly freely with the German civilians, causing considerable concern among senior officers. The process was facilitated by the number of German-speaking troops, children of fairly recent immigrants. Orders prohibiting interactions were mostly just ignored.

For their part the German citizenry were puzzled by the non-fraternization order. Richard Derby was billeted in the house of an affluent family. "On Christmas Eve the family asked me on my return home in the evening to join their family party in the dining room. When I reminded them that our countries were still at war, that I was an American army officer billeted in their house, and that I was neither permitted nor had I any desire to have any social relations with them, they could not seem to understand my attitude."[34]

Occupation duty was difficult for men who thought they were waiting to go home soon, and were for the most part tired of military life. In the usual disjoint, officers wrote of the joy of conducting field exercises and drilling their troops in the snow and winter weather, while enlisted men griped about the futility.[35]

Captain Cates was typical of the officer attitude. "You know how if you ease up on people after a war, they soon go to pieces."[36]

Among the troops sports like football were far more popular, and numerous memoirs discuss competitions at length.

In May the Germans finally learned the full implications of the harsh terms the Allies were determined to impose. The news led to considerable concern about unrest and German attacks, and again detailed plans were issued, to be implemented upon receipt of the signal "Consolidate for movement". Troops were moved into defensive positions along the perimeters of the north bank enclaves. The occupation troops were ordered to stand by for continued fighting.

Gerald Thomas: "The only thing approaching excitement was in early June of the next year when the Germans were showing some reluctance in agreeing to the terms of the treaty of peace, they didn't want to sign it. They refused to sign it so we moved up to the edge of the neutral zone, ready to move on into and occupy the rest of Germany. We stayed there a couple of days when they saw the light and they signed."[37]

Such preparatory orders for a possible resumption of fighting continued to be issued for months.

A major problem was that in the aftermath of the war, food continued to be critically short for the German civilians. The occupying troops were supposed to consume only meat shipped in for the purpose, but craved fresh meat. Alfred Noble: "I know our non commissioned officers had gotten hold of a pig, and were going to have roast pig. I remember I got word of it, and I went in there just before the mess, where they had all gathered, and there was this roast pig, and right before the whole assembly I said, 'Let's have that pig, and take it right outside and dump it right in the garbage.' The whole pig. They'd been smacking their mouths about that for a long time. You could have heard a pin drop. So they didn't get any more fresh German meat after that. For years I've seen some of those people every now and then, and they 'd laugh about that pig! It got to be funny after about ten years!"[38]

Another issue that resurfaced when the troops had no one to fight was the old inter-service animosity over Belleau Wood and Château-Thierry. In general the two brigades of the Second Division were like squabbling children who unite in the face of outside criticism, but not so other divisions. One officer reported to Lejeune that as his troops marched by—under tight march discipline—lounging soldiers sang modified lyrics of a popular tune:

> The Marines have won the croix de guerre, parlez-vous?
> The Marines have won the croix de guerre, parlez-vous?
> The Marines have won the croix de guerre,
> But the sons of bitches were never there,
> Hinky dinky, parlez-vous.[39]

Grammatically the ditty is not good French. "*Parlez-vous?*" means "are you talking?", instead of "*comprenez-vous?*"—"do you understand?" But it was, after all, a nonsensical song.

The presence of the Marine aviators in France had always been the source of friction between the Army and Navy, and even the Navy was all too glad to be rid of them. The first contingent sailed away on November 22, with the entire contingent gone by mid-December.

Many of the aviation personnel were actually resentful of being sent home. Unlike ground troops, none had ever been given leave in Paris, or seen the exotic sights of Europe. If they could not sightsee, they just wanted to get home, and did not appreciate the spectacles at which they were the nominal guests of honor. In Newport News, Virginia, Mulcahy observed that "They must have got us there at least … an hour or two before anything was going to happen. And of course the men were tired of standing there, and nobody was enthusiastic about the parade anyway." The officer in charge mused, "I wonder what would happen if … I told these guys to throw these [borrowed] rifles in the drink."[40]

As the occupation force in Germany dwindled, the Marines were collapsed into a composite regiment that Pershing used for ceremonial purposes in Paris, London, and other cities. The men were hand-picked: at least 5 ft 10 in. tall, combat veterans, in good physical condition. The MPs in Brest required liberty passes to be presented on demand, and were strict in enforcing curfews and other orders until "General Pershing issued an order … 'Lay off the Composite Regiment'" His ceremonial guard eventually returned with Pershing aboard the luxury liner *Leviathan*.[41]

While at Brest many of the troops were awarded medals and decorations by the French. Later Hermle recalled one such ceremony. "We were decorated with the Legion of Honor … by a little, very short admiral, and [Division adjutant] Hanford McNeider, who was about six feet, decided that he wasn't going to be kissed by this admiral. He just stood tall with his head high.

"But that admiral had experienced that, I suppose. He put his hand behind McNeider's head and around his neck, pulled him down and smacked him on both cheeks. I stood alongside of him, and I wanted to laugh, it was so funny, there were about four or five of us being decorated who started to laugh, and I joined in the laughs.

"Very unmilitary."[42]

CHAPTER 16

Aftermath

When the peace treaty is signed, the war isn't over for the veterans, or the family. It's just starting.

KARL MARLANTES

With the end of the war there was tremendous public pressure to demobilize men, particularly reservists and duration-of-hostilities enlistees. The problem was that too-rapid demobilization would cripple the Corps for its remaining responsibilities. A November 20, 1918 order limited discharges to men who planned to continue their interrupted education, or who had urgent family responsibilities. On May 1, 1919 the reduction was further limited only to those who had urgent family financial responsibilities.

In August men of the Fourth and Fifth brigades arriving from France were given priority for discharge. Not until July 12, 1919 were orders promulgated to allow wholesale and rapid demobilization. By the end of the year virtually all the duration-of-hostilities men had finally been discharged.[1]

One of the great fallacies of modern American culture is that of extravagant homecoming parades that celebrate the return of troops from war. In reality most never experienced such events. On August 8, 1919 the brigade, which now included men who had seen no service in France, paraded in New York under the supervision of Major General Lejeune. On August 12 the brigade, under Brigadier Wendell Neville, was reviewed by President Wilson. The returning Marines were reassigned to Quantico, and on August 18, the Fourth Brigade was returned from Army to Navy service.[2]

Returning men found a terrible disjoint between what they had experienced, and what civilians knew of war from the jingoistic and sanitized media accounts. Editor George Pattullo recounted the tale of a war correspondent cornered by two elderly ladies who urged him to "tell them everything.... And all the dreadful sights you saw, too.... Isn't it awful what those Germans do? We've just been reading about the way they treated some of our boys they took prisoner. It's hard to believe human beings could ..."

"What've they been up to now?"

"Why, they kicked some of our boys who were prisoners!"

"Oh, well," remarked the correspondent tolerantly, "things like that are apt to happen in war, you know. Everybody's doing it. It's dog eat dog."

"What?" they cried I horror. "Our boys act that way? Oh, we'll never believe it. They're too noble."[3]

While most Marine ground units had returned to the US after the brief occupation of the Rhineland, the Fifteenth Separate Battalion remained in France until September 3, 1919. Originally designated the Provisional Battalion, the battalion was composed of men from both the Fourth and Fifth brigades and the Twelfth Separate Battalion. Their primary duties were ceremonial, but the battalion remained on standby for any possible problems arising from the Schleswig-Holstein Plebiscite.[4] On December 7, 1919 the battalion left Brest aboard the *Henderson*, the last unit to depart France.[5]

With the armistice the need for new manpower—and female Marines—ended abruptly, though the last woman would not be officially discharged until 1922. The last official review of the women Marines was held on the White House lawn, with Commandant Barnett and the Marine Corps Band ("The President's Own") in attendance. Josephus Daniels's gaffe would go down in history. Corporal Elizabeth Shoemaker: "We stood in front of him in our uniforms listening to every word of his eloquent speech; He said we had been good Marines and he was proud of us; Then, in his closing statement he said, 'We will not forget you. As we embrace you in uniform today, we will embrace you without uniform tomorrow.' All down the file of men standing at strict attention, the line broke, and everyone roared with laughter. The Secretary of the Navy forgot he was talking to women."[6]

Appendix: Equipment and Weapons

The deadliest weapon in the world is a Marine and his rifle.

GENERAL JOHN J. PERSHING

The Marine's uniform and equipment differed in several respects from his Army counterpart, and detailed illustrations are included in other publications.[1]

The dapper Marine Corps uniform was a point of considerable pride. Made of good quality forest-green cloth, and custom tailored, it was a powerful recruiting tool. Enlisted men's rank badges were backed with red felt, and in that era second lieutenants—like privates—did not wear rank badges; the only indication of their rank was an elaborately knotted officer's cord on the campaign hat. The wide-brimmed felt campaign hat was typically worn with a four-cornered Montana peak, although a fore-and-aft Stetson peak was often worn, particularly by officers and NCOs. There was a cotton tropical service uniform, but in keeping with the practices of the day the green dress uniform was also the temperate climate combat uniform; the user just added very light-tan canvas leggings, 782 (web) gear, and weapon. The canvas web gear was not that of the Army, but made to Marine Corps specifications in their own depots. There was no helmet.

After arriving in France Marines were issued British Mark I helmets—often called the Brodie helmet after its designer, but that name actually applied only to the original limited-production model—to replace the hat, and the fore-and-aft overseas cap replaced the rigid barracks cap since it could be conveniently folded and tucked into the belt. One issue with the overseas cap that caused considerable confusion was that Marine Corps officers transferred the traditional scarlet and gold braided trim from the campaign hat to the overseas cap.

The British helmet was quickly superseded by a similar American-manufactured M1917 model, but most Marines referred to both types by the generic "tin hat". The M1917 was overall sturdier and offered somewhat better protection, the most noticeable feature being the sand-textured exterior. When the Fourth Brigade was forced to wear Army uniforms, many Marines brazed the metal eagle-globe-and-anchor (EGA) from the campaign hat onto the front of the helmet. It was also common to paint the regimental symbol, a black EGA superimposed on a colored diamond, with the regimental number (V or VI) in the center.

The most unique helmet décor belonged to "Pvt. Clem D. Evans, known as 'Red Blanket', a Creek Indian from Oklahoma, enlisted in the 74th Company, 6th Marines. At Belleau Wood he found some peacock feathers which he attached to his helmet with a band made from a bandoleer. At Soissons and Blanc Mont 'when I was going over the top I put the feathers on my helmet; when we came out of the line, I slipped them into my haversack.'"[2]

Unfortunately the forest-green color of the pre-war uniform was very similar to that of German uniforms. For this reason, and to simplify logistics, as uniforms wore out they were replaced by Army uniforms of coarse brownish-drab wool. The Marines hated this uniform. The coarse wool chafed, particularly around the high collar, and it came in standard and usually baggy sizes, giving the wearer a run-over-and slept-in look.

When the drab Army uniform replaced the early Marine Corps uniform, many individuals went so far as to transfer distinctive items like buttons (which featured the older Marine Corps emblem, a fouled anchor with an arc of stars above), and rank badges to the new uniform.

Replacement uniform items were replaced only when they became unserviceable. The Corps had developed mobile laundry vehicles, but in France the individual could either find a civilian to launder clothing, or wash it himself. Personal hygiene was often relegated to a lower priority, and John Aasland recorded in his diary "Sept. 22 (Sunday): Had inspection of underwear. We did not have to take it off, only open shirts and let the officer see how dirty it is."[3]

Army Private John Hughes of the division's Third Brigade wrote that before an attack "Everybody got busy and cleaned up. We always tried to clean our clothes, especially our underwear, before going up as we surely would need the change at the front." [4]

Once in combat, cleanliness became a secondary concern. Brigadier James Harbord wrote that in the fighting in Belleau Wood, in the summer heat, "One of my majors did not have his clothes off for seventeen days. I merely happen to know of his case, but it is no exception." [5]

There was no lightweight rain gear, only the heavy issue greatcoat which was too hot, heavy, and bulky for general wear. Many officers purchased civilian "trench coats", but enlisted men usually just suffered through downpours. Corporal John E. Aasland wrote that "Getting wet the other night, so awful wet, and being inactive the day afterwards, has just sapped all our strength and I am all in."[6]

Few items are of such practical interest to infantry as socks and boots, and the procurement system did not serve the Marines well. Marines went to France with low-topped, lightweight leather boots that were well suited to garrison duty and had proven serviceable enough in short expeditionary campaigns. The glutinous mud and constant wet of the trenches quickly destroyed them. As an interim solution the Marines were issued French shoes, and the French supply system had to do the best it could to accommodate larger and particularly wider American feet. James Rendinell: "They asked us what size we wore, then they gave us just one size 19 by 21 French style. It is American style No. 11. You can put them on either foot and they fit just as good. We could not line up for inspection. You are supposed to get your toes in line, but with these French shoes when your toes were in line your shoes stuck way out beyond." [7]

The US Army had similar problems and experimented with several types of heavier boots; the first and inadequate effort was the M1917 trench boot. The troops were eventually issued the M1918 "Pershing boots", or "little tanks". These were low-topped boots made of heavily oiled russet leather, with a durable beef-tallow waterproofing called "dubbing". The triple-stitched, triple-layered sole was studded with hobnails for better traction in wet conditions with a heavy iron plate under the toe, and a U-shaped heel plate to reduce wear.[8]

In the last days of the war the Marines were issued poorly made British boots that quickly disintegrated under any use. American troops also described the use of wooden French *sabots* (clogs). Period photographs document the extensive use of a variety of civilian waterproof rubber boots, ranging from low top "gumboots" to thigh-length fishing waders.[9]

There were never enough socks to supply changes, and Walter Gaspar recalled that in prolonged combat "You'd be surprised what a relief it is, [to] just turn your socks inside out or change them from one foot to another."[10]

At the beginning of the war Marine enlisted men wore distinctive canvas leggings that laced up the outside on the leg. These, and most of the other 782 gear, were made of a light tan canvas very different from the darker and brown-tinged Army issue. The canvas leggings were quickly replaced by Army-style wrap puttees in dark cloth. Although many officers, including generals, wore the standard cloth puttees, many purchased the popular Stohlwasser leggings. These were hard leather leggings that fastened with spiral straps and buckles around the lower leg.

Like most soldiers, the Marine infantryman was burdened with a load that would have broken a mule. The items of most immediate need were attached to the M1910 cartridge belt, which incorporated ten ammunition pouches: each pouch held two five-round stripper clips for the rifle. Metal eyelets on the belt allowed attachment of the bayonet, fighting knife, a cloth pouch holding a one quart (0.94 l) canteen and metal drinking cup, field dressing pouch, plus compass, wire cutters, and other odd items. Rifle grenadiers were issued belt pouches for the grenade discharger cup that fitted over the muzzle of the rifle. The loaded belt was supported by two belt suspender straps which transferred part of the load to the shoulders, but their primary purpose was attaching the M1910 haversack.

The haversack was not a simple bag but a monkey-puzzle of straps and buckles that opened out into a cross-shaped canvas sheet with slots, straps, pockets, and other gizmos for holding various items. It was far better suited to "junk on the bunk" inspections than actual field use. In the Field Marching Pack, or "heavy" pack, configuration the Marine carried spare clothing, a change of underclothes, housewife (sewing kit), emergency rations, toiletry items, personal items like foot powder, mail and writing supplies, a towel, jellied alcohol ("Sterno"™) for cooking, and tobacco or candy. A shelter half (tent) with a single pole, five wooden pegs, guy rope, and wool blanket was rolled and secured as a lower extension to the haversack. Strapped to the outside of the pack were the M1910 or M1918 metal mess kit with two metal pans and knife, fork, and spoon, an entrenching shovel or two-piece M1910 mattock (in theory issued in equal numbers, but the shovel was more common). All this weighed some 60 pounds (27 kg).

In the attack most of this gear was placed under guard and left behind to be recovered later. The light "assault pack" included bare necessities like emergency rations, ammunition, and items like extra socks, but no blanket or heavy clothing, reducing the weight to about 20 pounds (9 kg). In protracted operations this created hardship as the men were short of even basic necessities.

Occasionally suggestions were made to allow the men to carry blankets and make "rebel rolls", a rolled blanket tied together at the ends, and worn diagonally over one shoulder. (A very common recruiting poster depicted this arrangement). By a quirk of Marine Corps regulations, the rebel roll was considered a distinction of officers, so the idea went nowhere.

No provision was made for carrying hand grenades, so they were typically carried in a sandbag or any other available sack, or in pockets. A grenade vest with pouches was issued in extremely small numbers, but no evidence indicates it as ever issued to Marines in World War I.

In addition each Marine was issued two gas masks, the French M2 one-piece mask and protective hood, carried in a semicircular pouch attached to a shoulder strap, and the British Small Box Respirator (SBR) worn in a pouch around the neck. Lieutenant Clifton Cates thought the M2 "had some kind of chemical on it that wasn't any good." The M2 was designed to counter the first generation of poisonous gases, and was a simple ill-fitting hood with layers of absorbent cotton impregnated with neutralizing chemicals. The problem was that the M2, though designed for extended wear, was easily damaged.

The SBR was soon replaced by the American Corrected English (CE) mask in three sizes for a better fit, and with a record card that made it easier to determine when the filter needed to be changed. For both the English and American masks, the mask was pulled out from a carrier pouch, and the filter canister remained in the pouch connected to the mask by a flexible tube. Cates was not impressed by either, and thought that "In fact, the respirators we had about half of them were defective."[11]

Like most infantrymen the Marines were not equipped with any other type of protective gear. That was reserved for the division artillery, who handled shells that all too often were defective or leaked. Army Private John A. Hughes described a battery position firing mustard gas. "It was some type of liquid gas: when you shook a shell the gas inside would make a noise as though it were full of water. However, it was exceptionally strong as we were allowed only 25 shells at the gun at one time. All of us had to wear oilskin pants and coats, also hot rubber gloves and our gas mask at alert. We looked more like fishermen than soldiers. At 6.00 A.M. we started firing. It surely turned out to be a hot day, especially with the extra uniform on. Those not needed to fire the guns were busy hauling shell. The heat and smoke were awful."[12]

Officers generally carried a musette bag, a large purse-like shoulder bag adopted from the French, as well as map cases, compass in a belt pouch, and the binoculars that made them a target.[13] Officers also wore a "Sam Browne" belt, a narrow leather strap diagonally across the chest, further distinguishing them as targets. The Sam Browne was not actually an authorized uniform item, and many officers were resentful of having them summarily stripped away by provost marshals upon their return to America. This item eventually was approved, and remains a feature of the officers' dress uniform.

As an automatic rifle section leader, Corporal John Rendinell carried "a 60 pound pack, [plus] rifle, bayonet, machete, trench knife, .45 Colt,

220 rounds of ammunition [for the Chauchat automatic rifle]. The weight grows the further you go till it bends your back like a U." [14]

The Marine's basic weapon was the bolt-action 30.06 M1903 "Springfield" rifle, named after the arsenal where it was first manufactured, though wartime production also came from other factories. The Springfield is often described as the most accurate general-issue rifle ever made, and it remained in service through World War II as a sniper rifle. The original issue heavy russet leather sling tended to swell and rot under wet conditions, and was replaced by a canvas sling. This weapon was fitted with the 16 in M1905 bayonet.

Many veterans preferred the pump shotgun as a close-quarter weapon, and procured such weapons from stores issued to troops on interior guard duty. From mid-1918 Marines were issued the M1917 trench gun, a militarized version of the 12-gauge Winchester M97 shotgun with a six-round magazine, sling, and bayonet mounting lug. The weapon sprayed nine .32caliber balls, but the use was limited by swelling of the paper cartridges. This was later remedied by the issue of brass cartridges. Marines armed with the shotgun were issued a box-like canvas ammunition pouch for the belt. The Germans considered the shotgun a "terror weapon" and promised that anyone caught with a "trench broom" would be summarily shot.

Over the years the Marines had experimented with a wide variety of machine guns. The ultimate choice, the reliable Lewis machine gun, was easily recognized by the drum magazine atop the weapon, and its large cooling jacket. The Lewis was renowned for its reliability, and used the same ammunition as the M1903 rifle which simplified logistics, but it was in great demand to equip aircraft.* The ground Marines were reluctantly forced to give up the Lewis in favor of the French Chauchat automatic rifle and the heavy 8 mm Hotchkiss M1914 machine gun.

---

* There was a rumor(see Wise, *A Marine Tells It To You*, p. 179) that Brigadier William Crozier, Chief of Army Ordnance, was engaged in a dispute with Lewis and vowed that no Lewis guns would be used. Since the reassignment of guns was negotiated between Crozier and Winston Churchill, it was most likely unfounded.

Clifton Cates: "Well, they claimed that they needed the Lewis machine guns for the planes and Chauchat was the best thing they had which wasn't worth a hoorah."[15]

The Chauchat automatic rifle was officially designated the Fusil Mitrailleur Modèle 1915 CSRG. The American version, redesigned to use ammunition common with the 30.06 Springfield rifle, was the Automatic Rifle, Model 1915 (Chauchat). Few of the 30.06 Chauchats actually reached American troops, and the few that did were so unreliable they were discarded in favor of the French 8 mm weapon. By any name, it was absolutely despised by the Marines.

The weapon was the first practical automatic weapon designed to be carried and fired by one man, with an assistant and ammunition carriers, but its problems were many. The semi-circular magazines that fitted underneath the weapon were open on one side, allowing dirt and debris into the spring-driven feed mechanism, and this caused about three-quarters of the failures of the weapon to fire. The operator also had to be careful to limit fire, as the weapon was prone to stoppages when overheated. Walter Noble thought "That was another jammer: if you could get through a clip without jamming, you were good!" The bipod designed to steady the weapon was flimsy, as was most of the construction. Lieutenant James M. Sellers described it as appearing to be "made out of cigar boxes and tin cans."[16]

Each infantry half-platoon had an automatic rifle section with a corporal, two automatic riflemen, two assistants, and two ammunition carriers. The job of the ammunition carriers was not only to carry the bulky ammunition, but load loose rounds into the spare magazines.

Although the weapon itself was relatively light at 9.07 kg (20 pounds), the heavy ammunition bags, up to 60 pounds/27.2 kg, were suspended from narrow straps that dug painfully into the shoulder. James Rendinell described training with the weapon. "Each squad has 2 automatic rifles and 4 ammunition bags of 25,000 rounds to carry. We take turns carrying the ammunition bags.

"When they checked up after a hike my squad had only 1,800 rounds left all told. What a bawling out they give us. Each of the boys throwed away a couple of handfuls every time it come his turn to carry. I throwed plenty away myself."[17]

Derided by some weapons experts as the worst machine gun ever made, the cardinal sin of the Chauchat in Marine Corps eyes was its gross inaccuracy. Lieutenant Graves Erskine complained that "With this damn thing, it was like a hose, you never knew where it was going to go, so we had no respect for that weapon, and we thought we'd been given a pretty dirty deal."[18]

The cone of dispersion at its woefully short effective range of 220 yards/200 ms was simply enormous. Lieutenant Clifton Cates stated that even clamped into a vise the cone of dispersion was 25 feet/7.6 m. In other words, a skilled user could perhaps hit a two-story building.[19]

Officers, NCOs, and heavy weapons crews were issued side arms, most commonly the familiar M1911 semi-automatic pistol. Another common issue weapon was the .45-caliber M1917 revolver, and officers carried a very wide variety of privately purchased side arms.

The Hotchkiss heavy machine gun, with a tripod that allowed it to be used against ground targets or raised for anti-aircraft use, weighed 100 pounds (45 kg) without ammunition or tripod. Roland McDonald, who served in a machine gun company, complained that "it was like you were carrying a 75 [cannon] on your back."[20]

Unlike the Lewis it could not be fired without its tripod. Awkward 24- or 30-round stripper clips that waggled from the left side required frequent changes, and greatly slowed the sustained rate of fire to 120 rounds per minute.

An unexpected problem was the packing cases for the long stripper clips. These heavy, awkward, gray-painted wooden boxes had steel-reinforced corners, but "The bottoms of the strip containers are not substantial enough for a long advance where they receive tough handling by tired men." It was not uncommon for a company to abandon some of the heavy boxes, with a runner detailed out to remember the position in case of need. Unsurprisingly, these unattended ammunition dumps had a tendency to disappear before being reclaimed.[21]

The Chauchat and the Hotchkiss were replaced in the last months of the war by the Browning Automatic Rifle (BAR) and the M1917 water-cooled Browning machine gun respectively. The delay in release was purportedly due to fears that the Germans would copy some of the innovative features of the weapons.

The BAR was everything the Chauchat was not—rugged, reliable, and accurate. It was issued with a special belt that had a cup-like fixture on the right side to hold the butt of the weapon steady for "marching fire" in the assault, and pouches for the 20-round box magazines. The assistant gunner was provided with a belt that had more magazine pouches, and there were additional ammunition carriers to supply the prodigious number of rounds fired.

The M1917 machine gun was heavier than the older Hotchkiss, primarily because of its sturdier tripod and water-cooling system. A huge advantage was that it was belt-fed, eliminating the awkward stripper clips. The belts not only simplified loading, but eliminated the frequent changes of clips that slowed the sustained rate of fire.

The heaviest weapons used by the Marines were the British 3-inch Stokes mortar and the French-designed 37 mm M1916 trench gun. The mortars were used in very small numbers, six per regiment. The M1916 was a small cannon, the same one mounted in the French FT light tank. The M1916 trench gun had detachable wheels for long-distance movement and its own small ammunition caisson. Both were useless under combat conditions and the heavy weapons were hand-carried. With the wheels detached, the 342-pound (155 kg) weapon was carried by men using handles mounted on the trails, and a carrier pole that plugged into a socket on the front of the mount. In action the weapon rested on trails and a front monopod. Ammunition carriers lugged 16-round, 8-pound (3.6 kg) metal ammunition chests with high-explosive or canister ammunition. Despite its weight, the trench gun was a useful and popular weapon, except among those who had to carry it.[22]

Machine-gun and mortar sections were supplied with two-wheeled carts that could be pulled by draft animals on long marches, or more typically by men.

The Marine Corps had both horse-drawn field artillery, which had been deployed to Mexico, and large-caliber fixed coastal guns of the advanced base detachments. Only two of the latter were deployed outside the United States, to defend the seaplane base in the Azores. The Marine Brigade in France had no artillery, but direct artillery support was provided by the Army's Twelfth and Fifteenth Field Artillery regiments with French 75 mm field guns, the general support artillery of the Seventeenth Field Artillery with 155 mm howitzers, and the heavy mortars of the 2nd Trench Mortar Battery. In addition the Marines were quite often supported by French corps artillery, with 75 mm field guns, 155 mm howitzers, and long-range 170 mm guns.

The Marine Brigade was strictly leg infantry, utilizing only horses and mules to draw machine-gun carts, and a variety of wagons from cargo carriers to the field kitchens and water wagons—called water buffaloes by the Marines, for unknown reasons.

Ambulances, both motor vehicles and horse-drawn, were supplied by the Second Sanitary Train. Staff cars of various types, and motorcycles with sidecars for couriers and occasional transportation of officers were provided by the division motor transport section.

The single motor vehicle organic to the brigade was the Sixth Marines' Ford Model T truck equipped as an ambulance. The truck had been purchased and donated by three wealthy women, Mrs. Elizabeth Pearce, Mrs. Charles Childs and Miss Willard (first name unknown). The truck became known as the "Elizabeth Ford" or less often "Tin Lizzie". Interestingly, photos taken at Quantico show the name misspelled as "Elizaberth".[23]

Food, or the lack of it, was a constant and nagging concern, and food and other supplies were often a haphazard affair. In April 1918 Louis Jones was battalion quartermaster for 1/4, and found that even in a *bon secteur* like the Toulon/Les Eparges training area "We had a French engineer depot from which we drew our little cars [hand carts] to take rations down to this battalion [1/6], and you couldn't select the time you were going to get them. The French gave you those cars at certain times, so the Germans had us timed, and we went down this long road with these things one night and they shot the hell out of us. They had to come back, and I took a ration baggage wagon down this long road leading to this place where we dumped the rations, which was near where we then had our front lines. They didn't hit us, but they made life a little miserable with their shell fire down there." In the pre-dawn hours of the next morning the supporting troops, including Jones's supply section from the Headquarters Company and the 74th

Company of 1/6, were subjected to a four-hour chemical attack that injured everyone, killed several men, and landed Jones in the hospital for two months.[24]

An Army innovation welcomed by the Marines was the horse-drawn field kitchen. The wood-fired stove was equipped with large integral kettles and a simple oven. Worton recalled that "The cooks would cook right while we were on the march. And they were marching right behind us, cooking.... But looking back on it, it was pretty damn good food, compared to what I had out in the Pacific [in World War II] when we had nothing but Spam [TM]....

"I suppose some of this damn stuff might have been horse meat. Whatever it was, we never knew, and it was damn good. It was hot, which we needed in those days."[25]

In hurried movements to the front, even cooking by the field kitchen fell by the wayside. Corporal Daniel E. Morgan (77th Company) wrote that on the way to Belleau Wood, the cooks were preparing chickens when the word came to march into battle. The cooks just dumped everything into the trash. Days later, when they came out of the fighting, the famished Morgan "walked over to the basket where we left the chickens, and not having any food, took a bite out of a chicken's leg, uncooked: indeed we all had to eat the chickens without cooking them or starve."[26]

The horse-drawn company field kitchen could prepare only simple foods like soup or the ubiquitous slumgullion, but little else. Bread—typically hard rolls—was prepared by special bakery units, and distributed as best the supply system could manage. Both were distributed in the mess line where possible, but in the trenches carriers had to lug large metal canisters to the forward positions. The slumgullion usually arrived cold, with a thick layer of congealed grease on top.

Lieutenant Clifton Cates thought that "The supplies were very, very poor. Of course, we carried what was supposed to be four days' emergency ration. It consisted of four boxes of hardtack [unleavened crackers made with flour and salt], some bacon, I guess a pound of bacon, sugar and coffee. To start with we had bully beef [French Madagascar brand corned beef] and then later when we couldn't get that we had that doggone terrible Argentine canned beef that nobody could eat. [The

Argentine concoction was actually a beef stew with a soggy, tasteless vegetable mush]. They'd go hungry before they would eat it.

"Oh, it was terrible. When we were in action, we'd never, at any time, get over one meal a day and we'd get that at night. They'd bring it in under cover of darkness. Of course, we'd get that one meal—the details would get pretty badly shot up bringing it in—but we'd get it and it really would be pretty good. Mostly steak and mashed potatoes."[27]

Food carrier duty was considered hazardous in the extreme. The shiny metal cans might attract the attention of the enemy in the form of machine-gun or artillery fire. During the fighting at Belleau Wood on June 27, 1918, Corporal Joseph Rendinell (97th Company, 3/6) wrote in his diary that "A detail of thirty went back for chow. I wonder who won't come back? Food is cooked about 4 miles back of our lines and they have to go and get it. The only time we get water is when the water cart does not get hit and that is might seldom. We hold pebbles in our mouth to keep it moist.

"That ration detail came back with eleven men. The other nineteen killed or wounded."[28]

The company mess wagon could also prepare a rare treat called "trench donuts", fried bread balls coated with sugar. The Red Cross, YMCA, and Salvation Army also distributed (or sold) things like coffee, hot chocolate, donuts, candy, chewing gum and other comfort items, but these were rarities in the front lines.

Each man carried an emergency ration of hardtack biscuits and canned "monkey meat". The nickname derived from the fact that the primary brand was Madagascar brand *boeuf boulli*. The French *poilus* had long since reasoned that there were more monkeys than cows in Madagascar, so the stuff it was more likely canned monkey (there are no monkeys on Madagascar). There were several canned concoctions lumped under the name, from corned beef to a hash with carrots or potatoes.

The monkey-meat and hardtack were intended as emergency rations, to be eaten only when authorized. In practice the famished Marines usually just ate it anyway.

But Joe Rendinell said "After eating a can of it you are ready to climb a tree. Four cans, and you would grow a tail. The poor French people would not eat it. It was South American beef & carrots & tasted like coal oil." Walter Gaspar said "some of it was just rotten, that's all. You couldn't eat it."[29]

Hardtack biscuits had been a staple of the naval and military diet for decades. Unleavened bread made from flour, water, and salt, the World War I variant came packed in cartons, and were typically subdivided into daily rations wrapped in paper. With no protection from the ubiquitous damp, the biscuits often became soggy or moldy after a few days. Near the end if the war the US introduced canned hardtack.

A variety of other foods could be purchased from French suttlers. Walter Gaspar said that "Most of us carried big slabs of chocolate—*Chocolat Meunière*—and you could put that between two pieces of French bread."[30]

Many men carried bacon tins, elongated cans with tight-fitting lids. Cured bacon kept fairly well, and the fat was a good source of energy. Bacon could be fried in the mess kit, and crumbled hardtack soaked in the grease to make "skillygalee".

Another staple often mentioned was canned tomatoes. The acidic tomatoes kept well, were good to prevent scurvy as a supplement to a diet short on fresh vegetables, and were a source of dietary salt.

There was inevitably a lot of scrounging as the Marines traded for local food, or just confiscated it. James Rendinell recorded in his diary that while in the trenches at Les Eparges "*March 23rd*—Baled water & mud out of trenches & at 11 o'clock we sneaked out & climbed on top of the chateau & got some honey from a bee hive. My face was a sight where the bees lit."[31]

By far the best food came when troops were billeted in French homes, or made friends with local families. Joseph Rendinell wrote home that "Last Sunday I went to church & Sunday night three of us had a swell super with a French family. We had roasted chicken, lettuce salad, French fried potatoes and a lot of other good things to eat. Oh boy, I ate till I could hardly move."[32]

Another consumable that immediately found its way into the American soldier's and Marine's diet was wine in all its forms. In American society of that era beer and liquor consumption was quite acceptable, even celebrated. But wine was considered the drink of the decadent rich and the derelict alcoholic, an attitude that still survives in the American vocabulary as the derogatory "wino". The troops had no such scruples, and copious wine consumption is described in most memoirs.

Lieutenant William Worton observed that "You couldn't have stopped it even if you wanted to. I mean the French were going to give it to our people. If they hadn't bought it, the French people … would wander through there, and you'd stop for 15 min for a rest period. Why, hell, these French farmers would be out giving these kids a bottle of wine and biscuits and cheese."[33]

But because of the public attitude, and the desire to think of the troops as virtuous heroes, wine was not officially mentioned. There exist few official photos of Americans drinking wine, and none were released by censors.

The fighting man's other great consolation was tobacco. Canned shredded Bull Durham brand tobacco and wrapping papers were "issued out like rations. However there were ready rolls available if you had the money." Chewing tobacco was also popular, since it could be used when the glow of a cigarette might make you a target for sniping or artillery fire.[34]

Endnotes

Chapter 1

1 Unless otherwise noted, the following is based upon Millett, *Semper Fidelis: The History of the United States Marine Corps*, pp. 171–174, 267–277.
2 Wise, *A Marine Tells it to You*, pp. 123–127.
3 Garvin, "History of the 49th Company," p. 2.
4 Image of document held by National Archives and Records Administration, www.archives.gov/education/lessons/zimmermann

Chapter 2

1 Cowing and Cooper, *Dear Folks at Home*, p. 3.
2 McClellan, *The United States Marine Corps in the World War*, p. 76.
3 Ibid, p. 11; the reader should note that there are significant discrepancies between these numbers and those in Millett, p. 288. See also Shulimson, p. 8.
4 Jones interview, pp. 6–7.
5 Rendinell and Pattullo, *One Man's War: Diary of a Leatherneck*, p. 4–9.
6 Figures are from McClellan, p. 9; Millett, p. 288.
7 Abbott, *Soldiers of the Sea*, p. 291.
8 Jackson interview.
9 Brown interview, p. 2.
10 Owen, *To the Limit of Endurance*, p. 2; Gilbert and Gilbert, *U. S. Marine in World War I*, p. 12.
11 Thomas interview, pp. 8–9.
12 Gilbert and Gilbert, p. 12; raw numbers are provided by McClellan, p. 16.
13 McClellan, pp. 10, 18.
14 Ibid, p. 10.
15 Ibid, p. 14.

16 Gaspar interview, pp. 1–9.
17 Silverthorn interview, pp. 2–8.
18 McClellan, p. 25.
19 Jones interview, pp. 6–7.
20 Rendinell and Pattullo, pp. 4–9.
21 Krulewitch, *Now That You Mention It*, pp. 25–26; Rendinell and Pattullo, p. 10.
22 Jensen interview.
23 Schilt interview, pp. 7–10, 12.
24 Brown interview, p. 3.
25 Rendinell and Pattullo, pp. 11–12.
26 Hemrick, *Once A Marine*, p. 16.
27 Jensen interview.
28 Rendinell and Pattullo, p. 16.
29 Schilt interview, p. 13.
30 McDonald interview, pp. 3–4.
31 Cowing and Cooper, p. 12.
32 Schilt interview, p. 11.
33 Cowing and Cooper, p. 8.
34 Rendinell and Pattullo, pp. 18, 21–24.
35 Manchester, *Goodbye Darkness*, p. 13.
36 McClellan, pp. 21–23.
37 Jones interview, pp. 2–3.
38 Peck interview, pp. 6–8,
39 Worton interview, pp. 3–11. For a brief history of the Massachusetts Naval Militia see https://en.wikipedia.org/wiki/Massachusetts_Naval_Militia. As it turned out, Worton was also the only graduate of the state's Military Academy to be commissioned as a U. S. Marine.
40 Wise, *A Marine Tells it to You*, 157–159.
41 Erskine interview, pp. 1–7.
42 Shepherd interview, pp. 117–118.
43 Cates interview, pp. 1–5.
44 Noble interview, pp. 2–5.
45 Ibid, pp. 2–5.
46 McClellan, p. 26.
47 Lejeune, *The Reminiscences of a Marine*, pp. 242–245.
48 Erskine interview, pp. 18–19.
49 Hermle interview, pp. 1–3.
50 Erskine interview, p. 12.
51 For a more detailed description of the company organizational structure, see Gilbert and Gilbert, pp. 10, 16–18.
52 Rendinell and Pattullo, pp. 27–28.
53 McClellan, pp. 27–28.

54 Silverthorn interview, pp. 10–12.
55 Cates interview, pp. 7–8, 10, 12.
56 Erskine interview, pp. 14–16.
57 Worton interview, pp. 17–18.

Chapter 3

1 McClellan, *The United States Marine Corps in the World War*, p. 30.
2 Second Division Association, *The Second Division American Expeditionary Force in France 1917–1919*, p. 239.
3 Wise, *A Marine Tells it to You*, p. 160.
4 Shepherd interview, p. 121; McDonald interview, p. 5.
5 Thomas interview, p. 7.
6 Wise, p. 160.
7 Gaspar interview, pp. 9–10.
8 Second Division Association, p. 240.
9 *Seattle* was originally the Armored Cruiser *Washington*, see https://en.wikipedia.org/wiki/USS_Washington_(ACR-11); McClelllan, p. 30.
10 Second Division Association, p. 240.
11 Garvin, "History of the 49th Company," p. 3.
12 Wise, p. 161.
13 McClellan, p. 30.
14 Wise, p. 162.
15 Thomas interview, p. 8.
16 Silverthorn interview, p. 15.
17 Broun, *Our Army at the Front*, p. 35.
18 Pershing, *My Experiences in the World War*, pp. 189–192.
19 Wise, pp. 168–171.
20 The dizzying swirl of officers and reorganization is summarized by McClellan, pp. 32–33.
21 Silverthorn interview, pp. 16, 18, 21–22.
22 Jones interview, p. 21.
23 Quoted in McClellan, p. 31.
24 Rogers interview.
25 Noble interview, p. 8.
26 Rogers interview.
27 Rendinell and Pattullo, *One Man's War: Diary of a Leatherneck*, pp. 30–33.
28 Worton interview, pp. 18–19.
29 Rendinell and Pattullo, pp. 38–41.
30 Ibid, pp. 42–43, 49–50.
31 Ibid, pp. 43–44.

32 Erskine interview, pp. 22–23.
33 Worton interview, pp. 19–20.
34 Cates interview, pp. 10–11.
35 Ibid, p. 10.
36 Worton interview, p. 21.
37 Erskine interview, pp. 24–25.
38 Ibid, p. 26.
39 Hermle interview, p. 7.
40 Cowing and Cooper, pp. 187–188. Fussell, *The Great War and Modern Memory* devotes a full chapter to this concept, pp. 155–190.
41 Erskine interview, pp. 27–28.
42 Shepherd interview, pp. 125–128.
43 Wise, p. 164.
44 Broun, *Our Army at the Front,* p. 75.
45 Wise, p. 165.
46 Erskine interview, pp. 21, 28.
47 Shepherd interview, p. 128.
48 Jones interview, p. 12.
49 Thomas interview, pp. 8–9.
50 Wise, p. 173.
51 Gaspar interview, p. 11–12.
52 Wise, pp. 173–174.
53 Rendinell and Pattullo, pp. 54–56.
54 Noble interview, pp. 13–14.
55 McClellan, pp. 62–64.
56 McClellan, pp. 34–35; *Pocahontas* was the former German liner *Prinzess Irene*, see www.google.com/#q=uss+pocohontas.
57 Lejeune, *The Reminiscences of a Marine*, pp. 247–248; see also Bartlett, *Lejeune*, pp. 68–72.

Chapter 4

1 For a brief summary and illustrations of World War I communications techniques see Gilbert, pp. 4–8.
2 Rendinell and Pattullo, p. 60.
3 Harbord, *Leaves from a War Diary*, p. 300.
4 Wise, *A Marine Tells it to You*, pp. 180–183.
5 Westover, *Suicide Battalions*, pp. 58–59.
6 Garvin, F. H., "History of the 49th Company," p. 3.
7 Record of Events Sixth Marines, March 1918 (v. 3, p. 3). Hereafter numbers in parentheses refers to volume and page number in preserved Second Division document at Grey Research Center.

8 Cates interview, p. 16.
9 Rendinell and Pattullo, *One Man's War: Diary of a Leatherneck*, p. 61.
10 Rogers interview.
11 Rendinell and Pattullo, pp. 61–63.
12 Shepherd interview, p. 35.
13 Thomas interview, p. 10.
14 Hermle interview, pp. 6–8.
15 War Diary, Fifth Marines, March 28, 1918 (v. 7, p. 2).
16 Second Division Association, *The Second Division American Expeditionary Force in France 1917–1919*, p. 241.
17 Cowing and Cooper, *Dear Folks at Home*, pp. 56–57.
18 Ibid, pp. 59–61.
19 Rendinell and Pattullo, p. 63.
20 Wise, pp. 180–184.
21 Rendinell and Pattullo, pp. 65–67.
22 Cowing and Cooper, p. 58.
23 War Diary Fifth Marines, April 20, 1918 (v. 7, p. 4–5).
24 Wise, p. 186.
25 Westover, p. 71.
26 "Report of Gas Attack," War Diary Sixth Marines (v. 3, p. 6).
27 War Diary Sixth Machine Gun Battalion, April 7, 1918 (v. 8, p. 3).
28 Rendinell and Pattullo, pp. 67-70.
29 Ibid, pp. 72–73.
30 Ibid, pp. 77–79.
31 Cowing and Cooper, p. 49.
32 Ibid, p. 71–72. This letter is a bit problematical in that the brigade was not "in the trenches" on this date, and there was no 29th Company in the Fifth Marines. The reference may be to the 49th Company, 1/5.
33 Rendinell and Pattullo, pp. 83–84.
34 Ibid, p. 6.
35 Garvin, p. 5.
36 McClellan, *The United States Marine Corps in the World War*, pp. 39–40.
37 Letter Major Frank Evans to Mrs. Charles A. Childs, June 22, 1918, quoted in Cowing & Cooper, *Dear Folks at Home*, pp. 114–115.

Chapter 5

1 Belleau Wood was a complex and protracted battle, and numerous books have been written about this single action. One of the most useful is Robert Asprey's 1965 *At Belleau Wood*, especially for its maps. The book is out of print but used copies are widely available.

2 Thomas interview, p. 11.
3 The administrative history of the "French Marines" is complex, but in World War I these were primarily three regiments of *Troupes Coloniales* of the French Army. Wise is probably referring to one of these formations.
4 Wise, *A Marine Tells it to You,* pp. 191–192.
5 Rendinell and Pattullo, *One Man's War: Diary of a Leatherneck*, pp. 91–92.
6 Noble interview, p. 21.
7 Cowing and Cooper, *Dear Folks at Home*, pp. 95–96.
8 Wise, p.193.
9 Catlin, *With the Help of God and a Few Marines*, p. 82.
10 Wise, p. 194.
11 Gaspar interview, p. 12.
12 Thomas interview, pp. 12–13.
13 Rendinell and Pattullo, p. 93.
14 McDonald interview, p. 7.
15 Cowing and Cooper, p. 97.
16 Catlin, pp. 84–85.
17 Asprey, *At Belleau Wood*, p. 112.
18 Rendinell and Pattullo, p. 93; Major Frank E. Evans in Cowing and Cooper, p. 97.
19 War Diary, Sixth Machine Gun Battalion in *Second Division Papers*, June 1, 1918 (v. 8, p. 6).
20 Erskine interview, p. 52.
21 Cates interview, pp. 41–42.
22 In German usage the 10th Infantry Division would be recorded as 10. Infanterie Division.
23 "Report of Operations, 6th Machine Gun Battalion, May and June, 1918" in *Second Division Papers*, Vol. 8, Quantico, p. 7.
24 Wise, p. 196.
25 War Diary, Sixth Machine Gun Battalion, June 1, 1918 (v. 8, p. 7).
26 Shepherd interview, pp. 130–131; Asprey, p. 115.
27 Wise, pp. 196–198; Asprey, pp. 114–119.
28 Williams was subsequently killed in action. Colonel Wise and an Army captain both later claimed the statement, and some even attributed the quote to Colonel Neville. See for example Asprey, p. 120.
29 Wise, pp. 198–199.
30 Second Division Association, *The Second Division American Expeditionary Force in France*, p. 252.
31 Many American sources state that the 43ème Division d'Infanterie received orders for a morning counterattack. We have used French records as a more definitive source.
32 Jones interview; Shepherd interview, interview, p. 9.
33 Wise, p. 200.
34 American Battle Monuments Commission, *2d Division Summary of Operations in the Great War,* p. 10.

35 Ibid, p. 10.
36 Wise, p. 201.
37 Ibid, pp. 201–202.
38 Shepherd interview, p. 131.
39 Wise, pp. 202-206.
40 Cowing and Cooper, pp. 98–99.
41 Thomas interview, p. 13.
42 Rendinell and Pattullo, pp. 93–94.
43 Catlin, p. 95.
44 McDonald interview, p. 7.
45 Cowing and Cooper, pp. 98–99.
46 Ibid, p. 77.
47 Ibid, p. 96.
48 Derby, *Wade In, Sanitary!*, p. 57.
49 Thomas interview, pp. 13–14.
50 Rendinell and Pattullo, pp. 94–95.
51 "Reports of Patrols, Nights of April 6–7, June 5–6, and July 4–5, 1918" in *Second Division Papers*, Vol. 7, Sixth Marines, Quantico, p. 9; Rendinell and Pattullo, pp. 95–96.
52 Ibid, pp. 7–8.
53 Second Division Association, p. 253.
54 "Brigade Order No. 2 June 6, 1918" in *Second Division Papers*, Vol. 2, Fourth Brigade, Quantico, pp. 5–6; Rendinell and Pattullo, p. 97.
55 "Reports of Patrols, Nights of April 6–7, June 5–6, and July 4–5, 1918" in *Second Division Papers*, Vol. 7, Sixth Marines, Quantico, p. 9.
56 Bisett, *Operations On the Western Front, May 22 To June 8, 1918*, pp. 359–360.
57 Second Division Association, p. 253.
58 "Field Order No. [blank], June 6, 1918" in *Second Division Papers*, Vol. 3, Fifth Marines, Quantico, p. 6; "Report of Operations, 6th Machine Gun Battalion, May and June, 1918" in *Second Division Papers*, Vol. 8, Sixth Machine Gun Battalion, Quantico, p. 7
59 Harbord, pp. 296–297.
60 Wise, p. 207.
61 Derby, pp. 64–66.
62 Wise, pp. 207–208.
63 Charles F. Hoffman Medal of Honor citation.
64 Longstreet, *Gunner Nice of the "Devil-Dogs"*, p. 14.
65 Brigade Field Order No. 2 was time-dated 1405 h. Brigade Order No. 2, June 6, 1918 in *Second Division Papers*, Vol. 2, Fourth Brigade, Quantico, pp. 6–7.
66 "Brigade Order No. 2, June 5, 1918" in *Second Division Papers*, Vol. 2, Fourth Brigade, Quantico, pp. 6–7; Erskine interview, p. 35.
67 Cates interview, p. 18.
68 Rendinell and Pattullo, p. 97

69 Cowing and Cooper, pp. 100–101.
70 Rogers interview.
71 The story first appeared in Gibbons, *And They Thought We Wouldn't Fight*, pp. 296–298. Whether Daly or another NCO uttered the iconic words has been dispute (see for example), but the tale has gone down in Corps history as Daly's words.
72 Rendinell and Pattullo, pp. 97–99.
73 Ibid, p. 99.
74 Catlin, pp. 118–122.
75 Rendinell and Pattullo, pp. 99–100.
76 Cowing and Cooper, p. 101.
77 Gibbons, *And They Thought We Wouldn't Fight*, pp. 296–297.
78 Cates interview, pp. 18–20.
79 Ibid, pp. 18–20.
80 Erskine interview, pp. 36–37, 45.
81 See several accounts in Clark, *Devil Dogs Chronicle*, and Hart, T*he Somme: The Darkest Hour on the Western Front*.
82 Erskine interview, p. 38.
83 John Henry Quick had won the Medal of Honor for action at Guantanamo Bay, Cuba in 1898. He stood in plain view amid a hail of enemy bullets and used semaphore flags to redirect shelling from the support vessel USS *Dolphin*, which was falling on nearby Marines.
84 Harbord, pp. 295–296.
85 Letter Major Frank Evans to Mrs. Charles A. Childs, June 22, 1918, as quoted in Cowing and Cooper, pp. 114–115.
86 Gibbons, pp. 296–298.
87 Rendinell and Pattullo, pp. 100–101.
88 Wise, p. 209; see also "Report of Operations, Second Battalion (Fifth Marines), June 2–26, 1918" in *Second Division Papers*, Vol. 7, Fifth Marines, p. 6.
89 Derby, pp. 67–69.
90 Wise, pp. 209–213; James Hennen Legendre, Distinguished Service Cross citation.
91 Erskine interview, pp. 38–39, 42.
92 Rendinell and Pattullo, pp. 101–102.
93 Rogers interview.
94 Shepherd interview, p. 128.
95 Gibbons, pp. 310–326.
96 American Battle Monuments Commission, p. 14.
97 Rendinell and Pattullo, pp. 101–102.
98 Ibid, p. 102.
99 Ibid, p. 103.
100 Erskine interview, p. 42.
101 Lejeune, *The Reminiscences of a Marine*, pp. 250–255.
102 Cates interview, pp. 21–22.
103 Erskine interview, p. 42.

104 American Battle Monuments Commission, pp.14–15.
105 Gaspar interview, p. 12.
106 Wise, pp. 211–212.
107 *Kriegstagbuch*, Deutsche Siebte Armee, June 8, and unnumbered Order, Ia/Ic, Deutscher 28. Infanteriedivision, June 8 as translated in American Battle Monuments Commission, *2d Division Summary of Operations in the Great War*, p. 15.
108 Thomas interview, p. 14. Several minor typographic errors have been corrected from the original transcript.
109 Lejeune, p. 252.
110 "Report of Operations, Second Battalion (Fifth Marines), June 2–26, 1918" in *Second Division Papers*, Vol. 7, Fifth Marines, p. 6.
111 Thomas interview, p. 15.
112 Ibid, p. 16.
113 "Report of Operations, Second Battalion (Fifth Marines), June 2–26, 1918" in *Second Division Papers*, Vol. 7, Fifth Marines, p. 6.
114 Derby, p. 235.
115 American Battle Monuments Commission, p. 17; "Report of Operations, Second Battalion (Fifth Marines), June 2–26, 1918" in *Second Division Papers*, Vol. 7, Fifth Marines, p. 6.
116 Cates interview, p. 23.
117 Ibid, pp. 23–25.
118 American Battle Monuments Commission, p. 17.
119 Westover, *Suicide Battalions*, p. 125.
120 Cates interview, pp. 23–25.
121 Erskine interview, p. 43.
122 Ibid, pp. 43–44.
123 Derby, pp. 72–73.
124 "Report of Operations, Second Battalion (Fifth Marines), June 2–26, 1918" in *Second Division Papers*, Vol. 7, Fifth Marines, p. 7.
125 American Battle Monuments Commission, p. 18.
126 Cates interview, p. 46.
127 Gaspar interview, p. 31.
128 Jones interview, p. 18.
129 Cates interview, pp. 25–26, 39.
130 "Report of Operations, Second Battalion (Fifth Marines), June 2–26, 1918" in *Second Division Papers*, Vol. 7, Fifth Marines, p. 7.
131 "Reports of Patrols, Nights of April 6–7, June 5–6, and July 4–5, 1918" in *Second Division Papers*, Vol. 7, Sixth Marines, Quantico, pp. 9–11.
132 Rendinell and Pattullo, pp. 111–112.
133 Ibid, pp. 112–113.
134 American Battle Monuments Commission, p. 19.
135 Rendinell and Pattullo, p. 115.
136 Ibid, pp. 114–115.

137 Ibid, pp. 126–127.
138 Erskine interview, p. 51.
139 Rendinell and Pattullo, pp. 116–117.
140 "Report of Attack by 3 Bn. Night of [June] 23-24" in *Second Division Papers*, Vol. 7, Fifth Marines, pp. 10–11.
141 Rendinell and Pattullo, pp. 118–119.
142 Ibid, p. 119.
143 Ibid, pp. 120–121.
144 Ibid, p. 122.
145 Ibid, p. 123.
146 Ibid, pp. 124–125.
147 Ibid, p. 129.
148 American Battle Monuments Commission, p. 23.
149 Cates interview pp. 28–29.
150 "Reports of Patrols, Nights of April 6–7, June 5–6, and July 4–5, 1918" in *Second Division Papers*, Vol. 7, Sixth Marines, Quantico, p. 12.
151 Rendinell and Pattullo, p. 131.
152 Ibid, pp. 131–132.
153 Ibid, pp. 133–134.
154 Ibid, pp. 134–135.
155 McDonald interview, p. 10.
156 "Report of Operations, Second Battalion (Fifth Marines), June 2–26, 1918" in *Second Division Papers*, Vol. 7, Fifth Marines, pp. 7–8.
157 Harbord, p. 294.
158 Cates interview, pp. 31–32.

Chapter 6

1 Lejeune, *The Reminiscences of a Marine*, p. 260; Pershing's cable is quoted in Bartlett, *Lejeune*, p. 73.
2 McClellan, *The United States Marine Corps in the World War*, p. 33.
3 Peck interview, pp. 31, 46–47, 49.
4 https://en.wikipedia.org/wiki/USS_Henderson_(AP-1); Manchester, *Goodbye Darkness*, p. 18.

Chapter 7

1 Martin, "Doctor William Crawford Gorgas of Alabama and the Panama Canal."
2 For the history and function of the Sanitary Corps, see http://history.amedd.army.mil/booksdocs/HistoryofUSArmyMSC/chapter3.html
3 McClellan, *The United States Marine Corps in the World War*, p. 83.

4 Brannen, *Over There*, p. 55.
5 Derby, *Wade in, Sanitary!*, p. 61.
6 Ibid, pp. 42–43. For numerous photos see www.google.com/search?q=thresh-foden+disinfector&sa=X&tbm=isch&tbo=u&source=univ&ved=0ahUKEwiOh_W20vbUAhWD8CYKHVmfCSIQsAQIKg&biw=1019&bih=878&dpr=1
7 Brannen, p. 36.
8 Derby, p. 31.
9 Jones interview, p. 14.
10 Derby, pp. 37–41.
11 For a brief description of the procedure, see https://en.wikipedia.org/wiki/Fluoroscopy#Early_era
12 Brannen, p. 50.
13 Derby, pp. 16–18, 28–29.
14 Ibid, pp. 58–59.
15 Gibbons, *And They Thought We Wouldn't Fight*, pp. 326–337.
16 Ibid, pp. 338–352.
17 Avery interview.
18 Rogers interview.
19 Derby, p. 26.
20 Rogers interview.
21 McDonald interview, p. 6.
22 Lejeune, *The Reminiscences of a Marine*, p. 255.
23 Longstreet, *Gunner Nice of the "Devil-Dogs"*, p. 14.
24 Thomas interview, p. 23.
25 Rendinell and Pattullo, *One Man's War: Diary of a Leatherneck*, pp. 105–107.
26 Ibid, p. 111.
27 Ibid, p. 110.
28 Erskine interview, pp. 57–58.
29 Cates interview, pp. 46–47. For an example of the practice (and its practical application) in early American military campaigns, see Gilbert and Gilbert, *Frontier Militiaman in the War of 1812*, p. 59.
30 Erskine interview, p. 67.
31 Brown interview, p. 10.
32 Manchester, *Goodbye Darkness*, p. 16.
33 Ibid, p. 18.
34 Morgan, *When the World Went Mad*, p. 110.
35 Longstreet, *Gunner Nice of the "Devil-Dogs"*, p. 14.
36 Rendinell and Pattullo, p. 107.
37 Ibid, p. 106.
38 Second Division Association, *The Second Division American Expeditionary Force* in France, p. 254.
39 Harbord, *Leaves From a War Diary*, pp. 303–304.

40 www.historynet.com/rest-in-peace-bringing-home-u-s-war-dead.html
41 Erskine interview, pp. 70–71.

Chapter 8

1 Rogers interview.
2 Harbord, *Leaves From a War Diary*, p. 280.
3 Pigman, *Operations of The 2nd Division (U.S.) in the Soissons Offensive, July 16th to 25th, 1918*, p. 446.
4 Jones interview, p. 17; American Battle Monuments Commission, *2nd Division Summary of Operations in the Great War*, p. 27.
5 Harbord, pp. 318, 320–321.
6 Second Division Association, *The Second Division American Expeditionary Force* in France, pp. 256–257.
7 Thomas interview, p.17.
8 Pigman, p. 447.
9 Thomas interview, p. 18.
10 Brannen, *Over There*, p. 31.
11 Harbord, pp. 322–323.
12 Ibid, p. 324.
13 Despite the name, this division was not composed of Moroccan troops, but by Tunisians and Algerian Zouaves and Tirailleurs. It was activated in Morocco in 1912, hence the name. It was the most decorated French unit of the Great War.
14 Second Division Association, p. 261.
15 Pigman, pp. 447–449.
16 Louis Cukela Medal of Honor citation; Matek Kocak Medal of Honor citation; James R. Nilo, *"World War I: 75 Years Ago: Attack on Soissons"*, www.mca-marines.org/leatherneck/world-war-i-75-years-ago-attack-soissons
17 Thomas interview, pp. 19–20.
18 Ibid, p. 18.
19 Erskine interview, p. 57.
20 American Battle Monuments Commission, pp. 27–28.
21 Thomas interview, pp. 19–20.
22 Ibid, p. 20.
23 Brannen, p. 31.
24 The German *Kommißbrot* was dark bread baked primarily from rye flour. By this stage of the war sawdust was sometimes added to compensate for flour shortages.
25 Second Division Association, p. 262.
26 Longstreet, *Gunner Nice of the "Devil-Dogs"*, p. 14.
27 American Battle Monuments Commission, p. 27.
28 Second Division Association, p. 262.
29 Jones interview, p. 18.
30 Second Division Association, p. 262; Brannen, p. 31.

31 Pigman, *Operations of the 2nd Division (U.S.) in The Soissons Offensive, July 16th to 25th, 1918*, p. 449.
32 Thomas interview, pp. 20–22.
33 Cates interview, pp. 32–34.
34 Brannen, p. 31.
35 American Battle Monuments, pp.31–32; Gaspar interview, p. 40; see also Brannen, p. 31.
36 Thomas interview, pp. 20–22.
37 Cates interview, p. 37.
38 Brannen, pp. 31–32.
39 Thomas interview, pp. 20–22.
40 Gaspar interview, p. 27.
41 Westover, *Suicide Battalions*, pp. 165–166.
42 Cates interview, p. 32–34. Widely quoted and sometimes sourced as Asprey, *At Belleau Wood*, the date even in the dubious attributions is given as 19 July, clearly at Soissons.
43 Brannen, p. 32.
44 Cates interview, pp. 34–36.
45 Rogers interview.
46 Longstreet, *Gunner Nice of the "Devil-Dogs"*, p. 14.
47 Brannen, pp. 33–34; Second Division Association, p. 263.
48 Cates interview, p. 36; American Battle Monuments Commission, p. 33; Jones interview, p. 18.
49 Gaspar interview, p. 25.
50 Erskine interview, pp. 49–51. The reader should be aware that in the first session of his interview, Erskine attributed this episode to the period after Belleau Wood, but later corrected himself.

Chapter 9

1 Hewitt, *Women Marines in World War I*, p. 4.
2 Millett, *Semper Fidelis: The History of the United States Marine Corps*, pp. 307–308; Hewitt, p. 1.
3 Hewitt, p. 11.
4 Anonymous, "Girl Joins Devil Dogs."
5 Hewitt, p. 6.
6 Ibid, p. 6, 9.
7 Ibid, p. 7.
8 Ibid, p. 9.
9 Cowing and Cooper, *Dear Folks at Home*, p. 17; Hewitt, p. 7. Wilchinski's account originally appeared in *The Recruiter's Bulletin*, v. 4, no. 12, October 1918.
10 Cowing and Cooper, pp. 15–24.
11 Anonymous, "Women Marines Anxious to Serve United States"; Hewitt, p. 16.

12 Ibid, pp. 19–25; anonymous interview, Marine Corps History Division.
13 Leibrand was a professional name. Born Lela Emogen Owens, her legal married name was Lela McMath, later Lela Rogers. She was a Hollywood script writer before becoming one of the first ten women Marines. She was later director of new talent at RKO Pictures, and was the mother of actress Virginia "Ginger" Rogers. (; https://womenmarines.wordpress.com/2013/07/26/lela-leibrand/)
14 Ibid, pp. 27–31.
15 Ibid, p. 36.

Chapter 10

1 Bartlett, *Lejeune*, pp. 70–73; Lejeune, *The Reminiscences of a Marine*, p. 287.
2 Derby, *Wade in, Sanitary!*, pp. 89–99.
3 There are few comprehensive overviews of the St. Mihiel campaign. Unless otherwise noted, the following general information is from Bonk, *St. Mihiel 1918: The American Expeditionary Forces' Trial by Fire*. An additional reference dealing specifically with the Second Division in far more detail is the American Battle Monuments Commission, *2nd Division Summary of Operations in the Great War.*
4 Excerpt from Pershing, "Final Report of Gen. Jon J. Pershing."
5 Ibid; Derby, p. 111.
6 Bartlett, p. 78.
7 American Battle Monuments Commission, p.40.
8 Jones interview, p. 16.
9 Rogers interview.
10 Lejeune, pp. 318–319.
11 Erskine interview, p. 61–62.
12 Rogers interview.
13 War Diary, Sixth Machine Gun Battalion, September 12, 1918, *Second Division Papers* (v. 8, pp. 8–9, 12).
14 Hermle interview, p. 9.
15 Lejeune, pp. 324–325.
16 Ibid, p. 325.
17 Derby, p. 114.
18 Lejeune, p. 328.
19 Rogers interview.
20 Ibid.
21 Erskine interview, pp. 62–67.
22 Brannen, *Over There*, p. 41.
23 Lejeune, p. 331.
24 Clark, *Hiram Iddings Bearss*, pp. 180–182.
25 War Diary, Sixth Machine Gun Battalion, September 15, 1918 (v. 8, p. 9).

26 Ibid, p. 11.
27 Lejeune, p. 333.
28 Excerpt from Pershing, "Final Report of Gen. Jon J. Pershing."
29 Derby, p. 121.
30 Citation quoted in Derby, p. 243–244.
31 Brannen, p. 43.
32 American Battle Monuments Commission, p. 48.
33 Thomas interview, p. 22.
34 Derby, p. 123.

Chapter 11

1 DelValle interview (summary), pp. 1–3.
2 Data from table in McClellan, *The United States Marine Corps in the World War*, p. 17.
3 Jensen interview.
4 McClellan, p. 59.
5 Jensen interview.
6 McClellan, p. 61.

Chapter 12

1 For a variety of reasons Blanc Mont is one of history's lesser-known battles. For more details the reader is referred to Gilbert and Cansière's 2018 *Blanc Mont Ridge 1918: America's Forgotten Triumph*, especially for its more detailed maps and bird's-eye views.
2 Gaspar interview, p. 38.
3 Lejeune, *The Reminiscences of a Marine*, p. 337.
4 Ibid, p. 342. For a more complete description of the background of this lesser-known campaign, see Gilbert and Cansière, *Blanc Mont Ridge 1918: America's Forgotten Triumph*.
5 Gaspar interview, p. 36.
6 Thomas interview, p. 22.
7 Hemle interview, p. 11.
8 Lejeune, p. 344.
9 Brown interview, pp. 6–8.
10 Lejeune, p. 348.
11 Ibid, p. 345.
12 Ibid, p. 350.
13 Second Division Association, *The Second Division American Expeditionary Force in France*, p. 274.
14 Lejeune, p. 346.

15 War Diary, Sixth Machine Gun Battalion, September 15, 1918 in *Second Division Papers* (v. 8, p. 20).
16 See Gilbert and Cansière, *Blanc Mont Ridge 1918: America's Forgotten Triumph*; Hermle interview, p. 10.
17 Brannen, *Over There*, p. 47.
18 Second Division Association, p. 275.
19 Brannen, p. 47.
20 Westover, *Suicide Battalions*, pp. 209–210.
21 Hermle interview, p. 10.
22 Derby, *Wade In, Sanitary!,* p. 133.
23 Second Division Association, p. 275.
24 Avery interview.
25 Derby, pp. 133–139.
26 Lejeune, p. 352.
27 Hermle interview, p. 10.
28 Second Division Association, p. 275
29 Brannen, pp. 47–49.
30 Hermle interview, p. 11.
31 Brannen, p. 50.
32 Westover, p. 210.
33 Longstreet, *Gunner Nice of the "Devil-Dogs",* pp. 14–15.
34 Westover, p. 211.
35 Thomason, Fix Bayonets, p. 190.
36 Westover, pp. 212–213.
37 Second Division Association, p. 275
38 Hermle interview, p. 11.
39 See https://en.wikipedia.org/wiki/Matej_Kocak
40 Derby, pp. 139–140.
41 War Diary, Sixth Machine Gun Battalion, September 15, 1918 (v. 8, pp. 21–22); Lejeune, p. 355.
42 Brown interview, p. 9.
43 Lejeune, p. 358.
44 Rogers interview.
45 Ibid.
46 Lejeune, p. 361.
47 Rogers interview.
48 Lejeune, p. 363.
49 Gaspar interview, p. 36.
50 War Diary, Sixth Machine Gun Battalion, September 15, 1918 (v. 8, pp. 21–23).
51 American Battle Monuments Commission, *2nd Division Summary of Operations in the Great War*, p. 67; Lejeune, p. 364.
52 Derby, p. 156; Second Division Association, p. 280.

Chapter 13

1 Unless otherwise noted, the following is derived from Johnson and Cosmas, *Marine Corps Aviation: The Early Years 1912–1940.*
2 Day interview, p. 4, 7.
3 Mulcahy interview, p. 9, 12.
4 McClellan, *The United States Marine Corps in the World War*, p. 71.
5 The account of Collings and his career are from his autobiography, *Just for the Hell of It*.
6 Day interview, pp. 7–8.
7 Collings, p. 57.
8 Day interview, p. 10.
9 Cosmas, *Marine Flyer in France*, p. 20, 29, 32.
10 Ibid, p. 63.
11 Ibid, p. 35.
12 McClellan, p. 71.
13 Collings, pp. 62–63. Geiger became a full general, and commanded the US Tenth Army after Army General Simon B. Buckner was killed in action on Okinawa in 1945.
14 Collings, pp. 64–65.
15 Ibid, pp. 69–70.
16 Ibid, pp. 70–71.
17 Ibid, p. 82.
18 Day interview, p. 13.
19 Ibid, pp. 13–14.
20 Collings, pp. 78–79.
21 The *DeKalb* was the former German passenger liner *Prinz Eitel Friedrich*, converted to an armed merchant cruiser in China. She then raided sea lines primarily in the Pacific. After capturing and scuttling eleven Allied vessels (one was the schooner *William P. Frye*, first US vessel sunk during the war), she was interned when she put into Newport News VA for coal. After the US declared war on Germany, on May 12, 1917 she was taken into US service and renamed *DeKalb*.
22 Collings, p. 88.
23 McClellan, p. 72.
24 Collings, pp. 91–94.
25 Ibid, pp. 95–101.
26 Day interview, p. 25.
27 Ibid, pp. 15–16, 25.
28 Ibid, pp. 16–17.
29 Mulcahy interview, p. 34.
30 Day interview, p. 20.
31 This is notation attached to most of the Navy Cross citations.
32 Rogers interview, pp. 35–36.

33 Navy Cross citation, Thomas L. McCullough
34 Mulcahy interview, pp. 31–32.
35 Navy Cross citation, Chapin C. Barr.
36 Navy Cross citation, Everett R. Brewer; Navy Cross citation Harry B. Wershiner.
37 Willock, *Unaccustomed To Fear*, p. 94.
38 Ibid, pp. 97–98.
39 Medal of Honor citation, Gunnery Sergeant Robert Guy Robinson; Medal of Honor citation Second Lieutenant Ralph Talbot.
40 Navy Cross citation, Harvey C. Norman; Caleb W. Taylor's citation is similarly but not identically worded.
41 Collings, p. 106.
42 Navy Cross citation, John K. McGraw
43 Day interview, p. 18, 21.
44 Ibid, pp. 22–23.
45 Unless otherwise noted, material cited hereafter is from Johnson and Cosmas, *Marine Aviation: The Early Years, 1912–1940*, pp. 13-14.
46 Christian Schilt interview, pp. 20–21.
47 Tierney, *A Brief History of Marine Corps Aviation*, pp. 2–3.

Chapter14

1 York, *His Own Life Story and War Diary*, p. 215.
2 Westover, *Suicide Battalions*, p. 242.
3 Lengel, *To Conquer Hell*, p. 69.
4 Lejeune, *The Reminiscences of a Marine*, p. 368.
5 Ibid, pp. 371–375.
6 Cates interview, p. 47.
7 Derby, *Wade In, Sanitary!*, p. 172.
8 American Battle Monuments Commission, 2*nd Division Summary of Operations in the Great War*, pp. 74–75.
9 Lejeune, pp. 382–383.
10 Hermle interview, p. 12.
11 Second Division Association, *The Second Division American Expeditionary Force in France*, pp. 281–282.
12 Lengel, p. 162.
13 War Diary, Sixth Machine Gun Battalion, September 15, 1918 in *Second Division Papers* (v. 8, p. 24).
14 Noble interview, p. 24.
15 Hermle interview, p. 12.
16 Ibid, p. 13.
17 Lejeune, pp. 382–386.
18 Second Division Association, p. 282.

19 Brannen, *Over There*, p. 55.
20 Lejeune, pp. 388–392.
21 Second Division Association, p. 282.
22 Westover, pp. 257–258.
23 Lejeune, p. 393; War Diary, Sixth Machine Gun Battalion, November 1, 1918 (v. 8, p. 24).
24 Westover, p. 259.
25 Lejeune, p. 400; Brannen, p. 55.
26 Lejeune, p. 411.
27 Garvin, F. H., "History of the 49th Company," p. 15.
28 Cates interview, pp. 44–45.
29 Hermle interview, p. 13; War Diary, Sixth Machine Gun Battalion, November 1, 1918 (v. 8, p. 24).
30 Lejeune, p. 402.
31 Garvin, p. 15.
32 Hermle interview, pp. 13–14.
33 Lejeune, p. 405.
34 Ibid, p. 405.
35 American Battle Monuments Commission, p. 96.

Chapter 15

1 "Report of Operations, Sixth Regiment, dated November 16, 1918" (vol. 7, pp. 60–61, 77).
2 Fifth Marines Field Orders, 12 November 1918, in *Second Division Papers* (vol. 3, p. 51).
3 Noble interview, p. 26.
4 Hermle interview, p. 14.
5 Cates interview, p. 48.
6 Peck interview, p. 50.
7 Avery interview.
8 Rogers interview.
9 Thomas interview, p. 23.
10 Derby, *Wade In, Sanitary!*, pp. 181–182.
11 Ibid, pp. 179–180.
12 Lejeune, *The Reminiscences of a Marine*, pp. 414–415.
13 Second Division Association, *The Second Division American Expeditionary Force in France*, p. 284.
14 Lejeune, pp. 417–418; Gilbert and Gilbert, *U. S. Marine in World War I*, p. 57.
15 Cates interview, pp. 48–49.
16 Gaspar interview, p. 26.
17 Thomas interview, p. 24.

18 Derby, p. 184.
19 Bartlett, *Lejeune*, p. 106.
20 Second Division Association, pp. 284–286.
21 Hermle interview, p. 15.
22 Cates interview, pp. 49–51.
23 Lejeune, pp. 419–420.
24 Jones interview, p. 23.
25 Rogers interview.
26 Ibid.
27 Thomas interview, pp. 24–25.
28 Cates interview, p. 52.
29 Ibid, p. 53.
30 Noble interview, p. 27.
31 Field Order no, 118, dated December 16, 1918 in *Second Division Papers* (vol. 3, pp. 77–82).
32 Derby, pp. 196–197.
33 Hermle interview, p. 17.
34 Derby, p. 199.
35 Gilbert and Gilbert, p. 57.
36 Cates interview, p. 53.
37 Thomas interview, p. 25.
38 Noble interview, p. 28.
39 Communication Captain Frederick G. Wheeler to Lejeune, March 29, 1919, as cited in Bartlett, p. 108.
40 Mulcahy interview, p. 35.
41 Cates interview, pp. 54–55; Gaspar interview p. 50.
42 Hermle interview, p. 18.

Chapter 16

1 McClellan, *The United States Marine Corps in the World War*, p. 80.
2 Ibid, p. 79.
3 Rendinell and Pattullo, *One Man's War: Diary of a Leatherneck*, p. vi.
4 As a provision of the Treaty of Versailles the citizens of the old Duchy were to have self-determination as to whether to remain as part of Germany or become part of Denmark. In a vote finally taken in early 1920, the northern part elected to become Danish, while the southern region remained German.
5 McClellan, p. 79.
6 Hewitt, *Women Marines in World War I*, pp. 40–41.

Appendix

1 See for example Gilbert & Gilbert, *U. S. Marine in World War I.*
2 Second Division Association, *The Second Division American Expeditionary Force in France,* p. 273.
3 Ibid.
4 Ibid, p. 276.
5 Harbord, *Leaves from a War Diary*, p. 307.
6 Second Division Association, p.273.
7 Rendinell & Pattullo, *One Man's War: Diary of a Leatherneck*, p. 64.
8 For surviving examples of this boot see www.worldwar1.com/dbc/l_tanks.htm.
9 See photos in Gilbert & Gilbert.
10 Gaspar interview, p. 34.
11 Cates interview, pp. 15-16; for further descriptions and illustrations see Gilbert & Gilbert, pp. 26, 53.
12 Second Division Association, p. 255.
13 For further details and illustrations, see Gilbert & Gilbert, pp. 8-9, 26-29, 52-53.
14 Rendinell & Pattullo, p. 55.
15 Cates interview, p. 14; Gilbert & Gilbert, pp. 21-22.
16 See Clark, *Devil Dogs Chronicle*, p. 105; Noble interview, p. 16.
17 Rendinell & Pattullo, p. 44.
18 Erskine interview, p. 33.
19 For more information on the Chauchat, see https://en.wikipedia.org/wiki/Chauchat, and Gilbert & Gilbert, pp. 8, 21-22.
20 McDonald interview, p. 11.
21 War Diary, Sixth Machine Gun Battalion, September 12, 1918 (v. 8, pp. 10, 18).
22 Gilbert & Gilbert, pp. 8-9, 23-26, 52-53.
23 See for example photos at www.mca-marines.org/mcaf-blog/2012/01/31/elizaberth-ford-model-t-truck-france
24 Jones interview, p. 13.
25 Worton interview, pp. 25-26.
26 Morgan, *When the World Went Mad*, p. 28.
27 Cates interview, pp. 45-46.
28 Rendinell & Pattullo, p. 124.
29 Ibid, p. 86; Gaspar interview, p. 32.
30 Gaspar interview, p. 32.
31 Rendinell & Pattullo, p. 61.
32 Ibid, p. 88.
33 Worton interview, p. 26.
34 Brannen, *Over There*, p. 41; Gilbert & Gilbert, p. 30.

Bibliography

Published source material

Abbot, Willis J. (2005) *Soldiers of the Sea: The Story of the United States Marine Corps*, Dodd, Mead, New York, 1918; reprint Scholars Bookshelf, Cranbury NJ.

American Battle Monuments Commission. (1944) *2nd Division Summary of Operations in the Great War*, Washington.

Anonymous, "Girl Joins Devil Dogs," Washington DC *Evening Star*, No. 27,140, Wednesday, August 14, 1918, p. 1.

Anonymous, "Women Marines Anxious to Serve United States," *Richmond Times-Dispatch*, Sunday, September 1, 1918, p. 2.

Asprey, Robert B. (1965) *At Belleau Wood*, G. P. Putnam's Sons, New York.

Bartelett Merrill L.(1991) *Lejeune: A Marine's Life, 1867–1942*, University of South Carolina Press, Columbia.

Bisett, D. A., *Operations on the Western Front, May 22 to June 8, 1918*, in Anonymous, *Monographs of the World War*, no publisher specified, undated; available online at www.benning.army.mil/library/content/Virtual/Donovanpapers/wwi/D521_U6_Monographs%20of%20the%20World%20War.pdf

Bonk, D. and Dennis, P. (2007) *Château Thierry & Belleau Wood 1918: America's Baptism of Fire on the Marne*, Osprey Publishing.

Bonk, D. and Gerrard, H. (2011) *St. Mihiel 1918: The American Expeditionary Forces' Trial by Fire*, Osprey Publishing, Oxford.

Brannen, Carl A. (1996) *Over There: A Marine in the Great War*, Texas A&M Press, College Station.

Broun, H. (1918) *Our Army at yhe Front,* Charles Scribner's & Sons, New York.

Clark, George B. (2005) *Hiram Iddings Bearss, U. S. Marine Corps: Biography of a World War I Hero*, McFarland & Co., Jefferson NC.

___.(2007) *The Second Infantry Division in World War I*, McFarland & Co., Jefferson NC.

___.(2013) *Devil Dogs Chronicle*, The University Press of Kansas, Lawrence KS.

Collings, K. (1938) *Just for the Hell of It*, Dodd, Mead & Co., New York.
Cosmas, Graham A. (editor) (1974) *Marine Flyer in France: The Diary of Captain Alfred A. Cunningham November 1917–January 1918*, History and Museums Division, U. S. Marine Corps, Washington D.C.
Cowing, Kemper F. (compiler) and Cooper, Courtney R. (editor) (2015) *Dear Folks at Home*, Houghton Mifflin, New York, 1919. Reprint available from Forgottenbooks.com.
Denig, Robert L., *Diary of a Marine Officer During the Great War*, Personal Papers Collection, Marine Corps History Division, Quantico VA.
Derby, Richard C. (1919) *Wade in Sanitary! The Story of a Division Surgeon in France*, G. P. Putman's Sons, New York and London.
Fussell, Paul (1975) *The Great War And Modern Memory*, Oxford University Press, New York and London (The war in British literature.).
Garvin, Frank H., "History of the 49th Company," manuscript, Library of Congress (William Frederick Nice Collection).
Gilbert, Ed. (2008) *Native American Code Talker in World War II*, Osprey Publishing, Oxford UK.
___.(2012) *Frontier Militiaman in the War of 1812, Southwestern Frontier*, Osprey Publishing, Oxford UK.
Gilbert, Ed. and Gilbert, C. (2016) *U. S. Marine In World War I*, Osprey Publishing, Oxford, UK.
Gilbert, Ed. and Cansière, R. (2018) *Blanc Mont Ridge 1918: America's Forgotten Triumph*, Osprey Publishing, Oxford, UK.
Gulberg, Martin G. (1994) A War Diary, Brass Hat, Pike NH.
Harbord, James G. (1925) *Leaves from a War Diary*, Dodd, Mead & Co., New York.
Hart, P. (2010) *The Somme: The Darkest Hour on the Western Front*, Pegasus Books, New York.
Hewitt, Linda L. (1974) *Women Marines in World War I*, History and Museums Division, U. S. Marine Corps, Washington.
Johnson, Edward C. and Cosmas, Graham A. (1977) *Marine Corps Aviation: The Early Years 1912–1940*, History and Museums Division, U. S. Marine Corps, Washington D.C.
Krulewitch, Melvin L. (1973) *Now That You Mention It*, Quadrangle Books (New York Times Book Co.) New York.
Lejeune, John A. (1930) *The Reminiscences of a Marine*, Dorrance & Co., Philadelphia.
Lengel, E. (2008) *To Conquer Hell: The Meuse-Argonne, 1918*, Henry Holt & Co., New York.
Longstreet, E. S., *Gunner Nice of the "Devil-Dogs,"* Asbury Park Sunday Press, September 10, 1933; see Library of Congress http://memory.loc.gov/diglib/vhp/bib/loc.natlib.afc2001001.1339. Note that initial page number is not preserved in this image.
Mahan, Alfred T. (1890) *The Influence of Sea Power upon History,* Little Brown & Co., Boston.

McClellan, Edwin N. (1920) *The United States Marine Corps in the World War*, Government Printing Office, Washington.

Manchester, William H. Jr. (1979) *Goodbye Darkness: A Memoir of the Pacific War*, Little, Brown & Co., Boston.

Martin, Thomas W. (1949) "Doctor William Crawford Gorgas of Alabama and the Panama Canal," text of address to The Newcomen Society of England, American Branch, New York.

Millett, Allan R. (1980) *Semper Fidelis: The History of the United States Marine Corps*, Macmillan Publishing, New York.

Morgan, Daniel E. (1931) *When the World Went Mad*, Christopher Publishing House, Boston.

Otto, E. (1930) *The Battle at Blanc Mont (October 2 to October 10, 1918)*, translated from the German by Martin Lichtenberg, United States Naval Institute, Annapolis MD.

Owen, Peter F. (2007) *To The Limit of Endurance: A Battalion of Marines in the Great War*, Texas A&M University Press, College Station TX.

Pershing, John J., "Final Report of Gen. John J. Pershing," Government Printing Office, Washington, 1919; available online at www.shsu.edu/~his_ncp/Pershing.html

___. *My Experiences in the World War, Volume 1*, Frederick A. Stokes Co., New York, 1931.

Pigman, M. K., *Operations of the 2nd Division (U.S.) in The Soissons Offensive, July 16th to 25th, 1918*, in Anonymous, *Monographs of the World War*, no publisher specified, undated; available online at www.benning.army.mil/library/content/Virtual/Donovanpapers/wwi/D521_U6_Monographs%20of%20the%20World%20War.pdf

Rendinell, Joseph E. and Pattullo, George (1928) *One Man's War: Diary of a Leatherneck*, J. H. Sears & Co., New York.

Second Division Association (1937) *The Second Division American Expeditionary Force in France 1917–1919*, edited by Oliver L. Spaulding & John W. Wright, Hillman Press, New York.

Shulimson, Jack (1976) "The First To Fight: Marine Corps Expansion, 1914–1918," *Prologue* (magazine), issue 8.

Thomason, John W. (1927) *Fix Bayonets*, Charles Scribner & Sons, New York.

Tierney, Elizabeth L. (1962) *A Brief History of Marine Corps Aviation*, Marine Corps Historical Reference Series No.18, Washington.

Trask, David F. (1993) *The AEF and Coalition Warmaking 1917–1918*, University Press of Kansas, Lawrence KS.

Westover, W. (1929) *Suicide Battalions*, G. P. Putnam's Sons, New York.

White, Lonnie J. (1984) *Panthers To Arrowhead: The 36th (Texas–Oklahoma) Division in World War I*, Presidial Press, Austin TX.

Willock, R. (1968) *Unaccustomed to Fear: A Biography of the Late General Roy S. Geiger, U.S.M.C.*, privately published, Princeton NJ.

Wise, Frederick M. (1929) *A Marine Tells it to You*, W. H. Sears & Co., New York.

York, Alvin C. and Skeyhill, T. (editor) (1930) *His Own Life Story and War Diary*, Doubleday, Doran & Co., New York.

Unpublished sources

Second Division Papers. Bound volumes available at Grey Research Center, MCB Quantico.

Interviews

(Suffixes are file numbers, USMC History Division, MCB Quantico.)
Avery, Cecil B., audiotape, self-recorded. HD12585.
Brown, Wilburt S., transcript. HD13910.
Cates, Clifton B., transcript. HD13923.
Erskine, Graves B., transcript. HD9422.
Gaspar, Walter S., transcript. HD9482.
Hermle, Leo D., transcript. HD14040.
Jenson, Albert L., audiotape; the story of his misadventures with the Scots soldiers was read aloud from the *Orkney Herald*, July 5, 1918. HD10288.
Jones, Louis R., transcript. HD9613.
McDonald, Roland L., transcript. HD14066.
Mulcahy, Francis P., transcript. HD14077.
Noble, Alfred H., transcript. HD14083.
Peck, DeWitt, transcript. HD`14091.
Rogers, Ford O., transcript. HD14109.
Rogers, William W., audiotape. HD9965.
Schmolsmire, Karl, transcript. HD13949.
Schilt, Christian F., transcript. HD9975.
Shepherd, Lemuel C., transcript. HD14135.
Silverthorn, Merwyn H., transcript. HD14142.
Thomas, Gerald C., audiotape. HD14163.
Women Marines Project, audiotape, unidentified interviewee. HD11493.
Worton, William A., transcript. HD14211.